The Secret Struggles of Kitigan Zibi Anishinabeg Leaders

The Secret Struggles of Kitigan Zibi Anishinabeg Leaders

Political Resistance from the Margins

Anny Morissette

LEXINGTON BOOKS
Lanham • Boulder • New York • London

Published by Lexington Books
An imprint of The Rowman & Littlefield Publishing Group, Inc.
4501 Forbes Boulevard, Suite 200, Lanham, Maryland 20706
www.rowman.com

6 Tinworth Street, London SE11 5AL, United Kingdom

French Edition: © Les éditions du Septentrion, 2018
835, avenue Turnbull Québec (Québec), Canada G1R 2X4

The author has chosen to donate her royalties to the Kitigan Zibi Cultural Centre.

British Library Cataloguing in Publication Information Available

Library of Congress Cataloging-in-Publication Data Available

ISBN 978-1-7936-4570-8 (cloth)
ISBN 978-1-7936-4572-2 (pbk)
ISBN 978-1-7936-4571-5 (electronic)

To the Kitigan Zibi Anishinabeg, a proud and distinct People

To my husband and parents

Contents

List of Abbreviations

AANDC	Aboriginal Affairs and Northern Development Canada
AANTC	Algonquin Anishinabeg Nation Tribal Council
AD	Archives Deschâtelets
ANC	Archives nationales du Canada
ARDIA	Annual Report of the Department of Indian Affairs
BAC	Bibliothèque et Archives Canada
CAM	Conseil des Atikamekw et des Montagnais
INAC	Indian and Northern Affairs Canada
MAINC	Ministère des Affaires indiennes et du Nord Canada
NAHO	National First Nations Health Organization
NIC	National Indian Council
NWAC	Native Women's Association of Canada
OMI	Oblate of Mary Immaculate
QNW	Quebec Native Women
RCMP	Royal Canadian Mounted Police
RLS	Rapport des cours de formation de leaders sociaux
RRSL	Résumé du cours de formation de responsables sociales "Leadership"

Acknowledgments

I would first like to thank the Kitigan Zibi Band Council for granting me permission on July 4, 2007, to conduct research in the community. I am grateful to the Band Council and the Cultural Centre for their interest in my study and their generosity in making available to me several past research studies conducted on the community with the help of anthropologists and consulting and legal firms,[1] as well as several documents, books, and archival photos. The use of documentation from the Kitigan Zibi Anishinabeg was crucial to ensure the inclusion of Algonquin voices in the historical reconstruction of their political daily life. My goal in this research was not to seek to be impartial, but to provide the perspective of the people of Kitigan Zibi on their past and present. It is a privilege to have had access to the community's oral history interviews, as they proved to be very informative, containing testimonies that were rarely or never heard within the community and in Quebec. In the spirit of the gift/counter-gift Anishinabe tradition, I gladly donate my royalties for this book to the Kitigan Zibi Cultural Centre.

Kici Migwetch to the Kitigan Zibi Anishinabeg, whom I cannot name in order to preserve their anonymity, but who have kindly shared with me their knowledge, their life experiences, their daily lives. Thank you to those who welcomed me into their family, as an anthropologist and then as a friend. I am also grateful to the individuals who allowed me to attend ceremonies, gatherings, and community activities. Special thanks to the families of David Decontie, Danielle, Bryan, Jenny-Lee, and Douglas, who first welcomed me into their home and then welcomed me with open arms and open hearts as a full member of their family.

I would like to sincerely thank Professor Marie-Pierre Bousquet and Professor Guy Lanoue for the wealth of their comments, their sound advice, their constant support, their confidence in my abilities, their time and their patience. Working under your direction has been very formative and a privilege. My gratitude also goes to Professors Bernard Bernier, Claude Gélinas, Karine Bates, and Mylène Jaccoud for their comments and constructive criticism. I would also like to thank Dr. Karl Hele of Mount Allison University for his confidence, his interest in my research, and his words of encouragement. Thank you to my colleagues at Saint Paul University and especially Dr. Anahi Morales Hudon, Dr. Heather Eaton, Sister Louise Charbonneau, Dr. Marie-Rose Tannous, Dr. Lorraine Ste-Marie, Former Dean Manal Guirguis-Younger, Amélie Larose, Julie Nantel Powell, and Pawel Mazurek for their invaluable support and their passionate exchanges that advance me as an academic and as a human being. I would like to express my gratitude to my former colleagues from the United Nations University, the UNESCO office in Europe, Ms. Nieves Claxton, Ms. Elizabeth Mvogo, and Mr. Marco Antonio Dias for believing in my doctoral potential. I would also like to pay tribute to the Oblate Fathers working in First Nations missions and at the Archives Deschâtelets who provided me with valuable documentation.

On a more personal note, I would like to thank my husband, who believes in me and encourages all my passions. I would like to express all my affection to my mother, my sister Line, and my sister France who have supported me since the beginning of my journey as an ethnographer. I am deeply grateful to my brother Nicolas, the "best friend of mine," who has been holding my hand on the path of life for forty-six years, rain or shine. My gratitude also goes to my niece Claudia and my brother Pierre. I also thank my aunt Sylvie who constantly shows interest in all my projects and great adventures.

Thank you to my precious friend Marie-Pierre who has been a beacon in the undertaking of this long-term career project and in my personal life, a light in difficult times. I would like to warmly thank her husband, Bryn, for his support of my academic and professional success and for his expressions of friendship. My thanks also go to the inspiring Nadia Ferrara who is a source of motivation and a luminous presence. I am also thankful to my friend Jorge Solis for all his artistic guidance. Thanks also to André Mowatt, Nadine Langlois, Floriant Dubé, Raymond Launière, and Gilles Ottawa who followed the evolution of this work and encouraged me.

This book is the result of a doctoral thesis from the Université de Montréal, which was made possible thanks to the financial support of the Centre de recherche interdisciplinaire sur la violence familiale et la violence faite aux femmes (CRI-VIFF), the Department of Anthropology of the Université de Montréal and the Girardin-Vaillancourt Program Scholarship of the Fondation Desjardins. This book was originally published in French by Éditions du Septentrion under the title *"La lutte se poursuivit en cachette": Le pouvoir des chefs et des leaders de la bande algonquine de Kitigan Zibi (Québec)*

(Sillery, QC: Septentrion, 2018). Thanks to Marie-Michèle Rheault of Éditions du Septentrion for her expertise and valuable editorial advice. I would also like to thank Kasey Beduhn, my publisher at Lexington Books, for her involvement and attentive guidance. My sincere gratitude goes to Hortense Bleytou for her editing support and for always being there when I need help. It means a lot to me.

NOTE

1. Among these, the Kitigan Zibi Band Council provided me with a series of oral history interviews with Elders and former chiefs of the band as part of their Global Research Project (Holmes et al., 1999). The purpose of this research was to compile existing documentation regarding surrendered or lost Anishinabeg lands in order to assist in future land claims (Holmes et al., 1999: i). In addition to land claims information, cultural and historical data that had been gathered, and little used, proved to be relevant to my research. Recognizing that this information coincided with my interview questions, the Kitigan Zibi Band Council provided me with transcripts of the oral history tapes with Elders and former chiefs, provided that pseudonyms were used to respect anonymity. This oral history reported by band members, whether or not they were direct witnesses to the events, presents the Anishinabeg vision and perception of their past.

Introduction

Over the past twenty-five years, within the Western world and liberal democracies, minority or marginalized groups, with their growing political and identity claims, have become unavoidable infra-state collectivities[1] for the leaders of nation-states. Canada has not been spared by this situation. Through their recognition processes, their quest for autonomy, their land claims, Indigenous peoples are among the obligatory infra-state interlocutors of Canadian governments. For anyone who is even the slightest bit curious to understand the political functioning of Indigenous Nations,[2] it is clear that there is a documentary void at the local level on the issue. Under these conditions, it is rather difficult to grasp concretely what the field of action of the First Nations[3] in the Canadian political context consists of. Since colonialism has marked, and continues to mark, the power relations between Indigenous peoples and the Canadian state (Green, 2004: 12), focusing on the official political structure imposed on First Nations peoples, the band council, appears to be essential as a starting point for answering this question.

In 1869, Canadian authorities assented to *An Act for the gradual enfranchisement of Indians, the better management of Indian affairs* (Canada, 1869). One of the purposes of this Act was to break the traditional political structure of the original inhabitants by introducing a male elective system[4] under the control of the "Superintendent General of Indian Affairs." For political scientist Paul Tennant (1985: 325), the government's intention was also "to undermine the authority and prestige of aboriginal leaders, thereby facilitating control over Indian communities by the agents of the dominant society." At that time, it was clear to Canadian government officials that traditional forms of First Nation government were undermining the goal of gradual civilization and assimilation of Indigenous peoples into Canadian society (Canada, 1996).[5] In 1876, this measure on forms of First Nation government was consolidated with the development of the *Indian Act*, which detailed, among other things, the structures and operating rules of the band council. Although its name may be misleading, the band council is not a political entity endogenous to First Nations. It is an imposed administrative and political apparatus made up of an elected, or hereditary, chief and councillors. This system institutionalizes First Nations political life by setting out in great detail the rules of election, eligibility for the position of chief and councillor, the procedures of the formal assembly, and the scope of the council's powers. The band council thus becomes the only political apparatus recognized by the Canadian authorities as being able to represent First Nations peoples, thus negating all other forms of First Nations political organizations.

Over the years, the band council has been adopted gradually, or by force (Dupuis, 1991: 47), by all First Nations collectivities in Canada. The year of adoption of this system varies from one First Nation community[6] to another, since each has a distinct political history. For example, as noted by anthropologist Josée Mailhot (1999: 77–78), the Innu of Sheshatshit did not begin electing a band council until the mid-1970s. Why so late? How did they get into politics before then? Since the adoption of this structure by First Nations groups, the way they govern themselves has, in principle, been based on external Euro-Canadian criteria (electoral procedures, election rules, fixed term of office for elected officials, by-laws, bureaucratic structure). Although band councils are local structures elected by community members, they remain under the aegis of the federal government, which has, as Renée Dupuis (1997: 5) notes, a power of "disallowance," a final verdict, a right of intervention.

During the 1960s and 1970s, Indigenous associations and organizations emerged at the local, regional and national levels (Charest, 1992: 58). However, these groupings are not entities legally recognized by the government as representing Indigenous peoples, as Renée Dupuis (1991: 35) explains:

> Governments also maintain relationships with national or tribal organizations. However, these organizations do not have the authority to engage the people they represent. This is a major limitation to their ability to act as advocates for their people to governments. This situation poses the opposite problem for governments, which are never certain of the authority of interlocutors representing a national group composed of more than one band.

Defined by the *Indian Act*, a band is a group of Indians for whom the federal government holds lands and moneys for their use and benefit (Dupuis, 1991: 35). In addition to this legal definition, what is a band?

Thus, there are two positions regarding the field of action of First Nations in the Canadian political context within social science research. On the one hand, some researchers (Flanagan, 2000: 95; Widdowson and Howard,

2008) consider that Indigenous people can only evolve within the Canadian framework, which they have moreover fully assimilated. In this sense, First Nations have no real power (Simard, 1983); they are content to suffer, react as victims, have a culture of "whiners" and are in reaction and not in action. Ghislain Picard, Chief of the Assembly of First Nations of Quebec and Labrador since 1992, adds nuances to these assertions: "It seems that we always rise up in the media to complain. We don't complain, we want to assert our rights, our existence and our land claims to people who very often don't know the content of these claims" (Miny, 2008: 23). Certainly, the political structure was imposed on First Nations. But a borrowing sometimes becomes so incorporated that one forgets that it is a borrowing. Do the First Nations nowadays know that this structure was imposed? Do they consider the band council to be a federal entity, or have they reappropriated this structure?

Other researchers acknowledge the existence of the Canadian hegemonic framework imposed on First Nations, but they consider that the latter resisted the imposition of the colonizing system and are not passive victims (Miller, 1991, 1996; Smandych and Lee, 1995: 74; Poirier, 2000: 137; Ponting and Voyageur, 2001). The band council is part of a government bureaucracy. Indeed, it reports first to a regional office and then to the headquarters of the Department of Aboriginal Affairs and Northern Development Canada.[7] In a bureaucracy, there is no power granted in the structure, but only small margins that do not call into question the efficiency of the system. By power, I mean the ability and possibility of an individual or group of individuals to influence, decide and act in one or more areas of interest (politics, justice, culture, education, health, etc.). Thus, some researchers believe that Indigenous peoples hold a margin of power and manipulate, to a certain degree, the margin in action (Poirier, 2000; Morissette, 2007). I agree with this view and consider, as Sylvie Poirier (2000) suggests with regard to the first inhabitants of Canada, Australia, New Zealand, and the United States, that Indigenous peoples "seek, with all the obstacles and ambiguities that this entails, to appropriate the technical and political means that had hitherto served to discriminate against them." From this perspective, what kind of leaders do First Nations peoples rely on to guide them in their decisions and collective governance and to tinker with an imposed formal system in their own way? Do the political practices of the First Nations actors reflect typically First Nations forms of leadership? Are these always linked to formal politics?

To answer these questions, it is essential to explore the first level of articulation of First Nation politics—that is, the local space of the reserve. It is within this framework that the band council's political apparatus acts. Also defined by the *Indian Act*, a reserve is land belonging to the federal government that is "reserved" for the exclusive use of a band (Dupuis, 1991: 48). A focus on local politics can undoubtedly lead to a better understanding of Indigenous macro-local and national political practices. However, is a focus on local-level official political frameworks sufficient to capture the political life of Indigenous nations? In his review of the book *Aboriginal Autonomy and Development in Northern Quebec and Labrador*, edited by Colin H. Scott (2001) and published in *Études/Inuit/Studies,* anthropologist Jean Rousseau (2003: 548) argues that there is a formal and essentialist vision of Indigenous politics centred on institutions, negotiations, and self-government. The institutional path appears to be a partial reality of Indigenous politics, bringing nothing to the Indigenous experience beyond institutions. This is why it is relevant to define and analyze, at the local level, the place of politics in the everyday life of a highly politicized[8] minority population.[9]

RESERVES, FIRST NATIONS VILLAGES?

The study of reserve politics goes much further than a typical study of village politics focused on local power in everyday life. While a village is a settlement pattern that emerges from a voluntary settlement movement, reserves are artificial creations designed by a dominant group (Lithman, 1984: 8–11) for the use of a "subjugated" group. The increased presence of diverse government services serving First Nations peoples in Canada clearly distinguishes a reserve from a village and contributes to the politicization of the community (Morissette, 2004: 21). The colonial actions of Canadian authorities toward Indigenous nations can be qualified as interference, since they have insinuated themselves into the organization of these societies at all levels (social, economic, political, legal, spiritual, educational, linguistic) through laws and institutions. The multiple upheavals and cultural changes brought about by the colonial presence created post-traumatic effects among Indigenous peoples. Historical trauma (colonization, sedentarization,[10] imposed acculturation processes such as residential schools[11]) has been blamed for the social problems and Indigenous malaise (Wesley-Esquimaux and Smolewski, 2004). The model of pathogenesis developed by Richard Scott and Selina Conn (1987) for the Naskapi of Davis Inlet, Labrador, suggests that political alienation is one of the factors that has contributed to manifestations of violence, suicide, alcohol and drug abuse, child neglect, abuse, and delinquency. When it comes to reserves, this negative acknowledgment of First Nations reality is inescapable. Far from wanting to deny this reality, this book presents reserve life in a different light by highlighting the positive aspects of its history, its achievements, and its contemporary experience.

Most of the time, the reserve is approached from a colonial point of view. But now that the semi-nomadic populations have been sedentary for more than fifty years, has the reserve been reappropriated by First Nations? The gradual decolonization of reserves can be envisaged by taking a closer look at the band's political universe, its political ways of doing things, and its various power relationships.

THE BAND CONCEPT

To describe Indigenous political organization in their work, anthropologists have focused on the key notion of hunter-gatherers,[12] the "band."[13] As Guy Lanoue (1998: 3) notes with regard to the Northern Athapaskans, the Algonquians of Eastern Canada have not figured prominently in investigations of theories of political evolution and social organization concerning hunter-gatherers. Nevertheless, it is interesting to note the breadth attributed to the concept of a band,[14] because in reality this formation does not seem to be of capital interest in the everyday life of Algonquian societies during the era of semi-nomadism. It should be remembered that at the time of the practice of this way of life, the Algonquians lived for most of the year in small groups, made up of mostly related individuals, on "a hunting ground." In the Quebec context a band is, generally speaking, a political and social grouping linked to a territory, whose members, gathered in subgroups, have common cultural traits—language, customs, beliefs. As early as the 1960s, a constellation of categories surrounding this concept was created by anthropologists in an attempt to adequately describe this sociopolitical system. These categories include, among others, the local band, the regional band (Helm, 1965: 361–85), the matrimonial exchange group (Hirbour, 1969: 59–61), the microband, the macroband, the regional group (Mailhot, 1993: 54), the structural band and the conjunctural band (Gélinas, 2000: 95–98). Group size, use of a location, number of individuals, degree of social interaction, marital arrangements, and kinship are criteria used to establish these classifications. These band definitions reflect the difficulties of studying, in scientific terms, heterogeneous sociopolitical universes on which raw data are nonexistent. Indeed, from the time of contact until the nineteenth century, only the chronicles of Westerners (for example, travelers, missionaries, trading post clerks) relate the Indigenous experience. The biased point of view of these authors cannot paint a fair cultural portrait with a deep understanding of First Nations societies during this period. Thus, it is not surprising to note that the anthropological definitions of the band seem rather mechanical and obscure the human, emotional, and subjective experience of belonging to this unit, its meaning and its functioning according to First Nation categories and knowledge. Beyond the reference to the "traditional" First Nation political world, the band becomes, under the *Indian Act* of 1876, a legal, administrative, and political entity, effective on the reserve and managed by a band council. The band's base is no longer territorial. No work has yet been undertaken to understand the day-to-day political functioning of the "band." The analysis of its leadership seems promising to grasp its articulation and its relational dynamics generated by various powers.

EVOLUTION OVER TIME OF THE POWERS
AND RESPONSIBILITIES OF THE BAND COUNCIL

It was with *An Act for the gradual enfranchisement of Indians, the better management of Indian affairs* of 1869 that the authorities introduced the duties and first powers of the band council along with this elective system. Thus, section 11 provided that the chief or chiefs were "bound to cause the roads, bridges, ditches and fences within their Reserve to be put and maintained in proper order." Section 12 described the band council's law-making powers, its first seven areas of regulation:

12. The Chief or Chiefs of any Tribe in Council may frame, subject to confirmation by the Governor in Council, rules and regulations for the following subjects, viz:

1. The care of the public health.
2. The observance of order and decorum at assemblies of the people in General Council, or on other occasions.
3. The repression of intemperance and profligacy.
4. The prevention of trespass by cattle.
5. The maintenance of roads, bridges, ditches and fences.
6. The construction of and maintaining in repair of school houses, council houses and other Indian public buildings.
7. The establishment of pounds and the appointment of poundkeepers.

The development of the 1876 *Indian Act* consolidated the operation, responsibilities, and regulatory scope of the band council. In 1879, the Act was amended to specify the objects of regulations and to include new ones, including "The repression of noxious weeds" (section 63). This amendment also gave a new power to elected officials, a legal power. The chief could now impose a fine or imprisonment for the violation of rules or regulations (section 10).

An Act to amend and consolidate the laws respecting Indians (Canada, 1880) would again increase the band council's regulation-making authority. Section 74 clarified that the band council could now make by-laws concerning the "religious denomination the teacher of the school established on the reserve shall belong to," "the construction and repair of school houses, council houses and other Indian public buildings," and "the locating of the land in their reserves, and the establishment of a register of such locations." Jacques Bertrand (2010: 86), who has examined the organizational architecture of the political-administrative relations between the Department of Indian Affairs and Northern Development and band councils, notes:

> These responsibilities of the band council in relation to public management will change very little, and the changes will reflect the environmental conditions under which the band council operates. Here we are referring to the management of forest or mineral resources. However, the control of these responsibilities is still subject to the consent of the Governor in Council.

Adaptation to local realities suggests a certain flexibility of the political-administrative apparatus. The federal government's power of disallowance over band council decisions, which is still in effect, nevertheless leaves little autonomy for elected officials at that time, with the exception of the legal capacity to take action in the event of noncompliance with regulations issued by the council, as Bertrand points out (2010: 87). Moreover, the decisions of the Canadian authorities continued to affect the traditional political structures of the first inhabitants. While previously, lifelong chiefs could continue to "hold the rank of chief until death or resignation" (sec. 72), *An Act to amend and consolidate the laws respecting Indians* limited their functions, requiring them to be formally elected to "exercise the powers of chiefs" (sec. 72; Bertrand, 2010: 85). Although they were not formally recognized as chiefs, this did not mean that they were no longer perceived as such or that they had lost all authority in the eyes of their band members. To compensate for this perpetuation of First Nations political customs, the amended section 72 would also allow the Governor in Council to impose the electoral system "for the good government of a band" without the prior consent of the band.

An Act for conferring certain privileges on the more advanced Bands of the Indians of Canada, with the view of training them for the exercise of municipal powers (Canada, 1884), also known as the *Indian Advancement Act*, would increase the powers of the band council in health and property taxation while giving the Superintendent General power to dismiss elected officials (Miller, 2004: 181; Bertrand, 2010: 29). It was not until 1906, however, that the provisions of the *Indian Advancement Act* were incorporated into the

Indian Act and applied to all bands (Leslie and Maguire, 1978: 104; Miller, 2004: 181).

Although amendments are made almost annually, the *Indian Act* has retained its basic structure from the 1880s to 1951 (Leslie and Maguire, 1978: 80). During this period, the regulatory fields of the band council made small gains. In 1930, band councils were given the right to legislate "control of public games and amusements on the reserve" (Leslie and Maguire, 1978: 123).

Following hearings and reports of the Special Joint Committee of the Senate and House of Commons established to study the *Indian Act*[15] from 1946 to 1948, the Act was revised in 1951 (Canada, 1951). At the political-administrative level, the 1951 amendments allowed for the inclusion of women in the elective system[16] and expanded the powers of the band council (Canada, 1952) by granting "more autonomy for the management of reserves" (Lavoie, 2007: 16) through control of the accounting and budgetary administration as well as its human resources (Bertrand, 2010: 94). As noted by Leslie and Maguire (1978: 150), this autonomy is largely related to the fact that First Nation approval became necessary for the Minister to manage band affairs, including expenditures "for purposes that will promote the general progress and welfare of the band or its individual members" (Canada, 1952).

The observance of law and order, traffic, providing for the health of residents, beekeeping and poultry raising, conservation, protection and control of game, the activities of hawkers and the management of unauthorized individuals on the reserve are introduced as new areas of band council regulation, thereby expanding the powers of the band council (sec. 80). A band council that had reached a "high degree of advancement" was also given economic authority in the area of regulation of taxation on reserve land (Bertrand, 2010: 91). According to the 1952 Annual Report of Indian Affairs (Canada, 1952), "The powers of band councils to make by-laws were broadened to correspond in a general way with those exercised by councils in a rural municipality." The municipalization of reserves continued in order to allow for their articulation in the Canadian governance model and eventually their integration into the Canadian public administration.

There are two positions regarding the 1951 changes, as summarized by Jacques Bertrand (2010: 90): "For some researchers, the IA [*Indian Act*] is seen as an impediment that perpetuates previous Indian laws. Others argue that the 1951 IA [*Indian Act*] allows members of the most dynamic band councils to enfranchise themselves by using the *Indian Act* to their advantage." I agree with the latter perspective, because it emphasizes a possible room for maneuver, or even action, which gives a glimpse of the attitudes and strategies of actors struggling with a law that they are trying to tinker with by playing into the "cracks" of the system it has established.

The second Joint Committee of the Senate and the House of Commons on Indian Affairs from 1959 to 1961 and the Hawthorn-Tremblay Report of 1967 continued the project of integrating First Nations into Canadian society begun in the first Joint Committee (Lavoie, 2007: 15–16). This orientation of Indian policy continued to influence the operation of the band council. The administrative function was gradually going to be added to the political and social control functions of the band council (Bertrand, 2010: 118). First Nations bands were gradually taking control of their own affairs. According to Charest (1992: 57), the process of the gradual takeover by the bands of their own affairs[17] would have emerged from the 1965 Department of Indian Affairs' community development program. The latter "aimed to help the Indian population acquire the skills necessary to manage local affairs" (Canada, 1973–1974: 36–38 in Charest, 1992: 57). For Bertrand (2010: 23, 30), this program in fact had "the objective of supporting the formation of a public service within the band council" that would "manage programs administered by INAC" in order to "help the Canadian government deliver adequate services to the Indigenous population." Locally, government control would gradually be withdrawn in the areas of health, education, social assistance, and economic development, leaving these responsibilities to the band council, as stated in the 1965–1966 Annual Report of Indian Affairs (Canada, 1965–1966: 46). During the 1970s, the scope of programs administered by the band council would increasingly include housing, utilities, policing, job creation, economic development (arts, crafts, commercial fishing, fur trade, guiding and outfitting services), business development, resource development (forestry, mining), and land administration (Canada, 1972–1973). The transfer of these responsibilities was to proceed at the pace of each band council (Canada, 1973–1974). To achieve this assumption of responsibility for local government, the government had, since the 1950s, offered various training courses to band councils and members (Canada, 1973–1974).[18] More than an intermediary or a government agency, this First Nation public service was going to develop and have its own colors and ways of doing things, as will be discussed in more detail in chapter 3.

During the 1980s, greater political capacity on funding and budgets was given to the band council, which became a "service producer" (Bertrand, 2010: 30, 32). While program decentralization continued, it made local reserve administration by the band council increasingly complex by increasing its responsibilities (Bertrand, 2010: 133). The amendments to the *Indian Act* introduced by Amendment C-31 (Canada, 1985) gave regulatory authority over band membership criteria[19] to both the band council and band members (Bertrand, 2010: 84). Amendment C-31 also increased the band council's powers in relation to taxation (Bertrand, 2010: 96) and the regulation of intoxicants (sec. 85), the residence of band members, and the rights of children, spouses, or partners residing with band members on the reserve (sec. 81).

The emphasis on band autonomy and economic self-sufficiency in the early 1980s (Canada, 1979–1980) would also mark the decade from 1990 to 2000. The Special Committee on Indian Self-Government and its 1983 report (Penner Report) were no strangers to this paradigm shift in Indian policy (Lavoie, 2007: 17). Faced with the increase in programs managed by the band council, its administrative organizational structure was taking shape through its various departments, or community file management committees, which had gradually emerged since the 1970s (Bertrand, 2010: 128, 139). During the 1980s and 1990s, government funding programs used by band councils defined a new framework for managing their political-administrative apparatus while ensuring their integration into the Canadian public administration (Bertrand, 2010: 150). Bertrand (151) summarizes the new administrative responsibilities of band councils as follows:

- Responsible for implementing the political and administrative accountability mechanisms defined in the funding agreements
- Accountable to its population for providing services and programs
- Responsible for providing progress and annual reports on the management of funding programs
- Responsible for managing funding programs at the community level
- Responsible for compliance with contractual agreements with the department
- Responsible for implementing the management framework defined in the funding programs
- Include the various reports that must be submitted in the management of funding programs
- Responsible for the establishment of a competent, effective, efficient, and independent public service.

The end of the twentieth century and the beginning of the new millennium marked a turning point in the relationship between Canadian authorities and band councils as Indian policy entered the era of "partnership." As Bertrand (2010: 116) explains, "The Indigenous public service becomes a partner in the development and achievement of the organizational objectives pursued by the Department of Indian Affairs." Notwithstanding the intent, this is an asymmetrical partnership since the objectives are set by the department, which, moreover, has the right to intervene on the final verdict. Despite the evolution of the band council's political-administrative apparatus and its growing integration into the public service and the Canadian socioeconomic system, the band council's powers are still governed by the *Indian Act*. Appendix 1 presents the current powers of the band council as established by the *Indian Act*. Within the context of this Act and in the face of the vagaries of colonialism that undermined their traditional sociopolitical system and its internal power dynamics, the Kitigan Zibi Anishinabeg have never been passive. Through protest and resistance, the Kitigan Zibi Anishinabeg have challenged and continue to challenge state power over Indian affairs.

THE KITIGAN ZIBI ANISHINABEG

The Algonquin community of Kitigan Zibi was chosen to illustrate the subject of this book. Kitigan Zibi is located in the administrative region of Outaouais (Quebec), 130 kilometers north of Gatineau.[20] The municipality of Maniwaki borders the reserve.[21] The River Desert (north), the Gatineau River (east) and the Aigle River (west) naturally border the community. Also known as the Maniwaki Reserve or River Desert Band, the Algonquins of this community refer to themselves under the ethnonym Kitigan Zibi Anishinabeg,[22] which means "the people of the garden river" (*kitigan*: garden; *zibi*: river; *Anishinabeg*: people) (McGregor, 2004: 324). According to the Indian Register,[23] there were 3,370 Kitigan Zibi Anishinabeg as of December 31, 2018. Of these, 1,647 lived in the community while 1,723 lived outside the reserved territory (McGregor, 2004). Originally, the reserve had an area of 45,750 acres of land, or 18,514.4 hectares (Frenette, 1993: 43). Between 1873 and 1917, transfers and sales, sometimes illegal, reduced the reserve by 3,652.2 acres or 1,478 hectares (McGregor, 2004: 208). The decline in reserve land was to continue until the 1960s (Holmes et al., 1999: 129). Lots of land were gradually reclaimed beginning in the 1940s (Holmes et al., 1999: 47). In 2018, the size of the reserve was 51,914.4 acres or 21,009 hectares. Land claims are still pending to recover several parcels of land formerly owned by the reserve.

The Algonquins are part of the Algonquian linguistic group that includes in Quebec the Cree (Eeyou), the Atikamekw, the Innu (or Montagnais), the Naskapi, the Abenaki, the Mi'kmaq and the Maliseet. Although the community of Kitigan Zibi is surrounded by French-speaking municipalities (Maniwaki, Béliveau, Bois-Franc, Messines), the language spoken on the reserve is mainly English. A portion of the band membership (approximately 35 percent) is bilingual English-French. The vernacular language, Algonquin, is alive especially among the Elders, who also master either English or French, but often all three languages. The next generation that attended residential schools experienced a break in the use of Algonquin. Only a minority of this generation relearned their vernacular language upon their return to the reserve. There are also specialists in the Algonquin language who ensure its transmission by working on its teaching. The language spoken by the speakers of Kitigan Zibi is not only a question of age groups but is also influenced by the cultural background of the parents and the level of school education. Mixed unions[24] are common on the reserve. It should be noted that the Algonquin language of Kitigan Zibi has particularities that are unique to this community. This sets it apart from the Algonquin spoken in other Algonquin communities in Quebec.

There are eight other Algonquin communities in the province: Lac-Rapide, Kipawa, Wolf Lake, Winneway, Timiskaming, Kitcisakik, Lac-Simon and Pikogan. The community of Kitigan Zibi is the largest and most populous of these communities. Among all these Algonquin bands, Kitigan Zibi has a certain political importance. Indeed, it is the host community for the head office of the Algonquin Anishinabeg Nation Tribal Council (AANTC). The AANTC is responsible for "the protection and advancement of the human rights of indigenous peoples, particularly those of the Algonquin Nation, and to provide support to the member communities in human resources management, policy, communications and construction." [25] This council is a figurehead of Algonquin power, as it includes a Grand Chief and a Vice-Grand Chief representing the Algonquin Nation, includes the chiefs of the member Algonquin communities, and has representatives for Elders, women, and youth. Among the Algonquin member communities, six are from Quebec (Pikogan, Kipawa, Kitcisakik, Kitigan Zibi, Lac-Simon and Winneway) and one from Ontario (Wahgoshig). Prior to the signing of Treaty No. 9 in 1906, the Algonquins of Wahgoshig[26] and those who would settle in Pikogan were part of the Abitibiwinnik band whose hunting territories covered areas in both provinces (Bousquet, 2001: 97). The treaty split the band in two (Bousquet, 2001: 97), but the claims of both parties are the same, hence their common affiliation with the AANTC. The AANTC is not the first or only tribal council representing Algonquins. It was created following the dissolution in 1991 of the Algonquin Council of Western Quebec,[27] which had been created in 1979 to represent the bands of Timiskaming, Winneway, Kipawa, Wolf Lake, Pikogan, Lac-Simon and Kitcisakik (Bousquet, 2001: 201). The Algonquin Nation Programs and Services Secretariat, which currently represents the interests of the Algonquins of Wolf Lake and Timiskaming, is the second tribal council created as a result of this dissolution (Bousquet, 2001: 201). Internal dissension has overwhelmed the Algonquin Council of Western Quebec (Bousquet, 2001: 201). The Algonquins of Ontario also form a negotiating team composed of ten communities in that province that claim[28] to be Algonquin.[29] It should be noted that tribal councils are federally funded bodies. The plurality of Algonquin Tribal Councils is due to differing land claim realities, understandings, and interests. Tribal councils are also juxtaposed with other associations, such as the Anishinabe Association and the Algonquin Development Association, which bring together bands from different councils (Bousquet, 2001: 202). As Bousquet notes, "Alliances are made and broken as band chiefs change" (2001: 202). Algonquin tribal politics is complex because chiefs criticize each other (Denoncourt, 2013), the chiefs of a divergent tribal council may take a position in favor of a chief whose band is not a member of the same tribal council (Huot, 2008), not to mention the fact that the delimitation and overlapping of the territories claimed by each band are at the heart of several disagreements. Despite the turmoil, the AANTC is the first tribal council to be referred to most often by authorities when they think of Algonquin superstructures—that is, structures above band councils.

Economically, Kitigan Zibi is also the Algonquin community with the most local infrastructures: beauty salon, physiotherapy clinic, grocery stores, gas stations, sports store, wood yards, printing store, translation center, snack bar, craft stores, transportation and cab companies. Several services unique to this Algonquin community are also offered to the population: funeral home, Wanaki Rehabilitation Center, Waseya Home for Victims of Domestic Violence, Nicholas-Stevens Center for Disabled Persons, Kiweda Home for Seniors. The presence of a national group defending their interests, a thriving economic infrastructure, and specialized services is perhaps a sign of the potential political power of this band.

INTERSTITIAL LEADERSHIP AT THE
HEART OF ANISHINABE POLITICAL IDENTITY

Despite the Canadian government's attempts to break the traditional political structure of the Algonquin people by introducing the elective and political system of the band council, one of its main protagonists is still present today: the chief. However, the power, spheres of influence, conditions, and rules of this role, as well as the qualities and criteria that designate this political actor have changed, thus transforming the forms of leadership[30] and their representations within Algonquin societies. The chief was not the only individual whose leadership was recognized among Algonquians. The end of the semi-nomadic way of life, the establishment of permanent villages, evangelization, and the formalization of politics diminished the importance and even annihilated some of these other leaders while creating others. Chiefs' political ways of doing things have also had to evolve and adapt to the context of the reserves and their institutions. In addition to the role of chief, other formal political leaders, such as band councillors, have also been established. Informal leaders are also present in the community, such as influential members of certain families or individuals involved at the community level. It is clear that Algonquin leadership is no longer the same. The lack of leadership and power among Algonquians has long characterized the thinking of Westerners. In spite of many advances in this area, this perception seems to be still entrenched today.

Analyzing interstitial leadership is the guideline of this book. This approach to leadership draws on both the interstitial perspective theorized by Homi Bhabha (1994) and Kimberly Springer's (2001) postulate about black feminist movements that pursue an interstitial politics commonly referred to as "politics in the cracks." For Homi Bhabha, who was interested in the development of identity among the colonized, a hybrid culture is formed in an interstitial space of negotiation between the ethnic identity of the colonized and that of the colonizer. I would not entirely agree with Homi Bhabha's interstitial perspective, as I believe that interstitial leadership is not a phenomenon of hybridity but rather a characteristic of Algonquian leadership: flexibility. Subjectivity seems to be crucial in the process of defining leadership in a context of social and political change, as the main protagonists at the heart of the transformation make choices, adopt behaviors, and rely on references at the expense of others, thus charting their own path toward a postcoloniality.

Kimberly Springer (2001: 155–56) notes that the collective identity and organizations of Black feminists emerged because their "voices and visions fell between the cracks of the civil rights and women's movements." Black feminists thus theorized and conducted their "politics in the crack" from the interstices of gender, race, and class struggle while inserting themselves into the fissures "of the dominant political opportunity structure as well as into the fissures created by other social movements" (Springer, 2001: 156–60).

For its part, interstitial leadership implies the observation of leadership at the intersection of several juxtaposed categories of classification (traditional authority, legal authority, chief representing the State, intermediate chief, anti-state chief)[31] and the cultural overlap of various traditions, values, and legitimacies through various spaces (imposed or symbolic) and various institutions (formal and informal).

The idea of interstitial leadership exists in relation to Indigenous peoples. Earle Waugh (1996) applied this notion to the religious and liminal leadership of missionary Roger Vandersteene who worked among the Cree. He argues that interstitial leadership is based on both a formal position within a religious tradition and an alternative conception of the sacred encounter, a theological fluidity that was possible within ritual (Waugh, 1996: 299). This fluidity seems possible beyond the special events at the heart of a society (the ritual)—that is, in ordinary, everyday life. Applying Waugh's premise to First Nations actors and the political field suggests that interstitial leadership would be based both on a formal position within a political tradition and on an alternative conception of the encounter of an *Other* political universe. Interstitial leadership emerges from the cracks of a formal system and the crevices of a traditional system under reconstruction.

The interest in interstitial leadership also brings nuances and openness to the study of leadership, as it takes into account ambiguities, contradictions, and paradoxes by considering them not as anomalies but as an integral part of everyday politics. Interstitial leadership makes sense and is an aspect of the political identity of the society in which it takes place. Leadership "in the cracks" is the First Nations margin of power, their manipulation of the Euro-Canadian and First Nations political system and universe.

NOTES

1. By infra-state collectivities I mean groups of actors at the local and regional level, present "below" a State in legal terms.

2. An Indigenous nation is an identity of collective membership linking a set of bands with shared boundaries, history, language, beliefs, and traditions. There are eleven Indigenous nations in Quebec.

3. The terminology used to refer to the "first inhabitants" of this country certainly bears witness to the evolution of currents of thought and "politically correct" attitudes in recent decades. Moving from "Savage," "Indian," "Amerindian" to "First Nation," they have been referred to, since 1982, by the Canadian constitution as "Aboriginal peoples" and, since 1985, by the National Assembly of Québec, as "Aboriginal nations" (Dupuis, 1995a: 21). At the international level, they are referred to as "indigenous, tribal or aboriginal peoples" (Dupuis, 1995a: 21). Because of its etymological meaning the globally accepted term *Indigenous*, "a native," replaced the denomination "Aboriginal" in the Canadian context. However, it should be noted that the traditional names used by Indigenous peoples to identify themselves should be preferred. These numerous appellations will be used alternately throughout this book. The terms *Whites*, *non-Indigenous* and *Euro-Canadians*, which designate Quebec's colonizers of European origin (French, English, Scottish, Irish, etc.) will also be used alternately.

4. Under this system, only Indian men twenty-one years of age and older have the right to vote, thus legally determining the end of Indian women's political participation (Canada, 1996). The consequences of Canadian laws issued against First Nations women will be discussed later.

5. See chapter 9, The *Indian Act*, Section 7, An Act to Provide for the Gradual Enfranchisement of Bands: Responsible Band Government, http://www.collection-scanada.gc.ca/webarchives/20071212235629/http://www.ainc-inac.gc.ca/ch/rcap/sg/sg23_f.html, accessed July 22, 2009.

6. The term *community* is highly variable in its uses. In spite of the fact that it is unfavourable, even ethnocentric, to want to apply a Western definition to Indigenous peoples, the expression community will gradually become commonplace to designate the sedentary Indian bands, the reserves. On the other hand, the term *community* perhaps has a more positive connotation than *the reserve*, which is considered, in many respects, an ethnic "ghetto" by First Nations peoples.

7. Indian and Northern Affairs Canada (INAC) changed its name in 2011 to Aboriginal Affairs and Northern Development Canada (AANDC). The previous name will be used when the pre-2011 period is discussed. Under the Government of Canada's Federal Identity Program, "The new title of the Minister and the department's new name better reflect the scope of the Minister's responsibilities with respect to First Nations, Inuit and Métis. It is also in keeping with practices of the department as, in recent years, the responsibilities of the department have expanded to include and better serve First Nations, Métis and Inuit peoples" (retrieved from the AADNC website http://www.aadnc-aandc.gc.ca, accessed June 8, 2012). In 2015, Aboriginal Affairs and Northern Development Canada (AANDC) was renamed Indigenous and Northern Affairs Canada (INAC). The Latter was dissolved in 2017 and replaced by two departments: Crown-Indigenous Relations and Northern Affairs; and Indigenous Services. It should be noted that only designations prior to 2015 will be used, since the data collected in this work ends in 2014.

8. In Canada, the legal or administrative definition of an Indian dates back to 1850 and stems from the *Act for the better protection of the Lands and Property of the Indians in Lower Canada*. This definition was later adopted and amended. Since 1876, the *Indian Act* has administratively defined who is entitled to Indian status, the criteria for band membership, as well as the territorial and financial parameters applicable to Indians and the regulation of Indian management and succession. The guardianship by Canadian authorities of First Nations peoples, who are considered minors in the eyes of the law, makes them a highly politicized population in all aspects of their lives.

9. See the work of James Frideres (1998), Noël Dyck (1985) and Adrian Tanner (1983) for an understanding of the minority situation of Indigenous peoples and relations with the Canadian state.

10. In general terms, sedentarization corresponds to the fixation on the ground of a population that had a nomadic lifestyle. In contrast, the latter is characterized by the movement of individuals over a territory.

11. Residential schools were institutions set up by the Canadian government and religious authorities. Their task was the training and acculturation of Indigenous children (Anonymous, 1957: 6). In Quebec, residential schools operated from the mid-1930s to the mid-1980s.

12. By hunter-gatherers, I mean peoples who live by hunting, trapping, gathering, and fishing.

13. The band is first of all a concept developed by researchers in an anthropological context where the obsession with the quest for origins still reigns and where it is fashionable to make typologies. The work of Radcliffe-Brown (1931), Steward (1936, 1955) and Service (1962) on the social organization of hunter-gatherers marks the beginnings of the theoretical history of the band and of neo-evolutionism (Lee and

Devore, 1968: 7; Taylor, 2002: 270). The term "band" is applied to the local organization, both social and political, of diverse groups, both in terms of numbers (25–300 individuals) and in terms of where they come from around the world (Damascus, 1968: 117). Until the 1970s, the concept was universalized (Testart, 2002: 136). A nomenclature that reflects only the dominant ideology developed surrounding diverse social and political groups under the general label of the same "society" (Desgent and Lanoue, 2005: 10). In this typological context, the band has a heavy ideological burden, since it categorizes individuals according to stages of "civilization" according to Western notions. Equal status is not accorded to these societies and their organizations are seen as inferior because they come from an *Other* universe that cannot be conceived in Western terms. As an example, George Peter Murdock's 1965 article "Algonkian Social Organization" presents in an evolutionary, general, approximate, all-encompassing, and unjustified way, the regional and typological classification of the social system of all Algonquian-speaking peoples in North America. Since the publication of the book *Man the Hunter* (Lee and Devore, 1968), multiple ethnological research studies have changed the terms of the debate relativizing band data. Researchers then realized that the concepts they were using did not correspond to the same realities (Hirbour, 1969: 1). It is certain that this terminological discrepancy contributed to the confusion surrounding the concept of band. As a result, hasty comparisons are no longer appropriate, and researchers are beginning to delve deeper into areas of investigation related to the band.

14. According to Rogers (1963: 24), there are as many definitions as there are authors on the subject of band.

15. For a history of the Joint Committee to investigate the *Indian Act*, see Leslie and Maguire (1978) and Émilie Guilbeault-Cayer (2016).

16. Chapter 4 will focus more on the inclusion of women in the official political life of their bands.

17. On the subject of the devolution of power to First Nations communities, see chapter 3.

18. Chapter 2 will explore Indian leadership courses and social leadership training.

19. On band membership rules adopted by bands and their implications, see, for example, Clatworthy and Smith (1992) and Clatworthy (2009).

20. Retrieved from the Algonquin Anishinabeg Nation Tribal Council website http://www.anishinabenation.ca, accessed March 8, 2013.

21. Retrieved from the Algonquin Anishinabeg Nation Tribal Council website http://www.anishinabenation.ca, accessed March 8, 2013.

22. *Anishinabeg* is the plural form of *Anishinabe*. *Anicinabek*, and its singular, *Anicinabe*, is a spelling variant of the same ethnonym. In this book, I use both the ethnonym *Anishinabe* and the word *Algonquin*. I use the vernacular term even though it is not commonly used in everyday conversation, as it is the term that is seen in internal documentation from the structures on the reserve and on the facades of the community's buildings. I keep the Algonquin name because the people of Kitigan Zibi still use it when they introduce themselves. It is also the most common name in literature on Indigenous peoples and is more easily identified by the non-Indigenous population to the people of Kitigan Zibi than the ethnonym *Anishinabe*.

23. Based on the Indian Register data as of December 31, 2018, from Indian and Northern Affairs Canada, http://www.ainc-inac.gc.ca, accessed November 3, 2020.

24. Mixed unions in Kitigan Zibi are composed of a band member and a partner from another Indigenous community (either from Quebec, Ontario, or the United States) or of Euro-Canadian origin.

25. Retrieved from the Algonquin Anishinabeg Nation Tribal Council website http://www.anishinabenation.ca, accessed July 16, 2009.

26. Ironically, the federal government registered the Wahgoshig reserve as Ojibwe and not Algonquin (Bousquet, 2001: 97).

27. The Algonquin Council of Western Quebec replaced the Association of Algonquin Chiefs and Councils created in the early 1970s (Riopel, 2002: 96).

28. For a history of Algonquin identity claims in the province of Ontario, see Bonita Lawrence (2012).

29. Based on the *Algonquins of Ontario Land Claim Negotiations* tab from the Ministry of Aboriginal Affairs and Northern Development Canada website http://www.aadnc-aandc.gc.ca, accessed March 8, 2013.

30. The definition of leadership has, of course, evolved over the years but has not reached consensus in the academic community (Northouse, 2012: 2). Nevertheless, the combination of different definitions of leadership offers an operational explanation of the notion. In short, leadership consists of the influence and motivation exerted by an individual, known as a leader, on a social group in the pursuit of a common goal and the taking of actions aimed at changing their situation (Collerette, 1991: 177; Bass and Bass, 2008: 15; Northouse, 2012: 4). For a discussion of the definition and evolution of the concept of leadership in anthropology and social sciences, see Anny Morissette (2013).

31. The observation of a relationship with the state, or the absence of one, is also a promising way to understand the type of leadership of contemporary chiefs. In a book devoted to leadership and political systems in the Pacific Islands, White and Lindstrom (1997: 10–17) consider that in contemporary times there are three categories of chiefs: (1) the chief representing the State; (2) the chief who acts as an intermediary and broker between the State and his locality; (3) the anti-State chief. These authors (White and Lindstrom, 1997: 17–18) argue that, in reality, the different categories of chiefs who seem contradictory can be juxtaposed, and this does not pose any problem for the local populations of the region. The juxtaposition of forms of authority and chiefs' categories reflects the need to break down dichotomies, polarizations, and divisions and explore their margins within the cultural reality under study. This method applied to the Algonquin context allows an opening in the treatment of leadership and the understanding of the role of chief by taking into account the nuances.

Chapter One

The Variability and Flexibility of the Kitigan Zibi Anishinabeg Leadership

The conditions, rules, and qualities that designated an Algonquian chief before and after the imposition of a Euro-Canadian political system are no longer the same. How do we analyze these changes? For Marc Abélès (1992: 25), who has made a major contribution to the development of political anthropology in recent years, legitimacy and representation are inevitable research orientations for understanding the conditions for the establishment and sustainability of political actors. Whether expressed in "words or deeds," as Abélès (1991: 245) points out, representation refers to the profile and symbolism surrounding an individual invested with the power of spokesperson by a group where he or she also embodies in person the identity of that group. According to Abélès (1991: 246), "through representation, atomized subjects become a political body in their own right." This reference to the body politic is relevant since it does not focus solely on official institutions, such as the State. How does one individual more than another come to be a legitimate representative of the body politic? Regarding the notion of legitimacy, Weber (1965) states that it refers to the character of an authority that is recognized by a society. Thus, an individual is designated in a role of authority because of qualities, abilities, values, and capital, to borrow the Bourdieusian expression, which are moral, cultural, and symbolic in nature. An individual in a position of authority may also have political leadership. The notion of political leadership refers to the skills and competencies of an individual, which are necessary to gather, lead, guide his or her community and decisions concerning its governance. What is the legitimacy of the leaders in Kitigan Zibi based on?

This chapter looks at the political history of the River Desert Band from the mid-nineteenth century onward. Among the Algonquins of the River Desert (Frenette, 1993: 43), as is also the case for other Algonquian groups (notably Gélinas, 2000: 82, and 2003a: 196; as well as Lebel, 2003: 23 for the Atikamekw, and Ouellette, 1977: 9 for the Crees), the band's political grouping was not fixed, but was in perpetual recomposition. Thus, there was a movement of individuals who were free to join one band or another according to their interests. This flexibility of political organization reflects fundamental characteristics of Algonquin politics as a whole: political flexibility and variability. Algonquin political organization and autonomy were going to be severely tested by the Euro-Canadians, their laws and imposed structures. Thierry Rodon (2003: 41), who was interested in Indigenous power in comanagement experience in partnership with the Canadian State, explains that "in the context of structures of domination, it is not a question of power sharing but rather of resistance to power, and the autonomy of a group is measured by its ability to resist the dominant power." The authors, in general, tend to speak of Indigenous protest and resistance when they were not passive in the face of Euro-Canadian processes of colonization. For example, Serge Laurin (1991), referring to the "Oka troubles," talks about the history of resistance. Hélène Bédard (1988: 111), who has documented the life of the Innu on the Betsiamites reserve in the years 1850 to 1900, even considers the reserve to be the site of the Montagnais resistance. For Bédard (1988: 111), "the strategies of domination, those of the state as well as those of the missionaries, gave rise to the emergence of a leadership of contestation." What is a leadership of contestation? According to Bédard (1988: 113), the Montagnais seizure of power in 1885, the abolition of the chain of intermediaries linking them to the State, the denunciation of missionary interference and the incompetence of the Indian agent, and the local police officer, the declaration of their situation of dependence, domination, and subjugation, as well as the articulation of their claims to sovereignty and autonomy constitute a leadership of contestation.

It is true that colonization implies resistance on the part of the colonized peoples. However, it is simplistic to speak of First Nations political efforts and First Nations leadership always in terms of "protest" and "resistance." All the more so since the term *resistance* denotes a character oriented towards victimization or a state of reaction. Sherry B. Ortner (1995: 176–77), who was interested in resistance and ethnographic denial, states: "If we are to recognize that resistors are doing more than simply opposing domination, more than simply producing a virtually mechanical re-action, then we must go the whole way. They have their own politics [. . .]" Although there is sometimes resistance, it is not the only driving force behind Indigenous politics. Any analysis on the subject would do well to stop seeing leadership in the dichotomy between resistance fighter and collaborator. It may be a First Nation leadership that agrees and adapts to situations, which corresponds to Algonquian culture. Political leadership among the Kitigan Zibi Anishinabeg was not created just in contestation and resistance, it is also based on various representations (traditional, spiritual, symbolic) at the interstice of several juxtaposed categories of leader type classification. The various representations have allowed Algonquins to preserve a political identity despite certain ruptures and transformations introduced into their society and the continual renewal of the function and role of leader.

Generally speaking, the Algonquian political actor representing the band is called the chief. Until the nineteenth century, the term *captain* was also used. "Captain" is a name of the French colonial administration that appeared as early as the seventeenth century in countries colonized by France. Referring to the Amerindian and Maroon Guyanese chiefs, also called "captains" at that time, Stéphanie Guyon (2009: 59) notes that the French administration "consecrated them as its interlocutors and relays in the populations concerned." It was the same for the Algonquians. In the same vein, the family name "Commanda," widespread among the population of the River Desert, is said to have originated from the term "commandant," also attributed by the colonial authorities. In his French-Algonquin dictionary, Father Georges Lemoine, OMI (1909: 126), translated "commandant" as *Okima*. In the Algonquin language, *Okima* means chief or captain (Cuoq, 1886: 296). According to the lexicon of Ernest McGregor (n.d., 12), a member of the Kitigan Zibi Band, the word is *Ogimà*. It is the term *chief* that was officially adopted from a legal point of view.

The Kitigan Zibi Anishinabeg territory will be discussed first in this chapter, as it is central to their cultural and political identity. It will be followed by a study of key figures in the history of the River Desert, including the first chief of Kitigan Zibi and some of his successors. Thus, the history of the creation of the reserve and its evolution will provide a first glimpse of the transformations of the role of chief (hunting group chief, so-called traditional chief, and band chief) and other leaders (shaman, sub-chief, and councillor) in this community. What place do past chiefs occupy in the Anishinabe daily life? What legacy have these leaders left behind?

THE LAND: THE FOUNDATION OF ALGONQUIAN POLITICS

From the period of contact to the establishment of the band council political system imposed by the *Indian Act*, the traditional Algonquian sociopolitical articulation was based on territory use. It was on the basis of family hunting territories[1] that intergroup interactions and matrimonial ties were articulated to form the social base and the territorial anchorage (symbolic and real) to the band. As the source of primary identity and of daily importance, family hunting territories were the foundation of the band's networking. As noted by Leroux and his collaborators (2004: 212) regarding the Algonquins, the hunting territory was part of a collective territory that was the foundation of a support and mutual aid mechanism, the band. Referring to Turner and Wertman (1977) about the Cree, Guy Lanoue, who has studied the Sekani of British Columbia, mentions that the political identity of hunting groups and bands (local and regional) prior to settlement stemmed "from a common interest, the claim to an ancestral land" (1990: 130). Among the Algonquins, as with other Algonquian groups, the boundaries of a family and a band's territory, although flexible, were known to all and governed according to principles (Davidson, 1928: 31–32; Frenette, 1993: 43, 45). For example, an individual could not hunt with impunity on territory belonging to another band member. Speck (1915: 4) and Davidson (1928: 32) mention that the delinquent hunter was punished by a shaman's casting a spell and sometimes by death. Only starvation allowed animals to be taken from someone else's territory (Frenette, 1993: 45). On the other hand, the trapping of fur-bearing animals was prohibited (Frenette, 1993: 45). Special permission to hunt within the territory of another family could be granted to a hunter "as an exchange of courtesies" (Speck, 1915: 4).

In the same vein, an Algonquian did not hunt on territory belonging to another band either. Thus, prior to sedentarization and mass arrival and colonization by Euro-Canadians, Anishinabe territory was a political space, that is, a territory occupied by Algonquins and recognized by other First Nations. However, in order to preserve a territory, it was still necessary to continue to occupy it. For Lanoue (1990: 131), "the non-occupation of land is seen as an invitation to short-term 'visits' from outsiders, which can easily lead to conflict or even long-term claims if not addressed by band members." In his article on the Abenakis of the Mauricie region, Claude Gélinas (2003a) clearly demonstrates the appropriation by the Abenakis of the Atikamekw and Algonquin territories abandoned in this region. Thus, the Algonquian traditional territory was also a political territory. What was the extent of the River Desert Band's political territory? At the end of the 1920s, ethnologist Frank Speck (1929) traced its boundaries[2] as shown on the map. He states (1929: 98, 100): "The Indians now comprising the River Desert bands are the collected debris of the Algonquin proper who, by clear evidences of tradition and history, resided until 1850 on lower Ottawa river and north of the St. Lawrence eastward to and beyond Montreal."

The management of this political territory and the relations between the hunting groups was not carried out on a daily basis because the Algonquians only gathered during summer gatherings. Since he had excellent knowledge of the territory (for example, geographic boundaries and wildlife management) and of both non-human[3] and human entities within it, it was up to

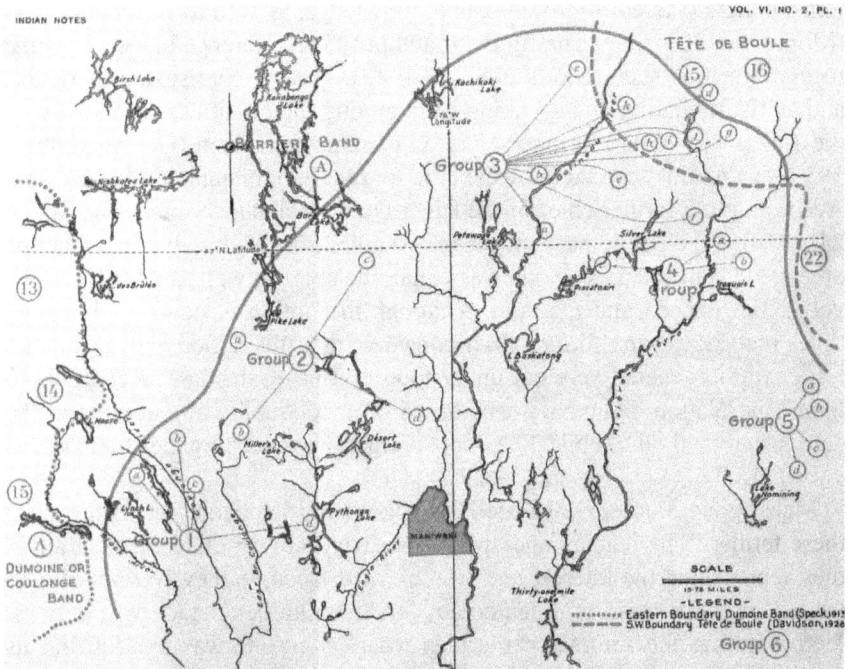

Figure 1.1. **Political Territory of the River Desert Band in 1927 and 1928. Groups 1 to 5 correspond to the different groups of River Desert hunters and their locations (Speck, 1929: 111-112). Group 6 is a remaining group of Algonquins from Lake of Two Mountains (1929: 117). The lower-case letters correspond to the names of the hunters (1929). The uppercase letter A refers to hunters from neighbouring Algonquin bands (1929: 113). Numbers refer to hunters later documented by Speck. For a more detailed explanation of this legend, see Speck (1929).**
From Gatineau and Nispissing Sheets, Nos. 9 and 10, Topographical Maps, Natural Resources Intelligence Service Ottawa

the chief to guide the band in decisions on its governance and to reach a consensus.

The authority of the chiefs was thus closely linked to the territory. This authority had a moral rather than a formal basis (Morissette, 2007: 128) and was not coercive. Moreover, Father Jean-Baptiste Proulx (1892: 211) considers that the authority of the chiefs was nominal. With regard to the Algonquins, Roland Viau (1993: 120–21) mentions that "individuals were masters of their decisions and behaviour and were not intended to be anyone's subjects, and therefore were not coercive." This corresponds to Hannah Arendt's description of the notion of authority, which states (1972: 140, 163, in Bousquet, 2009: 57) that it "implies an obedience in which men keep their freedom." It should be noted that authority can find its legitimacy in traditions, customs, beliefs (sacred or profane), and knowledge, as well as in social values (Morissette, 2004: 13). The figure of authority is a reference in a society that recognizes it as such (Morissette, 2004: 13). Having charisma, experience, and skills in hunting and speaking were among the qualities associated with the Atikamekw chief during the period of semi-nomadism (Gélinas, 2003a: 193–94), and this seemed to be the case for other Algonquian groups as well. According to a former chief of the River Desert (telephone interview, March 24, 2010), the chief at that time was not a more important individual than the others. He states that everyone was equal, the chief as well as the Elders, the youth, the women and the men. Although the notion of equality[4] is sometimes recognized, the former chief considers that this notion and Algonquin leadership in general were not understood by Euro-Canadians. According to him, First Nation democracy was based on this equality among all and the consensual method of collective decision-making guided by the chief and his knowledge.

McGregor (2004: 25) also defines Algonquin democracy at that time in these terms: "The leaders and spokesmen were not absolute rulers. Rather, they represented the interest and welfare of the people they were chosen to lead. This is the basis of a democracy." Algonquin democracy was only effective during the summer gatherings where everyone was present, but its decisions were active during the rest of the year. For example, decisions on the collective management of the territory and its resources were taken during the summer gatherings and their implementation took place throughout the fall, winter, and spring when semi-nomadic families returned to the forest. Respecting these decisions was crucial for the well-being of the entire band. Thus, band members ensured that the renewal of species was protected and that episodes of famine and incursions by other groups on band territories that could have been left unoccupied were avoided.

For some of the Algonquins who would make up the River Desert Band, the Sulpician mission of the Seigneury of the Lake of Two Mountains (Oka)[5] was a summer meeting place where they lived two months a year (Joly de Lotbinière, 1993: 56). It was in 1717, under the French Regime, that the king granted the Seigneury to the Sulpicians "for the maintenance of the Christian Algonquins and Iroquois" (Canada, 1912: 12–13, in Frenette, 1988: 101; McGregor, 2004: 107). Among the "domiciled" Indigenous in Oka, that is Indigenous converted to Catholicism, from 1721 onward one finds mainly Algonquins, Nipissings, and Agniers (Mohawks) (Frenette, 1993: 41; McGregor, 2004: 109). As early as 1763, the Algonquins and Nipissings, wishing to protect their territories from invasion by settlers, approached the colonial authorities (St. Louis, 1951: 7, 9, in Frenette, 1993: 41). At the beginning of the nineteenth century, colonization was progressing along the

Ottawa River due to the growth of the forestry industry (Joly de Lotbinière, 1993: 59). Previously, the Algonquins had no real contact with the Whites on their family territories. With the progression of Euro-Canadian immigration and economic development in the region, it became increasingly difficult for Algonquins to exercise their way of life on their territories (Joly de Lotbinière, 1993: 59).

Among the family groups that occupied a hunting territory in the region surrounding the River Desert (Kitigan Sibi)[6] was that of Luc-Antoine Pakinawatik[7] (McGregor, 2004: 167), spokesperson for the Algonquins of the Gatineau River (Frenette, 1993: 40). As early as the 1830s, Luc-Antoine Pakinawatik, his brothers François Passenjewa and Antoine Pijiw, as well as other Algonquins, cleared land, made gardens, and erected cabins not far from the Hudson's Bay Company[8] trading post (McGregor, 2004: 167; Frenette, 1993: 40–41). At that time, tension was high at Lake of Two Mountains (Day, 1978: 790; Day and Trigger, 1978: 795; Hessel, 1987: 93; Marinier, 1980: 31, Pariseau, 1974: 83–84, in Frenette, 1993: 41, 43). Marie-Pierre Bousquet (2001: 94–95) summarizes well the reasons that explain the departure of the Algonquins from Oka and the creation of the River Desert Reserve:

The Iroquois rebelled against the influence of the Catholic priests and brought in Methodist priests. The Algonquins decided to go and found with their priests a new Catholic mission (Speck, 1923: 226).

Beginning in the 1840s, the Amerindians of Oka tried to emancipate themselves from the tutelage of the diocese of Montreal and to reclaim the land on Lake of Two Mountains that they considered their own. They decided to cut wood on the mission lands to sell, without the consent of the Sulpicians. . . . As the climate was deteriorating, the Algonquins agreed to move to live on reserved land next to the parish of Assomption-de-Maniwaki, opened by the Oblates in 1844.

Bishop Guigues, the Oblate bishop of the new diocese of Bytown, put pressure on the government authorities to open a reserve for the Algonquins to make them sedentary Catholic farmers (Gaffield, 1994: 229).

The Algonquins continue to live in a semi-nomadic way, travelling up the Ottawa Valley to go trapping. [. . .] Agriculture and forestry were already encroaching heavily on their hunting grounds (Larose, 1988: 162). The chief of the Algonquin community of Oka . . . , Antoine Pakinawatik, therefore demanded that land be reserved exclusively for the Algonquins (Black, 1989: 63).

The efforts made since 1845 by Luc-Antoine Pakinawatik to obtain a land reserved for the Algonquins culminated in August 1853 with the creation of River Desert Reserve Number 18 (McGregor, 2004: 170–72). In 1853, there were twenty-eight Algonquin families established on this site and, in 1854, about twenty-five families lived there year-round (McGregor, 2004: 178, 182, 183). In fact, it was in the summer of 1854 that the first Algonquin families from Lake of Two Mountains settled on the reserve (McGregor, 2004: 178).

LUC-ANTOINE PAKINAWATIK, WAMPUM KEEPER

The demands of the Algonquins of Oka for a reserve not only followed the Euro-Canadian way of doing things by way of petition but also took on a First Nation political color. To claim the territory of the reserve from the authorities, Luc-Antoine Pakinawatik used, according to Arthur Einhorn (1974: 76), a First Nation political document: a wampum belt. Decorated with shell beads, wampum belts served several functions: "pledge, message bearer, reminder, fetish, proposal of marriage, ornamentation, tribute, 'blood-money,' ransom, document of peace and/or war, present, conciliation, condolence, symbol of leadership, religious activity and political document" (Speck, 1919: 32–56, in Einhorn, 1974: 83). Joly de Lotbinière (1993: 55) describes how wampums were also used as diplomatic objects exchanged following agreements (Joly de Lotbinière, 1993: 55). They symbolized the commitment of two parties (ibid.). The arrangement of shell beads on the belt evokes events and ideas (55). Thus, each pictographic (e.g., human figures) and geometric (Lotbinière, 1993: 55, a hexagon, a diamond) motif is a key to deciphering the meaning of the wampum and its use (Einhorn, 1974: 79). There are three wampum belts in Kitigan Zibi, one dating from approximately the 1400s and the other two from the 1700s (McGregor, 2004: 315–17). Arthur Einhorn[9] (1974) and Pauline Joly de Lotbinière (1993) have documented various interpretations attributed to the River Desert's wampums. Replicas of these wampums are on display at the community's cultural center, which is a sign of their historical importance to the Kitigan Zibi Anishinabeg. There is no doubt that these belts are material and ideological witnesses of the political heritage. But has the government recognized the validity of the wampum belt presented by Luc-Antoine Pakinawatik to claim the territory of the reserve? With the little information available on this subject, it is difficult to further clarify the role played by the wampum in the creation of the reserve. However, the historical and ethnographic data collected clearly show that wampum belts were, and still are, flagship symbols of leadership for the Algonquins of the River Desert. Indeed, not anyone can become a wampum keeper.

The "wampum keeper" is the person who oversees the protection, conservation and interpretation of these shell belts. Jean-Marie Therrien (1986: 17) notes that "the Amerindian chief is the depositary, the guardian and the interpreter of the shell belts: he must circulate this richness, this collective memory." Being a wampum keeper is not just an honorary role or simply a symbolic function, it is a social responsibility towards a community. Luc-Antoine Pakinawatik[10] was the keeper of four wampum belts that were passed down to him through heredity (McGregor, 2004: 219). This made him a custodian not only of artifacts, but of Algonquin history. Luc-Antoine Paki-nawatik was designated as the first chief of the reserve. His role as wampum keeper may have played in his favor in this nomination. Two other reasons for choosing Pakinawatik as chief of the band are stated by McGregor: "The lands around the River Desert region were the traditional hunting territories of Luc-Antoine Pakinawatik's family line, so it was with this respect that he was chosen by the River Desert Algonquins to become their first chief" (McGregor, 2004 : 219); "Also, Pakinawatik's efforts helped to establish the River Desert reserve, and so he had already demonstrated the capacity for the chieftainship role" (McGregor, 2004: 178). Moreover, Pakinawatik was what is known as a "second chief" or a "sub-chief,"[11] a role within the Algonquian groups that will be discussed in greater detail later, at the Lake of Two Mountains Mission (Gidmark, 1980: 17, in Joly de Lotbinière, 1993: 59; McGregor, 2004: 169). This political past and the experience gained from this position certainly contributed to recognition by his peers.

Luc-Antoine Pakinawatik was also a hereditary chief, a role passed down by his father. The function of chief was also hereditary among other Algon-quian groups, including the Atikamekw (Davidson, 1928), the Abitibiwinnik (Poiré and Moreau, 1840: 57) and the Montagnais (Lips, 1947). According to Davidson (1928: 25), only a few exceptional conditions meant that patrilineal transmission was not respected. However, Davidson does not specify what these exceptional conditions were. Claude Gélinas (2003b: 193) suggests that he was probably referring to a situation where "a chief had no sons or when the sons of a chief were too young or unfit to succeed him." With re-spect to the Mistassini and Lac-Saint-Jean bands, Lips (1947: 400) mentions that in the absence of a son, the brother of the hereditary chief succeeded him and specifies that in the absence of an heir, a new chief was elected. Claude Gélinas (2003b: 193) proposes, with regard to the Atikamekw, that the hereditary transfer of the role of chief should be a common practice at the hunting group level and that the Atikamekw may have wanted to extend this practice to the band level. It is possible that this was the case for the other Algonquian groups. Nevertheless, it can be assumed that the legitimacy of hereditary chieftaincy rested on the fact that the son could benefit from the knowledge and experience of the father and that he enjoyed the proximity of this moral authority which could influence him and, at the same time, train him as a future chief. It appears that not all Algonquin communities[12] prac-ticed hereditary chief role.

THE END OF THE HEREDITARY CHIEF ROLE

Following Pakinawatik's death in 1874, controversy surrounded the first election of the River Desert Algonquins, as evidenced by the Department of Indian Affairs' archives and the band's ethnohistory (BAC, RG 10, vol. 1934, file 3567; McGregor, 2004: 220–21). According to McGregor (2004: 221), John White, the Indian agent[13] responsible for implementing Indian policy on the reserve, "set the election for September, but did not inform most of the Algonquins, who were making ready to return to their winter hunting territories." According to McGregor (2004: 220), Agent White wished to have Simon Odjick elected, but his motive was unclear. A letter written to the Minister of Indian Affairs by Father Régis Déléage, OMI, a missionary working in Maniwaki, corroborates the facts stated by McGregor and offers a clue as to Agent White's motive (BAC, RG 10, vol. 1934, file 3567). In his letter, Father Déléage not only suggested that the department not hasten the election in the absence of the Algonquins but suggested that Agent White wanted to elect a leader who "would share his views." (BAC, RG 10, vol. 1934, file 3567) Despite the sudden death of Agent White, his successor, Agent C. L. Baudin, still held the election in September and Simon Odjick was elected at the expense of Peter Tenasco (McGregor 2004: 221). In her book on the Algonquin chiefs of the River Desert, Jenny Tenasco (1986: 2), also a member of the Kitigan Zibi community, writes: "Chief Peter Tenasco, being the late Chief Pakinawatik's son-in-law, was next in line to be the next Chief." Frank Speck (1929: 118), who conducted research within the band in the 1920s, makes a similar point, but with an additional nuance: "The nephew of this chief, on his sister's side, Peter Tenasco [. . .], married Paki'nowatik's daughter, a case of cross-cousin marriage in the ruling family. Incidentally, Peter Tenasco would have assumed the hereditary rank had this form of headship been continued. The elective system was adopted at this period." Thus, it is clear that the hereditary handover could also extend to a son-in-law and/or nephew. Furthermore, McGregor notes an additional reason for choosing Peter Tenasco as Pakinawatik's successor chief: "With the title of wampum Keeper, Peter Tenasco would also assume the chieftaincy of the River Desert Algonquins [. . .]" (McGregor, 2004: 220). This excerpt confirms that being a wampum keeper was a sign of legitimization of an individual's leadership.

Given the circumstances that naturally pointed to Peter Tenasco as Pakinawatik's successor, what could have motivated Simon Odjick to run for chief? Simon Odjick was an Algonquin belonging to a group of families from the Lièvre River,[14] including the Tshishkanti (Decontie), the Shishib[15] (Whiteduck), the Commandant, and the Jacko-Natawesi (McGregor, 2004: 220). This grouping was formed by a split of the Algonquins of Oka that occurred shortly after the 1800s (McGregor, 2004: 220). McGregor (2004: 220) explains the departure of this group as follows: "They had enough of the Sulpician priests at Oka and, as recent evidence might indicate, they also had enough of the pro-Catholic Algonquins at Oka." Unable to obtain their own reserve, these families joined the River Desert Algonquins between 1870 and 1885 (2004: 181). But the Catholic influence was once again very strong at River Desert and the Algonquins of Lièvre River wanted their traditional way of life and beliefs to be respected (2004: 220). According to McGregor (2004: 220), it was for this reason that Simon Odjick had run for chief. Given that the traditional way of life and beliefs are at odds with Catholic ideals and beliefs, it is not surprising in this context that Father Déléage, OMI, had an unflattering view of the new Chief Simon Odjick and the group he represented: "The other group was a collection of all sorts of Indian tribes and various Métis. . . . They were the most wicked, drunkards, immoral, etc." (Archevêché d'Ottawa, *Registre des lettres de Mgr Duhamel*, p. 53, in Carrière, 1968: 137). Dissatisfied with the results and the manner in which the election was conducted, another group of Algonquins on the reserve protested in writing to Indian Affairs (BAC, RG 10, vol. 1934, file 3567; McGregor, 2004: 221). It is often mistakenly believed that the grouping of individuals on a reserve is homogeneous. In reality, it is the amalgamation of several microgroups that, although they have cultural similarities, sometimes have divergent views and ways of doing things. In addition to the Lièvre River subgroup that joined the Algonquins of Lake of Two Mountains to form the River Desert reserve, there are also the Gatineau River subgroup, the River Desert subgroup, the Baskatong Lake subgroup (including the Smith, Tolé, and Carl families) as well as the Coulonge River subgroup (Speck, 1929; Frenette, 1993: 41–43). In 1873, there were still sixty-six Algonquins remaining at Lake of Two Mountains (Frenette, 1993: 43). In 1929, Speck (1929: 116) notes that documentation concerning the families living there remained to be done. It was in January 1878 that Indian Affairs held new elections at River Desert, and this time Pakinawatik's nephew and son-in-law, Peter Tenasco, was elected (McGregor, 2004: 221). The choice to hold the election in January seems surprising. Were not the majority of Algonquins, once again, on their winter hunting territory at that time?

This controversial first election on the reserve raises several interesting points. First of all, we note that long before the *Indian Act* was established in 1876, the Indian agent orchestrated elections at River Desert. He was certainly trying to gain control over the band's affairs. But what is particularly noteworthy about this episode in Algonquin political history is that nowadays, in the chronology of Kitigan Zibi chiefs found at the band council, on the internet site and in books written by community members, Simon Odjick does not appear as the chief who succeeded Pakinawatik. Simon Odjick's mandate from 1874 to 1878 is overlooked. The chronology of the band chiefs grants the mandate from 1874 to 1884 to Peter Tenasco. Despite Simon Odjick's election, did the Algonquins of the River Desert consider Peter Tenasco their legitimate chief? Is this omission a way to challenge the election again or to deny Simon Odjick's role as chief? Simon Odjick's leadership was certainly appreciated, as he obtained a second term as chief from 1884 to 1890. This was followed by another term as leader by Peter Tenasco from 1890 to 1896. One could thus say that at this period the power within the reserve oscillated between the Lièvre River group and the River Desert group. Jenny Tenasco (1986: 4), in her chronology of chiefs of the reserve, after also omitting Simon Odjick's first term and indicating Peter Tenasco as the first elected chief of the reserve from 1874 to 1884, however, specifies in his second term: "Previously, he was recorded as being Chief for only three years." Does the lack of further explanation mean that the first election and Odjick's first term as chief is also erased from the collective memory of the Kitigan Zibi Anishinabeg? McGregor's account of that first election (2004) rectifies this omission. Thus, McGregor reappropriates the political history of the reserve and offers, through his explanation of this political episode, his Anishinabe vision of the events.

VARIATION IN TYPES OF LEADERS AND THEIR ROLES

Even if a leader continues in office, this does not necessarily imply that his or her leadership role remains the same. For example, after describing Peter Tenasco as wampum keeper and natural successor to the hereditary Pakinawatik chief, McGregor (2004: 225) refers to Peter Tenasco as an "Indian Affairs chief." What does this mean? First, it indicates that he was elected according to the principles of the *Indian Act* (2004: 225). At River Desert, the band council system as a political apparatus was also introduced in the early years following the passage of the Act in 1876. This is suggested by Tenasco (1986: 3), who mentions that there was a council meeting in 1884. Were the Indian chiefs collaborators? This does not seem likely, since the role was not a choice but rather imposed, and the First Nations had to deal with it. But this role does not imply that the chiefs in place did not have any room for maneuver in the system and did not represent certain Anishinabeg values. Despite the fact that the *Indian Act* was in force, the Anishinabeg criteria for selecting a chief still seems to have persisted since, as mentioned earlier, Jenny Tenasco (1986: 2) and Frank Speck (1929: 118) felt that the logical choice for Pakinawatik's successor was his nephew, his son-in-law. As was observed among the Atikamekw of Manawan (Morissette, 2004: 90–95), an individual's ancestry has an influence on the choice of a chief, notwithstanding the establishment of the *Indian Act*. It is difficult to describe in detail the range of Anishinabe criteria for selecting a chief since there is little data on the issue. But what is certain is that there appears to have been different types of leaders despite the legislated imposition of a different type of election, as this excerpt from a 1998 interview with Edward (then seventy-eight years old) shows:

> My dad, but my daddy he was different than the others he was, we call Indian Act Chief the one that goes in council with the people. Then my daddy was tradition. He had a whole group of people. [. . .] He was a chief of a tradition way and chief on a government way. He was doing two things (interview conducted in Kitigan Zibi November 11, 1998, Kitigan Zibi Anishinabeg Global Research Project).

John B. Chabot, the father of this Elder, served as chief for three terms: the first from 1920 to 1924, the second from 1924 to 1927 and the third from 1939 to 1951. Edward implies that his father was not only an elected chief under the *Indian Act*, but a traditional chief. According to Toby Morantz (2002a: 227), "The Indian Affairs chiefs were not necessarily the traditional chiefs; they served different functions." Based on Leacock's (1954: 21) work on the Montagnais, Rogers (1965: 277) also mentions the coexistence of two types of leaders: "He is termed 'government' or 'outside' chief in distinction to the 'real' or 'inside' chiefs who are the leaders of hunting groups." According to Morantz (2002a: 227), chiefs or traditional leaders were usually Elders, who possessed a certain wisdom and supernatural powers that made them highly competent hunters. Indian affairs chiefs, on the other hand, needed other qualities to intercede on behalf of the band with government officials (2002a 227). Claude Gélinas (1998: 27), who took an interest in the Atikamekw band chief in the second half of the nineteenth century, considers that the Atikamekw chiefs had to possess new requirements for this function, including diplomacy.

What does the position of traditional chief at the River Desert refer to? The Algonquins of the band do not all seem to agree on this question, as evidenced by the words of a former elected official in an interview on May 2, 2008 (Charles, sixty-three years old, Kitigan Zibi):

> There are different views on the issue of traditional leadership. In the old days, the way society was organized among the nomadic Algonquin people was not that there was a grand chief as such. [. . .] There used to be multi-family groups where you had about thirty people from a group hunting together with a leader of the group who was a good hunter and knew the territory well, and he still

leads the group. And if he doesn't do the job, the group puts someone else in. Then there is no guarantee that he will stay there all his life, but many times he is the one who stayed there because he was very knowledgeable. But sometimes there were automatic changes. The group gets together and then says that it doesn't work anymore and that it's going to take someone more knowledgeable, more articulate and who plans better and he replaces him quickly. [. . .] The first chief of the community that was founded in 1853 was recognized [. . .] as perhaps a traditional chief in a sense that they kept him for a long time and they tried to adopt a hereditary mode.

Since John B. Chabot "had a whole group of people," is it reasonable to believe that he was the chief of a multifamily group? In the data collected by Speck (1929) on the boundaries of hunting groups in the River Desert Band, we note the presence of a J. B. Jabot[16] on the Lièvre River basin (see Group 3-e, Figure 1.1.). Frenette (1993: 39, 41), who took over Speck's work in 1987 and brought new data on the use of this band's territory, confirms the presence of Jean-Baptiste Chabot at the head of a multifamily group. The 1924 census of River Desert families, compiled by the Department of Indian Affairs (Speck, 1929: 111), mentions the presence of a single J. B. Jabot. It is therefore Chief John B. Chabot. Following the gradual invasion of the Algonquin ancestral territories (notably by the forestry industry, colonization and sports recreation), Frenette (1993: 49) concludes: "The mode of occupation and use of the territory based on the system of family hunting territories was disturbed from the end of the nineteenth century to disappear completely at the end of the 1940s." Since the traditional leadership system was based on this form of land occupation, it is possible that this type of leadership in Kitigan Zibi may have declined along with the family hunting territory system. However, another possible explanation as to why Chief Chabot was considered to be a traditional chief is possible.

According to several oral history testimonies collected during the Global Research, there was a period without a chief in Kitigan Zibi in the late 1920s. Victor (eighty-three years old) remembers this episode:

Jean Baptist Chabot, Michel Côté, and Jim Brascoupe were the chiefs back then. We did not have a chief for a long time. Afterward, my father became chief.[17] [. . .] In the late 20's, around 1926 or 28, there was no chief or council. At that time, the people elected my father for chief. At that time, a traditional movement was introduced. Chief John Chabot became traditional and this caused a division amongst the people (interview conducted in Kitigan Zibi on December 7, 1998, Kitigan Zibi Anishinabeg Global Research Project).

The traditional movement referred to by this informant is the Six Nations movement. Born in the United States and southern Ontario, this movement quickly became successful in Canada and also in the River Desert (Bouchard, 1980: 210–11). It aimed to "recognize the sovereignty of the Indian nation" by advocating a return to traditional values (1980: 211). Through this movement, American and Canadian Indians wanted to be compensated by governments for encroaching on their territories and logging (Clermont, 1982: 116). They also wanted to take legal action for the breach of agreements between Indian nations and the British Crown (Joly de Lotbinière, 1993: 65). In his interview, Victor mentions that Chief Chabot has become traditional: does he imply that he was not traditional before? Becoming traditional in this case seems to refer to adhering to the Six Nations movement's line of thinking oriented toward traditional values and the protection of a past heritage. Thus, being a traditional chief in the sense of hereditary leadership, or chief of a family hunting territory, should not be confused with being a chief who adheres to a political philosophy of protecting tradition. However, there is nothing to prevent being both a family hunting territory chief and an adherent of a traditional political philosophy.

About Chief Chabot, Tenasco (1986: 10) writes: "It seems that the Chief was always fighting for our rights and reminded the people that it was important to keep our language and tradition." The struggle for indigenous rights and awareness of cultural preservation is not a recent phenomenon among the Kitigan Zibi Anishinabeg. Is that why the Six Nations movement has been popular on this reserve? In his memoirs, Father Joseph-Étienne Guinard, OMI, recounts the arrival in Obedjiwan of one of these messengers as follows: "They [Obedjiwan's men] sat on their heels and listened to a stranger sitting on a chair holding an old beaded headband in his hand and giving lengthy explanations of its value and meaning. At his feet was a chest containing headbands, necklaces, helmets, calumets, eagle feathers, papers and insignia" (Bouchard, 1980: 213). Father Guinard, OMI, who was in total disagreement with what he saw in this assembly, immediately interrupted this meeting. But, elsewhere, the movement was gaining followers. Father Guinard, OMI (Bouchard, 1980: 212), explains the spread of the Six Nations movement and the reasons why Kitigan Zibi finally found itself without a chief:

> The repercussions of this movement were first felt in Maniwaki, Lake Victoria, La Barrière. American Indians invited Canadian Indians to rise up and join them in a large rebel assembly in Brantford, Ontario. Several Indians from Maniwaki and the surrounding area joined together and traveled to attend the assembly. They returned completely fanatical and overzealously undertook a propaganda campaign aimed at enlisting other Indian villages in Quebec. Faced with the situation, the Department of Indian Affairs had to crack down. It dismissed Jean-Baptiste Chabot, then chief of Maniwaki, and declared the foreign troublemakers outlaws. The struggle continued in secret.[18]

It was on the margins, "in secret," that Chief Chabot's leadership continued. As Steven Bovee[19] explains about organizational behavior in business
management, "leading in the cracks" means exercising a subtle influence,
knowing how to find the right partners and favoring the use of the informal
rather than the formal to establish one's authority and legitimacy. Bovee's
comments apply to interstitial leadership in indigenous context, since the
Algonquins can exercise power over their own people by taking the right
partners, such as those involved in the Six Nations movement, and not going
through formal channels. Chief Chabot's hidden struggle is an indirect and
silent act of resistance. Chief Chabot's political legitimacy does not rest on
his position as elected chief, nor only on this underground practice of resistance, but on the symbols of Algonquin culture that he embodies and defends.

The removal of Chief Chabot from office by Indian Affairs was not well
received by the population of River Desert. In her book on the Algonquin
chiefs of the River Desert, Jenny Tenasco states (1986: 10): "The reserve was
divided during these years. Some band members wanted to do away with the
Indian Act and others did not." According to McGregor (2004: 279), "The
Indian Act was at the root of the political split. Pien Kijemite's followers
wanted the *Indian Act* removed from the community's affairs." In that vein,
Pien Kijemite's group wanted to return to traditional culture (2004: 280).
Who is this man?

THE POLITICAL MOBILIZATION OF A SHAMAN

Pien Kijemite is not designated as a chief under the Act or a sub-chief in the
Algonquin Chief Chronology.[20] Nor does he appear on the list of seventy-
eight chiefs of the River Desert family drawn up by Indian agent Ernest S.
Gauthier in the late 1920s (Speck, 1929: 108–10). In interviews on the oral
history of Kitigan Zibi conducted for the community's Global Research Project, the Elders interviewed about Pien Kijemite reveal very little about him:
"Well, me I've heard of his name many times, Old Chimmity, ya, ya! But
actually I can't say, I don't know where he was from this man. I don't know
if he was born in this reserve or probably from another area. I don't know"
(Terry, sixty-two years old, interview conducted in Kitigan Zibi on November 20, 1998, Kitigan Zibi Anishinabeg Global Research Project).

Although they say they remember him, comments about this man focus on
the lot he occupied on the reserve and the lady who took care of him because
of his advanced age. Where did Pien Kijemite come from, and what authority
did he use to lead this protest movement within the band in the 1920s? Only
McGregor (2004: 247–48, 251) paints a portrait of this man:

His name was Pierre-Kijemite Chevalier. He was an old man, but no one knew how old he really was. "Kijemite" was how the Oblate priests at Maniwaki heard and spelled Pierre Chevalier's traditional Algonquin family name, Kichi Mide, which translates in context to "Great Medicine Man." The Algonquins at River Desert knew him as either Pien Kijemite or Pien Chimity, which was a corruption of his proper surname. . . . The genealogical records indicate that Pien Kijemite was the grandson of the Algonquin warrior Amable Chevalier, the first Algonquin to be given a commissioned officer's rank in British colonial army during the War of 1812. Lieutenant Amable Chevalier was a military leader and obviously a great one, highly valued by the British to be awarded an officer's commission. As an officer, Amable Chevalier was entitled to regular pay for his military service and also to a military pension. To be awarded these benefits by the British gives some indication of Amable Chevalier's leadership qualities, a trait which was passed down to his descendants, one of them being Pien Kijemite. Whereas his grandfather was a military leader, Pien Kijemite was a spiritual leader. Amable Chevalier was a great warrior; his grandson Pien Kijemite became a great medicine man. . . . Pien Kijemite lived like a wanderer. He visited among the River Desert Algonquins, had tea with them, a meal and sometimes they laid down an extra bedding of straw for him to spend the night. It was believed that he did own a small shack, its location thought to be along Bitobi Creek in the darkly wooded area somewhere behind the Holy Rosary Church. For any man who preferred to live away from the watchful eyes of the Oblates and the Indian Agent, this area of Bitobi Creek made sense. . . . Pien Kijemite was a short, stocky man and he was elderly, so he did not have the physical capacity to fight the Eurocanadians. But he did possess spiritual power and it was this form of power that scared the Oblates and the Indian Agent. The RCMP could handle physical force, but not invisible spiritual force.

McGregor (2004: 251) also mentions that Pien Kijemite was the head of a secret society that performed traditional dances and ceremonies. He also questions the extent of Pien Kijemite's medicine man powers and whether or not he had reached the stage of shaman (2004: 252). Marie-Pierre Bousquet (2009: 57) notes that historically there are three categories of individuals among Algonquians whose leadership was recognized: chiefs (of bands or family groups), the best hunters, and shamans. According to the information gathered, although Pien Kijemite may not have been an Algonquin of the band, he was recognized as a leader, mainly because of his spiritual authority and powers. McGregor also suggests that, like the hereditary transfer of the role of chief, Pien Kijemite's ancestry provided him with legitimacy through the transmission of a certain reputation and leadership qualities, even though he and his grandfather did not exercise leadership in the same field.

For McGregor (2004: 248), it seems normal that some Elders in the community do not remember Pien Kijemite because, in the 1920s and 1930s, the Algonquins of River Desert were not constantly at home on the reserve.

Moreover, it seems curious that the information about Pien Kijemite shared by the Elders during the interviews on the overall research is so uninformative. This suggests that either the secrecy and confidentiality about this man and his past activities continues or that this man was truly a shaman. In the latter case, according to observations in various Algonquin communities, Algonquins do not speak openly and lightly about shamans. For them, shamans and shamanism are taboo themes. For example, no one would dare to talk about a shaman through modern means of communication such as the telephone or email. There is an appropriate time and place to talk about it. The wood is still today a privileged place to discuss it. And even in this environment, information is not transmitted to everyone. For example, it is rare for an Algonquin to discuss it with non-Indigenous.

Is it surprising to note that a spiritual leader, a shaman, can get involved in the political world by leading a political protest movement? Among Algonquian groups, shamans were not only responsible for relations with the supernatural world.[21] They also had a role of mediator between men. Shamans held disciplinary power[22] because their recognized authority gave them moral direction and regulation of the band. The words of Julius Lips (1947: 476–77) about the Montagnais-Naskapi bear witness to this:

In the life of the Montagnais-Naskapi, shamanism and all that goes with it play a very important role. In the present connection, however, we are not concerned with the religious or magic aspects of this institution but solely with the functions exercised by the shaman in the sphere of the customary law of the Indians. Also the social and economic functions of conjuring have been merely sketched, as far as they are directly connected with the legal aspect. In the realm of the law-enforcing agencies the shaman is one of the most important pillars. [. . .] Beside these factors of time and emergency there may, of course, exist additional reasons inducing an Indian to call upon a shaman in order to secure his assistance. It may be that an Indian prefers a settlement brought about by the shaman and therewith displays a stronger confidence in the powers or the personality of the conjurer than in any other law-enforcing official and that to him the world of spirits and their verdict is more real than that of any other legal body. Furthermore—and this is the most important point—an Indian who has succeeded in interesting a shaman in his case has thereby won a representative who is not only willing to make the complainant's cause his own but who is ready as well to assist him with all the magic powers which are at his disposal. [. . .] The informants' reports seem to prove that the law-enforcing agencies of the shaman, the chief and the Company manager are co-existing and that they function independently of each other. [. . .] The shaman does not administer justice, neither does he pronounce or execute sentence. All this is the task of the "court" of spirits which, however, stands to a higher degree under the influence and the ability of the shaman than would any other court with any other "lawyer." Certainly the proportion of cases turned over to the shaman is by far larger than that submitted to either of the other agencies. Since hunting is the center point of all Montagnais-Naskapi life these disputes mainly deal with infringements of the hunting rights and the hunting-grounds.

As a leader, Pien Kijemite represented not only Algonquin spiritual values but also the "traditional" Anishinabe system of law and its political ways.

In contrast to the Pien Kijemite group, who opposed and wanted to abolish the *Indian Act*, other members of the band, those who followed the precepts of the Catholic Church, wanted to remain faithful to the existing system established by the Act. In the face of Kijemite's protesters, can the other group of band members be considered collaborators in the system in place? At the heart of this political disagreement, two factions emerged, having not only obviously opposing political positions, but also different religious and cultural visions. Jane Dickson-Gilmore (1999: 432), looking at the emergence of factions among the Mohawks of Kahnawake, notes that the opposition between "heathens" and converts has shifted at the political level to a struggle between conservatives and progressives. By conservatives, she (1999: 430) refers to individuals who wish to preserve beliefs and lifestyles based on the old ways. Dickson-Gilmore sees progressives as people who saw the old Mohawk ways as having certain weaknesses that were at the root of their social problems. Thus, "these converts looked to the Jesuits for success where the old ways had failed, and to lead the Mohawk Nation into a future as prosperous and powerful as their past" (1999: 431).

Does the conservative/progressive dichotomy described by Dickson-Gilmore for the Mohawks apply to the Algonquins of River Desert? McGregor (2004: 280) hypothesizes that Catholics "felt a sense of security with the *Indian Act* because it enforced the prohibition of liquor inside the reserve and also because the *Indian Act* was a law that they had adopted and felt secure with." Although this hypothesis is in line with Dickson-Gilmore's remarks, it seems difficult to verify this postulate because of the lack of documentation relating to this event. Caution should be exercised before labeling a group of pro-legislators as progressive or collaborators without knowing the reasons for their position. Sometimes those who appear to be the most progressive use an allogenic system to preserve indigenous ways of doing things. Also, getting the most out of a system sometimes means taking part in it. This can put band members in uncomfortable positions. It is not surprising that the Catholics confronted the Pien Kijemite group because, as Bousquet (2009: 61) states, "the missionaries actively fought for the disappearance of the power of the shamans." According to McGregor (2004: 252), the Oblates and the Indian agent feared Pien Kijemite not only because he was considered to have supernatural powers, but also because the Algonquin strategy of assimilation would fail if the Algonquins abandoned Catholicism to join Pien Kijemite and his traditional teachings. The protest movement formed by Pien Kijemite is a clear indication that some River Desert Algonquins were not passive in the face of the imposition of Euro-Canadian laws and ways of doing things. They demonstrated resistance to the new ways of doing politics established by the *Indian Act* and questioned the power of Indian Affairs by wanting to abolish this law. Among other Algonquins, McGregor (2004: 252) considers that "Pien Kijemite and his followers did their part to help retain a connection with the traditional Algonquin heritage." Despite the introduction of elections under the *Indian Act*, are there still traditional ways of selecting a chief?

SELECTION AND ELECTION OF A CHIEF

Toward the end of the nineteenth century, Gélinas (1998: 33) mentions that an individual did not impose himself as chief among the Atikamekw: "We did not take power, we received it." In his article on the laws within the Lac-Saint-Jean and Mistassini Bands, Julius Lips offers a possible answer. For Lips (1947: 401), public opinion plays a considerable role in the choice of a chief:

> The election ceremony took place only at the summer place and it could happen that the band remained without a chief for quite some time until public opinion had taken sufficient shape to point to a desirable candidate. A well esteemed tribesman then recommended the "choice of the people" and told the others about the good qualities of the proposed chief. Provided that nobody opposed him this man was elected by acclamation. If more than one highly qualified Indian seemed equally desirable for the office, the oldest would be given preference.

Based on the data collected, being approached by Elders to become chief also appears to be a traditional form of legitimate leadership selection among the Anishinabeg. The most experienced individuals according to custom thus recognize the abilities and qualities of a potential leader who can guide them adequately while ensuring the well-being of the community. This practice continued in Kitigan Zibi until the 1970s, as this excerpt shows: "Then when I returned to the community I was asked if I was interested in becoming a chief. . . . There was an older gentleman who approached me and saw me as a prospective chief" (Charles, sixty-three, Kitigan Zibi, May 1, 2008). This form of appointment by Elders is not unique to Kitigan Zibi. According to information gathered from another Algonquin community in Quebec, this practice was still in use in the 2000s. However, in the latter case, the individual approached by the Elders did not run for election to the band. Even though this Algonquin custom persists, the introduction of elections under the *Indian Act* has led to an electoral process. What does it look like in the River Desert? Elders interviewed during the community's Global Research Project recalled:

> They all gathered to appoint the Chief by a hand vote. Then they united as in to back up the one that they chose (Victor, eighty-three years old, interview conducted in Kitigan Zibi on December 7, 1998, Kitigan Zibi Anishinabeg Global Research Project).

> There was no book work. Those that didn't like the vote did not raise their hand. Those who said, ok, raised their hands (hand vote). Gauthier style around 50 years ago. They just raised their hands never mind that voting at the time and those opposed just sat there (Alexander, seventy years old, and Emma, age unknown, interview conducted in Kitigan Zibi on December 3, 1998, Kitigan Zibi Anishinabeg Global Research Project).

The Gauthier referred to in this excerpt is Ernest Gauthier, an Indian agent on the reserve from 1913 to 1939. Beck (1947: 216), who was present in the community in 1943, provides the following clarification of the election:

> At present, everyone reaching the age of twenty is considered to have reached his majority. From this age until death, he is allowed to vote for the chief, who rules for three years under the auspices of the agent. This title is more honorary than anything else, apparently, as his only power is to speak occasionally for the tribe when necessity demands it.

Several researchers have also found that in their early days, chiefs elected under the *Indian Act* held little power within the formal political system (Rogers, 1965: 276–77; Morantz, 2002a: 229; Gélinas, 2003a: 195–96). Frideres (1998) even uses the term "Puppet Chief" to describe this position. For Rogers (1965: 277), the reasons why the chief has lost power and authority lie in the fact that he no longer has multiple roles. The chief is no longer a religious leader, he is no longer responsible for the redistribution of goods, he has only the support of his band, he has no "policing" power, and he must call on external authorities (Rogers, 1965: 277–78). Finally, band members may have direct access to other authority figures, such as the Indian agent, without the intermediary of the chief (Rogers, 1965: 278). Morantz (2002a: 229) notes that although the chief no longer had real power, he still had a ceremonial role. Thus, his status within the community remained important (2002a: 229).

The role of leadership will undergo several other notable changes during the twentieth century and will be discussed again in the next chapter. Similarly, the system of raised hands as a method of election has become obsolete. According to Marshall (fifty-eight years old, translator, in Oliver's December 7, 1998, interview conducted in Kitigan Zibi, Kitigan Zibi Anishinabeg Global Research Project), the first ballot-based election was used to elect Ernest McGregor in 1970. It has been the same since then. While the introduction of the *Indian Act* changed the role of chief, it probably also contributed to the transformation of the role of sub-chief among the Kitigan Zibi Anishinabeg.

FROM SUB-CHIEF TO COUNCILLOR

What is a sub-chief? It is difficult to answer this question since there is no specific literature on the subject and several terms (second chief, next to chief, assistant chief) within Algonquian populations also seem to be related to it. McGregor (2004: 181) provides a historical background of the role of sub-chief of the River Desert: "It is not documented when the Algonquin political system changed to the concept of chief and sub-chiefs, but it becomes apparent at Oka somewhere after 1763, no doubt influenced by the British who, like the French, felt that the traditional collective decision-making process of the Algonquins was too slow."

McGregor (2004: 197) argues that the introduction of the military chain of command by British commanders to the Allied Indians, as well as the subdivision into platoons and the style of fighting as infantry soldiers, would not be unrelated to the establishment of a chief and sub-chief system: "After the War of 1812, the British maintained this structure of subordinate commanders in its political dealings with First Nations, and it is from there that the Chief and sub-chief system evolved." Unfortunately, McGregor does not mention his documentary sources. The hypothesis seems plausible since these denominations were common in English-speaking Africa and the Pacific. The terms *governor* and *lieutenant governor* were also introduced to refer to Penobscot chiefs in the Maine region of the United States at the same time.[23] Today, these terms have been replaced by the terms *chief* and *sub-chief*.[24] The chief and sub-chief system also extended to the Pacific Northwest coast, as evidenced by its presence among the Snoqualmie in the mid-nineteenth century (Tollefson, 1987: 124). Finally, data show that there were sub-chiefs among the Algonquins of Oka and this role continued when the River Desert Reserve was established (Tenasco, 1986). The first chief of the reserve, Luc-Antoine Pakinawatik, who had been a sub-chief of Oka (Gidmark, 1980: 17, in Joly de Lotbinière, 1993: 59; McGregor, 2004: 169), had as sub-chiefs, until his death, his two brothers François Passenjewa and Antoine Pijiw

(Tenasco, 1986: 1). Jenny Tenasco (1986: 13) notes, in her chronology of chiefs, the presence of sub-chiefs in the band until 1939, that is until the end of Chief Abraham McDougall's term. With the election of Chief John B. Chabot (1939–1951), his third mandate, the term *councillor* appeared (1986: 14). Did the councillors replace the sub-chiefs? Is it the same role and type of leadership? Before answering these questions, it is worthwhile to look more closely at the role of the sub-chief.

What qualities did a sub-chief possess? At the 1933 Manawan elections, Father Guinard, OMI, mentions the selection of assistant chiefs among the Atikamekw and that the latter "have been wise for they have chosen three men [a chief and two assistants] of good character and morals and I think the most intelligent of the band" (AD, 1933, in Gélinas, 2003b: 256). The Atika-mekw seem to have applied similar selection criteria to choose their leaders, whether they were chiefs or sub-chiefs. The sub-chief, like the chief, does not seem to have any power over other band members, as Cooper (1926a: 617, 1926b: 138, in Gélinas, 2003b: 196) noted in Obedjiwan in 1925: "there is a chief of the band with two assistant chiefs, but such political authority as exists is very limited." These qualities can certainly be extended to sub-chiefs in other Algonquian groups. At the heart of the data, it is not always obvious to distinguish sometimes between chiefs and sub-chiefs, as their roles are similar. A former elected official testifies to this:

> Clearly, the chief in the past, you didn't have a structure the way we have it today, in the sense, an issue was formed, we had sub-chiefs. It was the chief and the sub-chief but basically the same role in the council. You know, if the chief wasn't there the sub-chief would act in his place and even to this day, that can be delegated with council members (Charles, fifty-three years old, interview conducted in Kitigan Zibi on December 7, 1998, Kitigan Zibi Anishinabeg Global Research Project).

It seems to be part of the duties of a sub-chief to act as a substitute for the chief in his absence. For example, Marshall (fifty-eight years old), who was a translator and liaison officer for the Kitigan Zibi Anishinabeg oral his-tory interviews, wondered whether sub-chiefs were proxy chiefs (Elisabeth, seventy-four years old, interview conducted in Kitigan Zibi on November 20, 1998, Kitigan Zibi Anishinabeg Global Research Project). Similarly, Alex-ander notes: "As far as I remember, when William was chief, and if William could not attend, John Lambert Cayer would replace him at the meeting and that's what I call a second chief" (Alexander, seventy years old, interview conducted in Kitigan Zibi on December 3, 1998, Kitigan Zibi Anishinabeg Global Research Project). Speck (1915: 20), who documented the Timigami

Band of Ojibway origin in Ontario in the summer of 1913, made similar findings about the second chief[25] function, while providing further clarification:

> Under the old regime the head chief and the second chief[26] had about the same
> rank. If one was absent on a hunting expedition, the other would officiate. Their
> duty was to regulate contact between the band and neighbouring bands or tribes
> and the government. They were always supposed to be planning for the interests
> of the people in one way or another. They took care of widows and orphans and
> it was their duty to preach occasionally on the rules of the camp or upon topics
> in which they thought the people need instruction or encouragement. In this
> lecturing the second chief would generally do the talking, announcing that the
> chief had so and so to say. Should any member of the band behave in a way that
> was considered offensive or detrimental to the band, in other words, do wrong,
> the chief would call a meeting of all the men who would discuss the matter and
> decide what reprimand or punishment to administer. The second chief would
> publicly announce the result.

Another relevant feature pointed out by Speck (1915: 22) about the Timigami Band is that the second chief becomes first chief upon his death. The
experience gained as a sub-chief is therefore not a negligible aspect of ap-
pointing a chief. But at the River Desert, there is no longer a chief for life
at the same time observed by Speck. Thus, after having been chief for two
terms, Simon Odjick was sub-chief under three different chiefs from 1896 to
1917 (Tenasco, 1986: 5–7). Abraham McDougall was sub-chief from 1933
to 1936, during the mandate of Chief Patrick Brascoupé, before being elected
chief from 1936 to 1939. The same is true for William Commanda and Ernest
McGregor who served as councillors before becoming chief. But not all sub-
chiefs or councillors necessarily become chiefs.

Whether he has a similar role, the same rank, whether he replaces the
chief or not, the sub-chief is difficult to discern from the chief, because the
sub-chief is sometimes called "chief." For example, Toby Morantz (2002a:
226), reporting on the speeches of the Cree chief and second chief elected
in Waswanipi in 1934, mentions: "Both the chiefs addressed the band."
In his article dealing with scapulimancy at the River Desert, Speck (1927:
167) mentions Michel Buckshot as one of the chiefs of the band during his
research in 1926–1927. According to data collected by Jenny Tenasco (1986:
11), Michel Buckshot appears to have been a sub-chief during the term of
Chief Simon Odjick (1927–1933). Could there have been one or more chiefs
at the River Desert at that time? Were they different types of chiefs? It seems
that researchers tend to put the word chief in a much more closed category
than what the Algonquins do. In 1943, Horace Beck (1947: 261), who accompanied Frank Speck on his research at River Desert, tells of the elections:
"Formerly, one chief was elected. However, this practice has been somewhat

altered until now three chiefs are elected by majority vote." Beck's remark, however, goes against the words of a former elected official:

> There may have been some cases where people hunt, name themselves chiefs. There has been over the history were people call themselves tradition chiefs and there's elected chiefs. Some confusion that rises sometimes but as long as I can remember, at least from the formation of the reserve, there was only one chief that was formally recognized (Charles, fifty-three years old, interview conducted in Kitigan Zibi on December 7, 1998, Kitigan Zibi Anishinabeg Global Research Project).

Three Elders[27] interviewed for the Global Research Project also confirmed that they were not aware of more than one chief in the community at any one time. However, during Chief Peter Tenasco's second term from 1890 to 1896, Jenny Tenasco (1986: 4) notes: "Since the council remained in their meetings from morning until evening and others who travelled from far, Chief Tenasco requested, for the first time, to have expenses paid for visiting Chiefs." What does the term *visiting chiefs* refer to? Are they chiefs from outside the community or are they chiefs from the family hunting territory of the band passing through the community? Although the event in question is the band council where internal band affairs are generally discussed, the participation of foreign chiefs is not excluded. If the visiting chiefs correspond to the chiefs of the family hunting territory, this designation is in line with Charles' comments. The term visiting chiefs perhaps puts into perspective the fact that some chiefs still live on their territory most of the time and only occasionally come to the reserved territory. If this is the case, it is possible that, until the first half of the 1890s, the Algonquins of River Desert still had several individuals in their group who they considered as leaders. Regarding the Atikamekw, Father Guéguen, OMI, also noted in 1885 that there were two chiefs at Weymontachie (Baribeau, 1978: 87, in Gélinas, 1998: 29). The remarks of Gélinas (1998: 30) may explain the phenomenon:

> Until the late 1820s, there was no single chief among the people of Weymontachie. Still in the process of consolidation, the band at that time had several chiefs, each leading a hunting group. It was not until 1834 that the title of chief was associated with a single individual [...]. [...] In fact, the function of band chief must have been latent within the group, ready to emerge when the context was appropriate. It was only a projection of the role of hunting group chief on a larger scale.

For the Innu, leadership rested on the shoulders of the individual with the best knowledge required by the situation (Ezzo, 1988: 52). Thus, it is possible that there may have been several leaders in Algonquian societies where age was often synonymous with experience. But were these leaders all chiefs? Claude Gélinas (2003b: 190) mentions that the Atikamekw of Weymontachie, Coucoucache, and Manawan elected a band chief in common in the late 1880s. From 1870 to 1891, Coucoucache and Manawan were considered sub-groups of the Weymontachie Band. Witnessing such an election in 1887, Reverend Father Proulx writes (1891: 246, in Gélinas, 2003b: 190):

> Three candidates were in the ranks: Jean-Baptiste Boucher, outgoing chief, Charles Rikatadi of Coucoucache, and Joseph Rochelot of Manawan. The chief of Weymontaching commands all the others, he is the *kitchi okimaw*.[28] It was agreed that the one who gathered the most votes would be the great chief, the other two remaining his assistants. Rikatadi obtained 26 votes, Jean-Baptiste 12, and Rochelot 4.

Is it possible to believe that the River Desert sub-chiefs were leaders of sub-groups of the band? McGregor mentions something that contradicts this hypothesis. Discussing the group from the Lièvre and Rouge Rivers, he writes: "They were traditional in their thinking and they immediately entered a power struggle with the chief and sub-chiefs system installed at River Desert" (2004: 181). Does this mean that the function of sub-chief was alien to these two traditional groups? Is the position of sub-chief among the Kitigan Zibi Anishinabeg an Ojibwe or an Iroquois influence? The information gathered by Davidson from the Atikamekw of Obedjiwan in the late 1920s provides a possible answer. According to this author, the position of sub-chief suddenly emerged in Obedjiwan: "The natives gave no explanation for the creation of the positions of these two sub-chiefs, except the generalization that the chief needed some assistants" (Davidson, 1928: 27). Davidson considers the large population of Obedjiwan at that time, 144 individuals, to have been a determining factor in the creation of the sub-chief role. However, in his view (1928: 27), the establishment of this position may have been the result of diffusion from the southwest. Davidson (1928: 27) provides clarification in a footnote: "The institution of having assistant chieftains is much more regular and permanent in the Ottawa valley[29] and may be of Iroquoian derivation." This Iroquoian origin of the sub-chiefs[30] is very relevant given that the Kitigan Zibi Anishinabeg come from the Lake of Two Mountains Mission that they shared with the Iroquois, the Mohawks.

Another possibility of a foreign origin is possible to explain the emergence of sub-chiefs. There may be a link between the system of chiefs and sub-chiefs and the system of "trading captains" and lieutenants documented by Toby Morantz (1982, 1983, 2002a) among the Crees of Eastern James Bay. Introduced by the Euro-Canadians in the eighteenth century during the fur trade,[31] the trading captain system refers to the Indian leaders responsible for bringing groups of Indians with their furs to the trading posts (Morantz, 1982, 1983: 129). In James Bay, Morantz (1977: 78) mentions that trading captains are identified from 1744 to 1815. After 1815, the captains were designated as leaders or principal men (1977: 79). Morantz (1983: 135) notes that this system was not developed among the Crees but was supposedly imported. Did the terms and function of captain or lieutenant create, through the economic pressure of the fur trade, leaders among the Algonquians where none existed before? It should be noted that it was the individuals at the trading posts who designated captains and lieutenants based on the amount of furs these men brought and the influence they had on other Indians (Francis and Morantz, 1983: 44). But a man could become a trading captain despite questionable moral qualities (Francis and Morantz, 1983: 44): "Even Indians who were deemed untrustworthy or idle were made captains." Unlike the traditional leader who was chosen for a short period of time to perform a specific task based on his skills, being a trading captain was a lifelong position (Francis and Morantz, 1983: 44). Also, those who were designated as captains were relatively young individuals[32] (Morantz, 1977: 81). The trading captain system thus interfered with the sociopolitical organization of the Crees, their leadership system (Morantz, 1983: 135), and its values. It is conceivable that this economic leadership led to a new division of roles among sociopolitical actors and to social stratification.

Francis and Morantz (1983: 42) report that trading captains and their lieutenants were rewarded with military dress. This is evidenced by the words of a Hudson's Bay Company employee, Edward Umfreville (1790: 59, in Francis and Morantz, 1983: 42–43): The clothing consisted of

> a coarse cloth coat, either red or blue, lined with baize and having regimental cuffs; and a waistcoat and breeches of baize. . . . He is also presented with a white check shirt; his stocking are of yarn, one of them red, the other blue, and tied below the knee with worsted garters; his Indian shoes are sometimes put on, but he frequently walks in his stocking feet; his hat is coarse, and bedecked with three ostrich feathers of various colours, and a worsted sash tied round the crown; a small silk handkerchief is tied round his neck; and this completes his dress. The Lieutenant is also presented with a coat, but it has no lining; he is likewise provided with a shirt and a cap, not unlike those worn by mariners.

Yet, McGregor (2004: 181) notes that the British also distinguished chiefs and sub-chiefs by providing them with jackets, hats, novelty items, jewelry, and buttons. During the election among the Atikamekw of Weymontachie in 1887, Reverend Father Proulx (1891: 235) also notes the presence of an honorary object distinguishing the chief: "The silver medal is attached to the chest of the newly elected." According to Gélinas (2003b: 200), the Atikamekw displayed the official decorations they had received as early as the 1870s. Through economic means, that is through unequal access to resources, amenities and positions, is it possible to believe that the notion of Western-style power could have appeared at the same time in Algonquian governance? Morantz (1977: 86) hypothesizes that trading captains were the precursors of "governments chiefs," that is, chiefs elected under the *Indian Act*.

In the same vein, it is conceivable that the title of sub-chief corresponds to the councillor role set out in the Act. Referring to the 1916 Huron elections in Lorette, Patrick Brunelle (1998: 36) reports: "In his report, Agent Bastien states that 'in accordance with the authorization you gave me . . . to elect a chief and five sub-chiefs for the Huron of Lorette tribe, [. . .] [I posted] a notice on the door of the Huron Village church on the 17 [December] announcing that the election would take place on December 28.'"[33]

In addition to formalizing and redefining the role of band chief, the *Indian Act* may also have been intended to transform and include other types of leaders in the formal political organization. Whether he is a chief of a hunting group, a trading captain, or a councillor under the *Indian Act*, a sub-chief is an individual who is considered a leader among his people. The importance is not so much to discover exactly where this political role comes from but what it conveys about a traditional feature of Algonquin politics: political flexibility and variability. Algonquins are continually renewing themselves politically within their system. This is not an effect of acculturation, hybridity, or modernity but a matter of tradition. Sylvie Poirier (2001: 112) notes: "However, just because the Atikamekw no longer practice semi-nomadic way of life does not mean that they have totally abandoned the practices, knowledge, and values of their ancestors." The same analysis can be made about the Kitigan Zibi Anishinabeg and their political universe.

THE END OF TRADITIONAL SKILLS IN A BAND CHIEF

While some traditional values, knowledge, and practices persist, other traditional skills for being a chief have ceased. Jenny Tenasco's 1986 chronology of Kitigan Zibi chiefs is very useful in portraying the chiefs of the reserve and their skills in the twentieth century, as this author also documented and compiled a summary of each chief's accomplishments. There is no need to duplicate here the events surrounding each chief's mandate. However, elements put forward by Tenasco help to capture the role of chief at different times by revealing certain characteristics associated with leaders.

In the early 1900s, it was exceptional for an Algonquin chief to master both French and English in addition to the Algonquin language. Such was the case for John Cayer, chief of the River Desert from 1917 to 1920 (Tenasco, 1986: 8). According to Tenasco (1986: 8), he was thus able to translate for those who did not speak French or English. However, what appears to be crucial is that, by speaking three languages, Chief Cayer is able to interact adequately with a variety of interlocutors who deal with people on the reserve: government representatives (e.g., the Indian agent) or the town of Maniwaki, Euro-Canadian employers, missionaries, and others. (Tenasco, 1986: 8). William Commanda, chief from 1951 to 1970, is also a native Algonquin speaker and has learned French and English on his own (Bousquet, 2001: 388). Ernest McGregor, elected from 1970 to 1976, was so proficient in languages that, following his mandate, he published three editions of an Algonquin language dictionary (McGregor, n.d., 1987, 1994). Recognized by linguists, Ernest McGregor's lexicographical works are an outstanding contribution to the field (see, among others, the review by O'Meara, 1993). The end of McGregor's mandate in 1976 also marked the end of the proficiency of the Algonquin language by the chiefs of Kitigan Zibi. The chiefs elected thereafter are bilingual in English and French or unilingual in English. However, learning the Algonquin language became a priority for Chief Gilbert Whiteduck, who was elected in 2008 (Thériault, 2011).

William Commanda is another example of a chief who had traditional skills related to the world of the forest. Raised in this environment, William Commanda was a recognized artisan (Bousquet, 2001: 388). He knew how to build a canoe and make snowshoes, baskets, and other objects of Algonquin material culture (Bousquet, 2001: 388).[34] In the mid-1970s, traditional skills related to the forest were no longer adequate or relevant to carry out the band's politics, which had become more complex. The following chapters will provide a portrait of a new type of leadership and contemporary politics.

Just as some traditional skills are becoming obsolete, a strong political symbol linked to the Algonquin chief also disappeared in the mid-1970s: the chief's headdress. Indeed, Ernest McGregor is the last chief of Kitigan Zibi to have worn such an ornament. In addition to Chief McGregor, Chief John B. Chabot, Chief Patrick Brascoupé, and Chief William Commanda wore the headdress. According to an online source on a First Nations website aimed at educating the public about the history of the Firsts Peoples of North America, author Lee Sultzman[35] notes: "In the 1800's, some Algonquin chiefs began wearing an impressive feathered headdress like their western neighbours the Sioux." Why did the Algonquins adopt a western headdress? Trudy Nicks (1999) links the Mohawks of Kahnawake's use of images and stereotypes of Indian life in the 1930s to tourism. She notes (Nicks, 1999: 303): "If the choice of representations accommodated twentieth-century tourists' expectations, it was also an authentic expression based on a long history of negotiating

Figure 1.2.   Chief Ernest McGregor, the Last Chief of Kitigan Zibi to Wear the Head-dress
Courtesy of Stephen McGregor, Eric McGregor and the Kitigan Zibi Anishinabeg Cultural Centre

intercultural encounters with Europeans." Not only could tourists expect to see a chief wearing a headdress, but also Euro-Canadians as a whole.

The imposing feathered headdress may be a cliché, but it is undeniably a symbol associated with the Indian chief, a typically Indigenous material political heritage. The wearing of such finery in public ceremonies was not unique to the chief of Kitigan Zibi. Other Algonquin chiefs from Quebec communities also wore it. Several reasons may explain why the chiefs of Kitigan Zibi no longer wear the headdress: personal choice, outdated fashion, rarity of the accessory. The headdress may also represent an imposed symbol designating the official and nontraditional chief, or the traditional chief who wants to become an official chief in the face of Euro-Canadians. In both cases, symbolism emerges from a Euro-Canadian hegemony. It is important to remember that hegemony is much more than domination. It is an ideological construct of the dominant group adopted by the subordinate group, which exercises a re-politicization of the symbol and reproduces, by the same token, the initial system in which dominant and subordinate evolve (Lanoue, 2011: 91). But this symbolic transformation remains a relevant process because, on the one hand, it allows the subordinate group to modify the rules to some extent despite their continued participation in power games (Lanoue, 2011: 91). On the other hand, this transformation taking place in everyday life (Lanoue, 2011: 91) leads us to take a close look at the banal practices of daily life.

THE DAILY OMNIPRESENCE OF PAST CHIEFS

In the daily life of Kitigan Zibi, past chiefs are always visible in both private and public spaces. In fact, several homes on the reserve visited have a copy of Tenasco's (1986) book *Algonquin Chiefs of the River Desert Band*. The past chiefs are also visible in the band council where their portraits adorn the walls of the administrative offices' passageway.[36] The presence of the chiefs is not only a recognition of past leaders; it also represents the political history of the community. As well, a plaque in honor of the chiefs is placed outside the main entrance of the band council.

The affixing of a commemorative plaque contributes to the construction of memory (Sauber, 1993). According to Sauber (1993: 725), "because of their special position, in full view of everyone, they are a way of writing or rewriting history on the public place." This no doubt explains the omission on this plaque and within the official chronology of Simon Odjick's first controversial mandate following Pakinawatik's death.

Having a plaque and the portraits of the chiefs at the band council is a strong symbol when we know that any stranger dealing with the community necessarily transits through this place which is at the heart of everything on the reserve (Morissette, 2004: 97–98). Is the affixing of a plaque and the portraits of the chiefs a political gesture? For Sauber (1993: 725), "plaques are always a political issue." In fact, they are the physical witness to an intangible political heritage. Not only do they recall the men who contributed politically

Figure 1.3.   The Omnipresence of Past Chiefs
Anny Morissette, June 2007

Figure 1.4.   Past Chiefs, a Political Heritage on the Public Place
Anny Morissette, June 2007

to the advancement of the community through their skills and know-how, but they also show the popular choice of band representatives by band members. The text inscribed on the plaque also implies a political message:

> Kidji takwenimindwà anishnàbeg ka pi ogimawidjig Kitigan Zibi anishnàbe akìng kà ako kijeningdagwak 1854 kichi agindàsowin. With great pride and dignity we the people of the River Desert Band commemorate our Algonquin chiefs who have been our leaders since our reserve was established in 1854.

The use of the vernacular language affirms first of all the collective identity of the people of this place and their Algonquin origin. This use of the Algonquin language is a political gesture, a public expression of cultural belonging, a claim to cultural continuity specific to the inhabitants of this reserve. The text brings to the forefront the pride of a people and confirms that the people of the River Desert Band have recognized that their chief is an Algonquin and not a Euro-Canadian since the creation of the reserve. Thus, the message in a way rejects the guardianship of Algonquins by Canadian law. To tourists and visitors, the commemorative plaque affirms that there are still Indian chiefs today, that they are not folklore despite the changes in their role and functions.

Chief Pakinawatik is omnipresent in Kitigan Zibi. Every time an individual from outside the community visits, he is necessarily told about Pakinawatik, the founder of the reserve. A priori, the notion of foundation does not exist among Algonquians, who were semi-nomadic. Speaking of the elements of a theory of foundation, Harris Memel-Fotê (1991: 266) notes: "An action by which something radically new comes into the world, the foundation presupposes one or more founders and a soil. It then consists of a process that produces an object." With Pakinawatik, this notion of foundation emerges among the Algonquins: sedentary life begins on a reserved land. Pakinawatik is not only the historical founder of Kitigan Zibi, but he is also the symbolic character of the victory over the invasion of the settlers. Indeed, his group left Lake of Two Mountains to live on its own reserve, a land that the Euro-Canadians could not appropriate. Despite the historical and symbolic importance of Pakinawatik, its name was not passed on to other chiefs. Among the Algonquin people, it was customary upon the death of a chief to symbolically "resurrect" him by giving his name to his successors. Rémi Savard (1996) has drawn a detailed portrait of the Tessouat Algonquin lineage. This custom was not perpetuated in the case of Pakinawatik: there was therefore a political break. This does not mean that Pakinawatik is no longer important in terms of identity.

In everyday life, Pakinawatik is also omnipresent in a very particular way at the heart of the personal identity of the Kitigan Zibi Anishinabeg. It is frequent that the informants we met, who are in their fifties and over, mention their kinship with this illustrious character. This form of self-presentation is not new to Kitigan Zibi. During his stay in the community in 1943, Beck (1947: 260) notes about one informant:

> Mrs. Buckshot, who was eighty-one years old when we stayed with her, was the wife of Michel Buckshot, deceased, once chief of the tribe. Formerly a Golden Lake Indian, she is the granddaughter of Paganowatik (Lightning hit tree), who was the last true "life" chief and brought the band here seventy years ago from Lac de Deux Montagnes. He is considered one of the great men of the tribe.

What does this reference to Chief Pakinawatik mean? By this affiliation, the Anishinabeg demonstrate the continuity of the lineage of the first chief of the reserve as well as the continuity of their presence. By introducing themselves in this way, the Anishinabeg benefit from a symbolic capital. In a way, it is prestigious to be associated with the founder of the reserve. One could go so far as to say that showing kinship with Chief Pakinawatik also legitimizes an individual's position as a political leader. Indeed, whenever the former elected chief William Commanda was introduced to a crowd, or named in a written article, it is mentioned that he was the great-grandson of Pakinawatik. However, apart from Pakinawatik, the Kitigan Zibi Anishinabeg display their affiliation with only one other past chief, William Commanda. This is indicative of his importance to the community and its history. William Commanda was one of the best-known Algonquin chiefs of this century in America and internationally.

CONCLUSION

The study of Anishinabeg political actors—that is, hunting group chiefs, so-called traditional chiefs, band chiefs, sub-chiefs, and shamans, shows the variability of political leadership among Algonquins and the existence of different types of leaders despite the imposition of a single chief's office by the *Indian Act*. In fact, the category "chief" is open to the Algonquin and reflects Anishinabe political flexibility. The changes in First Nations leadership and political processes have not been studied in this chapter as a cultural loss of the group experiencing the upheavals of colonization. On the contrary, the place of the free will of the actors involved, as well as the internal dynamics of the band, have been emphasized. The written protest of the election of Pakinawatik's successor and the mobilization by Chief John B. Chabot and Pien Kijemite demonstrate that the Kitigan Zibi Anishinabeg were not passive in the face of the imposition of Euro-Canadian political ways within the band. In fact, it is in political mobilization and action that Anishinabe identity and political culture flourish and become visible locally to various observers inside and outside the community. Confronting Euro-Canadians has cemented the community. The band has become sedentary and is learning to change its sense of community. It begins to be based on living together. Opposition to the Euro-Canadians therefore becomes more significant on the reserve because the Algonquins deal with them on a much more regular basis than before. The Algonquin experience of a new form of election, the transformation of forms of leadership, and the negotiation of Anishinabeg with various forms of legitimacy (territorial, moral, traditional, spiritual, symbolic, official) have demonstrated a distinct political culture where adaptation to each situation prevails. This flexibility is a characteristic of interstitial leadership and Kitigan Zibi Anishinabeg politics.

NOTES

1. It should be noted that the origins of family hunting territories have been the subject of numerous anthropological debates, notably for Speck (1915) and Leacock (1954). For a synthesis of the theoretical debates surrounding Algonquian territoriality based on the writings and hypotheses formulated by Frank G. Speck (1915), Frank G. Speck and Loren C. Eiseley (1939), Diamond Jenness (1935) and Eleanor Leacock (1954), see Leroux et al. (2004: 13–21).

2. Research carried out in 1987 by Jacques Frenette (1993), in collaboration with the community of Kitigan Zibi, has since redefined the extent of the band's territory.

3. In Algonquian beliefs, non-human entities refer in particular to nature spirits, animal masters and mythical beings (the Kokodi, small humans). On the subject of beliefs about animal masters and nature spirits, see, among others, the writings of Beck (1947), Leroux (1992) and Bousquet (2002) for the Algonquins, Adrian Tanner (1979) and Harvey Feit (2000) for the Crees, Peter Armitage (1984, 1992) and Denis Gagnon (2007) for the Innu. Among the authors who have taken an interest in mythical beings, see in particular Bousquet (2001) for a synthesis, Teicher (1960), Preston (1977) and Clermont (1978) on the Kokodi, Windigo, and Joly de Lotbinière (1993) on small humans.

4. The egalitarian ideal corresponds to the absence of power relations within a group of individuals, a society.

5. Over the years, the Sulpician mission of the Seigneury of the Lake of Two Mountains took the name Oka, which means walleye, the golden fish (Guinard, 1960: 129).

6. Sibi and Zibi are spelling variants of the same Algonquin word meaning "river." According to McGregor (2004: 338): "The 's' takes a 'z' sound when spoken in a compound form, as in Kitigan Zibi."

7. Pakinawatik, or Paki'nowatik, means either "Tree Split by Lightning" (Speck, 1929: 118) or "Tree struck by Lightning" (McGregor, 2004: 180).

8. According to Speck (1929: 115), this trading post was removed from Mani-waki in 1878 or 1879.

9. According to Einhorn (1974: 84), the use of wampum belts as an illustrated political document began to lose ground at the end of the eighteenth century to writ-ten documents. The main reason for this decline is that "the white man had proven himself incapable of 'remembering' what the wampum documents stated." (1974: 84)

10. Upon arrival at the River Desert, the Algonquins would have had a fourth wampum belt in their possession (McGregor, 2004: 219). According to McGregor (2004: 317), "What became of the fourth wampum belt is unknown."

11. According to McGregor (2004: 169), Pakinawatik was the sub-chief to Chief Basil Outik (Odjij), the Algonquin chief of Oka.

12. This seems to be the case of Pikogan in Abitibi.

13. The role of Indian agents on reserves and their impact on First Nations politics will be discussed in the next chapter.

14. Vincent M. Petrullo (1929), who visited this region in 1928, considered the individuals of the Lièvre River as forming a band.

15. *Shishib* means "duck" in Algonquin.

16. According to Speck (1929: 111), Jabot is pronounced Ca'bot. He states that it may be a surname of French origin, but "Father Fafard considers the possibility of its being an abbreviation of a name beginning with ca'bo 'through.'"

17. The father of this informant was Vincent Odjick, chief from 1927 to 1933.

18. This comment by Father Guinard, OMI, on the struggle that went on in secret was a source of inspiration for the title of this book.

19. Retrieved from *The Leading Edge* Journal, https://go.roberts.edu/leadingedge/all, accessed March 11, 2013.

20. Indigenous shamans are also called sorcerers or jugglers in ancient texts.

21. By supernatural world, I mean the beliefs surrounding the animal masters and the spirits of nature, as well as the ritual and divinatory practices for communicating with them. Divinatory practices include drumming, the shaking tent (see Flanerry, 1939; Rousseau, 1953; Vincent, 1973, 1977; Proulx, 1988; Dominique, 1989; Pres-ton, 2002), scapulimancy (see Speck, 1928, 1935; Tanner, 1978), and dreaming (see Vincent, 1976; Spielmann, 1993).

22. Among the types of power differentiated by Michel Foucault (1984) are sov-ereign power and disciplinary power. Sovereign power is vested in the monarch, who imposes his wishes on his subjects in an absolute and unconditional manner because he has the right to do so, even the right to cause death or to let live (1984: 258). Disciplinary power, for its part, is exercised by professionals in charge of institutions through mechanisms of surveillance, regulation, repression, organization, codifica-tion, and standardization of conduct. There is no sovereign power among the First Nations of Eastern Canada. But disciplinary power seems relevant when applied to Indigenous leaders, as some find their legitimacy in the organization and regulation of the band. The term *discipline* may seem problematic, since it can only be perceived in a negative form of constant reprehension. For this reason, the understanding of this word must stick to its etymology. The word *discipline* comes from the Latin *disciplina*, which means "teaching" or "moral guidance." This moral direction opens

the way more to the notion of authority, which, unlike power, does not use coercion to bring about men's obedience. Power and authority are not implicitly antagonistic, because a leader can hold both. But power and authority can generate different types of leaders.

23. Retrieved from Penobscot Cultural and Historic Preservation website http:// www.penobscotculture.com, accessed March 9, 2013.

24. Retrieved from Penobscot Cultural and Historic Preservation website http:// www.penobscotculture.com, accessed March 9, 2013.

25. Speck (1915: 21) also mentions the presence of a third man whom he considers to be a third official known as *"mi zi' nawe* 'Man who collects' (for the chief)." This man is responsible for collecting money and provisions for the chief's feasts, advice, and travel expenses, and is also responsible for distributing meat for the families in the camp (1915: 21).

26. According to Speck's data (1915: 21), the Timigami Band named the second chief *ani ke' o'gi ma*—that is, "Next to Chief."

27. They are Oliver (December 7, 1998 interview), Alexander (December 3, 1998 interview), and Arthur (December 3, 1998 interview).

28. According to Sylvie Poirier (2001: 100), *Kice Okimaw* is synonymous with "grand chieftaincy" and consists of a territorial government in place among the Atikamekw at the same time. As a flexible entity, Poirier (2001: 100) specifies that it could also be made up, in time and place, of an Atikamekw chief and chiefs from other bands of another nation (for example, the author cites the Innu and Cree nations). Unlike Gélinas, Poirier (2001: 100) does not consider Manawan and Coucoucache in 1881 to be sub-groups of Weymontachie, but rather full-fledged bands in the same way as Weymontachie and Kikentatch (Obedjiwan).

29. In this regard, Davidson refers the reader to the work of Speck (1915) in this region.

30. Fred Voget (1957: 373) describes the Iroquois sub-chief function as follows: "Each chief had an assistant or sub-chief who advised and acted as a kind of messenger and liaison agent." The Iroquois sub-chief also replaced the chief in his absence and acted as ambassador (Fenton, 1996: 32). This fits the description of this role for the Algonquians. While the Algonquians might have adopted the Iroquois sub-chief system, they did not incorporate its mode of selection. Among the Iroquois, as was the case with chiefs, sub-chiefs were chosen by clan mothers (Voget, 1957: 373).

31. The fur trade began in the eighteenth century and dropped considerably around 1935 (Gélinas, 2003a: 114).

32. Morantz (1977: 81) gives the example of an individual made captain at the age of thirty-six.

33. Excerpt from a letter from Antoine Bastien to J. D. McLean, Secretary of the Department of Indian Affairs, Ottawa, quoted in Pierre-Albert Picard (1916–1920).

34. See Gidmark (1980) on this subject.

35. Lee Sultzman, "The Algonquin," Snow Owl, http://www.snowwowl.com/ peoplealgonquin.html, accessed February 10, 2010.

36. In 2018, portraits of past chiefs were no longer displayed on band council walls but were present on the walls of the community's school. Some of them were also being restored at the Cultural Centre.

Chapter Two

Creating and Training Band Chiefs

The Euro-Canadian Vision of First Nation Leadership

Power relations were the basis of European colonial projects (Izard, 2002: 161). The political colonization of a people implied total interference by the colonizer, hence colonial domination. Within the colonial system, the sociologist Guy Rocher (1992: 580–81) states that "traditional political power is *redefined* and *reoriented*: it is no longer an autonomous authority, but a delegated authority, acting as an intermediary between the population and the colonial authority." Beyond the establishment of the *Indian Act*, how did Euro-Canadian authorities concretely *redefine* and *redirect* the basis of traditional First Nation political power—that is, the chief?

When a people is colonized, it is put in a marginal position with respect to power. As Memmi (2008: 105) notes, "the colonized is not free to choose between being colonized or not being colonized." The colonized has no choice but to deal with the system put in place by the colonizer. The treatment of the subject of the influence of colonial hegemony on the colonized has experienced an effervescence in academic circles since the publication of Edward Said's book *Orientalism* (1978). The creation of a discourse on the East by the West—that is, the discourse on the *Other*, extends generally to the colonial world. In order to legitimize its position as a colonizer, the latter had to demonstrate its superiority by negatively portraying the colonized, by showing what it was not, even imposing this stereotyped image in institutions (Memmi, 2008: 103, 106). This way of doing things, which dehumanized and depersonalized the colonized, justified the colonizer's efforts to change or even transform the colonized (Memmi, 2008: 103–4). Colonization was obviously not the same everywhere. However, the First Nations did not escape this creation of a discourse and a vision of them on the part of the Euro-Canadian colonizers. A First Nation person in general was portrayed as a savage, a polygamist, a drunkard, an immoral being. First Nations chiefs were not spared negative perceptions and Euro-Canadian criticism of their leadership until the mid-twentieth century. From a Euro-Canadian perspective, First Nation leadership was often perceived as ineffective or underdeveloped, lacking authority or having no real power. In order to respond adequately to the political demands of reserve life, Canadian authorities used missionaries, Indian agents and Indian Affairs directives to try to produce and train a Euro-Canadianized First Nation chief—that is, to create a First Nation leadership that suited them and represented the state. To do this, new forms of symbolic power related to the position of chief were introduced. Teaching the First Nations a way of conducting Indian politics by Euro-Canadian actors was done through decorum and protocols to be followed, election rituals, investiture ceremonies, and simulated demonstrations of political assembly. The colonizers' staging of power was aimed at the creation and perpetuation of a Euro-Canadianized First Nation political space, a renewed First Nation society where the chief was acculturated to Euro-Canadian standards. Beyond this typically colonial approach of imposing a political system, what do we know about the margins of power of local authorities and the freedom of manoeuvre of First Nations chiefs? Wim van Binsbergen (2003: 498–499), who has studied the decline and resistance of traditional chiefs in Zambia, notes that chiefs are constantly looking for room to manoeuvre by tinkering with old and new ways of doing things (498–99). African chiefs thus find themselves at the intersection of two systems (2003: 491). The situation of First Nations chiefs appears similar. However, the Zambian reality that van Binsbergen describes is the folklorization of a chief-king, derived from a historical cosmology, within a modernizing postcolonial state, hence the limits of the comparison. In fact, First Nations chiefs have never been sovereigns from a historical cosmology. Moreover, the reality that interests us is that of the techniques of colonization by the Canadian state and not the situation of a postcolonial state, the reality of which should already be proven.

This chapter will discuss First Nation leadership as seen by the colonizers and the influence of this vision on the people of Kitigan Zibi. The Euro-Canadianized conception of First Nation leadership did not suit the Algonquins. Having directly interfered in the management and implementation of government policy within the bands, Indian Affairs agents and missionaries left their mark on the collective memory and political history of the River Desert. Elisabeth sums up the community's feelings toward these Euro-Canadian actors well: "It was tough, it was tough. You couldn't, there wasn't much we could do. Between the Indian agent, the Department and the priest. They had us." (Elisabeth, seventy-four, interview conducted in Kitigan Zibi on November 20, 1998, Kitigan Zibi Anishinabeg Global Research Project). Placed at the interstice of official power, the Anishinabeg did not remain passive in the face of the Euro-Canadian vision and way of doing things in indigenous politics.

This chapter is devoted to the colonial actors who questioned the forms of leadership present within the Kitigan Zibi Band. It is divided into four parts. The first focuses on the Oblate missionaries, who were at once political allies of the First Nations, agents of colonial power on the reserves, and those responsible for Indian education in the residential schools. The second part deals with Indian agents, representatives, and official intermediaries of the government to the First Nations. The third part deals with police constables and law and order officials on reserves. The fourth part focuses on Indian leadership courses under the patronage of the Department of Indian Affairs. In the establishment of exogenous power within bands, there was an overlap in the jurisdiction of colonial officers. Thus, the presence of Indian agents gradually diminished the influence of the missionaries. The control of a band's official political affairs by colonial agents did not necessarily imply total control of its internal political dynamics and members. However, one cannot deny the influence of these agents on a form of traditional leadership that was already undergoing transformation as a result of the sedentarization of the Algonquians. For the federal government, the community development of a reserve depended on the chief. That is why it was essential for the authorities to educate the leaders to technically develop the reserves according to the Euro-Canadian village model and its community life. The political identity of a colonized person is defined in relation to the history of colonization. Interstitial leadership emerges from Euro-Canadian remodeling, the perpetuation of chiefs' control over their bands, and the emergence of a new system of First Nation leadership that fosters a new kind of leader.

MISSIONARIES AND THE OBLATE
INFLUENCE ON ANISHINABE LEADERSHIP

Arriving in Montreal in 1841, the Oblates of Mary Immaculate, a Catholic congregation of French origin, were officially entrusted with the care of the First Nations by the ecclesiastical and governmental authorities (Bousquet, 2001: 70). As early as 1849, Luc-Antoine Pakinawatik approached Bishop Eugène-Bruno Guigues, OMI, who was passing through River Desert, to have a permanent missionary among his people (Guinard, 1960: 66; Carrière, 1962: 77–88; Frenette, 1993: 42, Comité des fêtes du 150ᵉ de Maniwaki, 2001: 11). The establishment of a missionary was therefore a desire of the Algonquins and not an imposition by a religious authority. This request also testifies to the fact that Pakinawatik was "a man of faith" (Guinard, 1960: 66) and that he certainly saw advantages in having a permanent missionary close by on a daily basis. Could there be political advantages?

Regarding the Atikamekw, Claude Gélinas (2002: 37, 2003b: 73) states that the missionary was a useful ally and an effective intermediary between the Atikamekw and the political authorities. The missionaries also played a similar role for the people of the River Desert. In 1845, Father Thomas Clément, OMI, served as a translator for Pakinawatik, who wrote a petition to Lord Elgin, governor of Canada at the time, to obtain a reserve (McGregor, 2004: 172, 191). This petition did not receive a response (Frenette, 1993: 42). In 1848, the petition was sent again, but this time it was accompanied by a letter from Bishop Guigues supporting the Algonquin undertaking (Carrière, 1962: 85–88, in Frenette, 1993: 42). During Bishop Guigues's visit in 1849, the Algonquins entrusted him with a new petition requesting reserved land to be transmitted to the Canadian government (Lapointe, 2007: 7). The same year, Father Clément, OMI, also presented another request to Indian Affairs on behalf of the Algonquins (Carrière, 1962: 78, in Frenette, 1993: 42; McGregor, 2004: 191). According to McGregor (2004: 192), it was thanks to the support of Bishop Guigues that the Algonquins finally obtained a reserve on the River Desert. However, McGregor (2004: 172) suggests that Pakinawatik was the mastermind behind these petitions. The latter certainly showed perseverance and was able to find political allies to achieve his ends. But did the political visions of the First Nations go in the same direction as those of the missionaries?

According to Gélinas (2003c: 90–91), "administratively and ideologically, the missionaries walked hand in hand with the federal government and its policy of assimilation." Moreover, the missionaries' attitude toward the First Nations was marked by paternalism and a colonizing spirit. The missionaries had a strong desire to protect "the children of the woods."[1] Considering the First Nations people as children was not only the result of the mentality of the nineteenth century and the first half of the twentieth century. It should be remembered that they were minors according to the laws concerning them. Thus, the missionaries had assumed the role of "natural guardians of these minors."[2] Not only were the First Nations people considered by the Oblates as minors, but for some they were also inferior beings. In a 1922 letter addressed to the Department of Indian Affairs, Father Étienne Blanchin, OMI, wrote that the First Nations people were endowed with "physical and moral inferiority" (ANC, 1922, in Leroux et al., 2004: 63). The Oblate perception of inferiority of the First Nations people went hand in hand with the evolutionary conceptions of the time when the peoples of the world were evaluated according to Western notions of civilization. Achiel Peelman, OMI (1996: 36), who was interested in the Oblate vision of Native American cultures in

Oregon in the nineteenth century, notes that there are similarities between the missionaries of the nineteenth and seventeenth centuries: "In three centuries, the discourse on Native Americans has not changed!" As explained by Peelman (1996: 37), the Oblates also inherited the missionary concepts and practices of their predecessors—that is, they continued to apply the same techniques of evangelization and had a negative perception of Native American cultures and their spirituality. This context also seems to apply to the first half of the twentieth century. Consequently, from the Oblate point of view, the inferiority of the First Nations people made their evangelization, civilization and assimilation necessary.

To achieve this, the missionaries aimed to settle the semi-nomadic Algonquians by creating reserves and turning Indians into farmers. Although the Algonquins of the River Desert had expressed the desire to develop agriculture in their petitions requesting a reserve (Frenette, 1988: 217), the adoption of this way of life was perceived differently. Frenette notes: "For the Algonquins, agriculture presented itself as a last chance for survival" (1988: 217). Indeed, colonization and logging had greatly reduced access to Algonquin territories and their resources (1988: 217). Thus, Maniwaki was transformed, as early as the 1860s, "into an enterprise of 'Indian colonization' at the custody of the Oblates" (Laurin, 1991: 88). At that time, the missionaries were well established on the River Desert reserve (Frenette, 1988: 154). Moreover, Maniwaki had become a hub for the missionaries on their way to the workcamps and other First Nations missions such as those of James Bay and St. Maurice (Carrière, 1968: 117–48, in Frenette, 1988: 154). Several Oblates resided in Maniwaki and served the Algonquins of the River Desert.

Table 2.1 gives an overview of the missionaries in charge of the reserve. However, these missionaries were acting in the reserve far beyond their role as Catholic missionaries. With regard to the missionaries present in the Montagnais reserve of Betsiamites, Hélène Bédard (1988: 107) considers that they were the first agents of colonial power. For Toby Morantz (2002a: 73), they were the agents par excellence of Western society. They interfered intimately in the affairs of the band until they took full charge of Indigenous people, a framework that, through coercion, discipline, and submission, attempted to implant exogenous power (Bédard, 1988: 107). This assumption of responsibility by the missionaries was not always welcome at the River Desert, as this dispute reported by Gaston Carrière, OMI, shows (1968: 136) in *Histoire documentaire de la Congrégation des Missionnaires Oblats de Marie-Immaculée dans l'Est du Canada*:

in early January 1875, war broke out between Father Déléage and the Indians. The chiefs [Simon Odjick and the sub-chiefs chiefs] were writing to Bishop Duhamel to complain that the missionary, who was interfering in their temporal affairs, had caused them to lose a few hundred dollars (Archevêché d'Ottawa, *Registre des Lettres de Mgr Duhamel*, in Carrière, 1968: 136).

According to the testimonies collected,[3] the supervision by the missionaries was also part of the Anishinabe daily life in Kitigan Zibi through the constant surveillance of the members of the band by some missionaries, their public reprimands at Sunday Mass and the threat of ending up in hell.

Table 2.1.   Oblate Missionaries at the River Desert

Missionaries	Years
Mgr Eugène-Bruno Guigues	1849
Father Hercule Thomas Clément[a]	
Father Jean-Nicolas Laverlochère	
Father Hercule Thomas Clément	1850
Brother James Brady	
Mgr Eugène-Bruno Guigues	1851
Father Thomas Clément	1852
Father Louis Reboul	1855
Mgr Eugène-Bruno Guigues	1860
Father Louis Babel	1862–1866
Father Christophe Tissier	1864
Father Jean-Pierre Guéguen	1886–1898
Father Joseph-Étienne Guinard	1898
Father François-Xavier Fafard	1915–1939
Father Joseph-Étienne Guinard	1940
Father Louis-Philippe Martel	?–1959
Father Gérard Deschênes	1959–1981
Father Rémi Côté	1963–?
Father Réal Paiement	1978–1993
Father Gaston Saint-Onge	1992–2001
Father Kennedy	?
Father Eugène Lapointe	2007–2011

[a] Father Eugène Lapointe, O.M.I. (2007: 7), states: "In the documents, we often find the name Thomas as the only first name of Fr. [Father] Clément. But he always signs H. Th. [Hercule Thomas] Clément."
Source: Table based on the following sources: AD JA 61. A64R 27; Anonymous (1959a: 7); Carrière (1978: 48); Bouchard (1980: 69, 221); Frenette (1988: 142–43); Comité des fêtes du 150e de Maniwaki (2001: 11, 20, 39); Meredith (eighty-five years old, interview conducted at Kitigan Zibi on February 7, 2008), obituaries of the Oblates of Mary Immaculate.

How did the missionaries obtain such authority in Algonquian societies? First of all, they competed against the shamans, who, let's not forget, were political actors among the Algonquians. According to Bousquet (2009: 58–59, 61), it is by ridiculing their powers (for example, dialogue with the spirits of the supernatural, casting spells, curing diseases, predicting the future) that missionaries diminished, or even made the authority of the shamans disappear. Second, missionaries gained authority because they provided government assistance to the First Nations people and were intermediaries with the government, where they sometimes defended Indian interests.[4] Thirdly, they established themselves as authority figures through their religious rituals, which put them in the forefront by demonstrating their oratorical abilities. The religious rituals were also a demonstration of the spiritual power of the missionaries as well as their communal power to bring people together. Eloquence, spiritual power and convening skills were valued characteristics among Algonquian chiefs. For Bousquet (2009: 60), with the intensification of evangelization and government administrative control within First Nations societies in the mid-nineteenth century, the presence of missionaries and Indian Affairs agents changed the sense of authority and, consequently, the status of leadership. Moral authority was redefined and no longer rested solely with the chief. Legal and administrative authority was gradually imposed through Indian agents. The introduction of new power figures into First Nations daily life weakened the traditional authority of leaders and their status.

At River Desert, the presence of Indian agents as early as 1860, which will be discussed in the next section, certainly contributed to diminishing the political role of the missionaries. The missionaries, however, seemed to retain an indirect political role: instilling and applying the guidelines of Indian Affairs (through sermons and parish visits), governing community life, and calming First Nations spirits likely to bring about a political revolution. As discussed in chapter 1, the Six Nations movement and its ambition to recognize Indian sovereignty met with great success at River Desert in the 1920s. Has the return to traditional Indigenous values advocated by this movement undermined missionary authority over time? In the 1940s, Father Guinard, OMI, then a missionary on the reserve, noted the lack of piety of the Anishinabeg, the poor attendance at Mass and the few Indian visitors to his residence (Bouchard, 1980: 223). According to Mérédith, an Elder from the reserve (eighty-five years old, Kitigan Zibi, February 7, 2008), it was during the 1940s that the altar boys ceased to exist in the community when there were usually four to five boys in charge of altar service. This may suggest a weakening of the Catholic religion at that time because not all the children of Kitigan Zibi had gone to residential school. Moreover, if the people of River Desert no longer visited the missionary, it is because they may no longer have sought his advice and acted on their own initiative. During the 1940s, an Indigenous rights activist, Jules Sioui, visited River Desert a few times (McGregor, 2004: 280–81). Among his demands, he strongly encouraged First Nations to reorganize the leadership of their Nation (Sioui, 1943, in Mc-

Gregor, 2004: 281). In 1948, the sale of the Oblate farm, located on reserve land,[5] to a non-Indigenous person would raise a storm of protest against the missionaries in the community (Lapointe, 2007: 16). Even though the missionaries no longer held the role of political actors among the First Nations, they still assumed the role of creating and training First Nations political leaders according to their visions through the residential schools.

Residential Schools: Colonization and Division in Kitigan Zibi

The residential school system in Canada began in 1845 (Valaskakis, 2005: 105). Under the aegis of the government and thanks to its funding, the direction, management, and maintenance of these residential schools were entrusted to various religious orders (Catholic, Anglican, Presbyterian, United Church) (Valaskakis, 2005: 105–6). As early as 1885, the Oblates set up residential schools, which were then called industrial schools because they were dedicated to "preparing young boys and girls for the trades that were to ensure their subsistence: agriculture, construction and mechanics for boys, and domestic arts for girls" (Miny, 1995: 13). In Quebec, the Oblates were responsible for four residential schools[6] that operated from the mid-1930s to the mid-1980s (Bousquet, 2006; Bousquet and Morissette, 2008: 22; Gaudreau and Miny, 2003: 11). Intended for Indian children, these institutions responded to government policies:

> School attendance was of vital concern to the government, for education of the Indian child was a keystone of the civilizing process the reserve system was to perform. Since schools on the reserve were not well attended by Indian Children, they were regarded as ineffectual instruments of this process. Residential and industrial schools, which removed the child from the detrimental influence of uncivilized parents and Indian traditions, were regarded as better instruments of government policy (Tobias, 1983: 48).

Not all children in Kitigan Zibi[7] went to residential school. Comments from a former resident (Joseph, fifty-seven years old, Kitigan Zibi, February 17, 2008) indicate that family background was the deciding factor in determining whether or not an Algonquin child was sent to a residential school. If it was deemed harmful (for example, an undisciplined, unhealthy home where the parents were considered negligent by Euro-Canadian standards) by the missionary and/or Indian agent, the child would attend the residential school. A healthy and stable family environment and Algonquin children who functioned well in the surrounding school setting helped some to avoid residential schools. According to McGregor (2004: 282), approximately one hundred children from the River Desert attended residential schools between

1927 and 1960. They were dispersed in four residential schools located in two provinces: St. Mary's Residential School for Indian Children in Kenora, Ontario, Spanish Residential School in Ontario, the residential school in Saint-Marc-de-Figuery, Quebec, and the residential school in Pointe-Bleue, Quebec (McGregor, 2004: 282). In addition, some children in the community attended more than one residential school. Also, it should be noted that members of the same family were sometimes sent to different residential schools where the languages taught differed (French or English). On other reserves in Quebec, the attendance of children from one community at the same residential school created a bond, solidarity, and even a collective feeling between them through the common experience, the memory of places, events, and individuals present. According to my observations, the attendance of Kitigan Zibi's children at different residential schools has contributed to the opposite, that is, to dividing the community and families. Was this an ulterior motive of the authorities in dispersing the children from the reserve? If not, it proves the chaotic management of the bureaucracy surrounding the residential schools and the government's irresponsibility toward the children on the reserve. In the 1950s, Quebec imposed compulsory schooling for all First Nations children (Bousquet, 2001: 159).[8] What was the purpose of residential schools?

Residential schools were responsible for the education, training and acculturation of the Indian child (Anonymous, 1957: 6). According to Mary-Ellen Kelm (1998: 57), who became interested in residential schools in British Columbia in the early twentieth century, residential schools also had another purpose: to "reform the Aboriginal body" in Foucault's sense. In *Surveiller et punir*, Foucault (1975) focuses on the discipline of the body to right the mind. This reform of the body, which is emphasized in institutions such as prisons, schools, and hospitals, is carried out using various techniques such as surveillance, punishment, the use of a schedule, and exercise. At the Indian Residential School in Saint-Marc-de-Figuery, near Amos in Abitibi, in addition to academic training (history, geography, French, and mathematics), catechism, altar service, manual work, culinary arts, sports, drama, drawing, singing, dancing, and acting were also taught to the residents to "develop their talents and personalities" and to give them "a taste for instruction, order, beauty and cleanliness" (Lucas, 1966: 1, 4–5). According to a report card from the Pointe-Bleue residential school of 1961–1962, belonging to a former Algonquin resident of Kitigan Zibi, it is noted that hygiene was part of the instruction and that conduct, politeness, and cleanliness were also evaluated among the students. These subjects were taught in the classical colleges and convents of Quebec at the same time.[9] However, in the residential schools, the aim was not simply to train a professional workforce, but to transform the Indian into a Euro-Canadian citizen through the devaluation of his identity:

"We were taught that everything Indian was bad" (Marcelline Kanapé, Innue de Betsiamites, in Lepage, 2002: 30). To do this, authority and strict discipline were necessary to "train the savage" in being civilized: religious orders, strict schedules, marching in rows, dress code, adoption of Euro-Canadian behavior, and rules of good manners[10] had to be followed, failing which punishments and corporal punishment were inflicted (Ottawa, 2010; Bousquet, 2012: 181, 185–86). Developing future leaders was also part of the ambitions for Indian residents.

When it opened in October 1960, the Pointe-Bleue residential school welcomed Algonquin children from the River Desert among its two hundred residents (Anonymous, 1960a: 3). Within this residential school, boys' and girls' councils were elected, each headed by a chief and a "chieftain" (Anonymous, 1961a: 3).[11] These councils were effective for the duration of the school year. The boys' council consisted of a sub-chief, a religious counselor, a sports counselor, and a works counselor (Anonymous, 1961a: 3). The girls' council, on the other hand, was made up of female counselors, but they did not have specific areas of interest assigned to them (Anonymous, 1961a: 3). Historically, student councils and student groups often had a real political role (Lipset, 1968, 1971, in Bélanger and Maheu, 1972: 309). Although the 1960s is a very good reference point for student movements around the world, student political participation did not begin in the 1960s. Among other things, students were at the heart of the 1848 revolution in Germany and Austria, the overthrow of the Chinese Qing dynasty in 1911, anticolonial struggles in Asia and Africa, and the defence of freedom in Eastern Europe (Lipset, 1968: 1). As early as the 1920s, international student assemblies were organized (Lipset, 1968: 1). Missionaries had to be aware of the potential political power of student councils. But for them, student councils could be continuators of the kind of power that true political leaders had and not become counterpowers.

The public proclamation of the elected members of the boys' and girls' councils and their presentation were the occasion for a real celebration in September 1961 at the Pointe-Bleue residential school (Anonymous, 1961a: 3). An article in the Oblate journal *Vie indienne*, of December 1961, recounts the event where the raising of the reserve flag, a parade of 22 units, a snack, a vigil of song and dance were part of the festivities (Anonymous, 1961a: 3). Dignitaries and guests were present for the occasion, including the parish priest of Pointe-Bleue, the chief of the reserve, and the representative of Indian Affairs, and "circumstantial speeches" were made (Anonymous, 1961a: 3).

Among the photos accompanying the article is a photo of the boys' council and a photo of the girls' council. The photos show that students from these councils wore traditional, patterned fringed clothing, headdresses, and feather headbands (figure 2.1). Thus, the residents were taught decorum (ceremonial dress)—a symbolic world (flag), protocol (public presentation, distinguished guests, official speeches), and celebration (parade, feast) surrounding the election of their peer councils. This was the First Nations' introduction to the Western-style staging of the political world in all its ceremonial complexity, ritualization, and representation. This skill was perhaps essential to pass on to Indian children, as certain political expectations were expected of the residential school. These expectations, however, point to contradictions and even inconsistencies in Canadian colonization. As Bishop Marius Paré of Chicoutimi said during the official opening mass of the Pointe-Bleue residential school on May 3, 1961: "From this school must come out chiefs, an elite who will ensure the survival of your people" (Anonymous, 1961b: 1). According to Guy Rocher (1992: 581–82), in the colonial system, education was used to create "an evolved elite" that would work as administrative and technical executives and serve as a bridge between the colonized and the colonizers. For Diom Roméo Saganash (2005: 89), a Cree leader from Waswanipi and a former resident, it was necessary for Indigenous people to be "[transformed] into useful members of society."

To create these future leaders, this Indian elite, the Oblates provided them with a Western-style academic formation to help them cope with Euro-Canadian society. According to J. R. Miller (1996: 418, 430), the residential

Figure 2.1. Pointe Bleue Residential School Girls' Council Ready for Parade
AD

schools were thus able to transmit talents that enabled the First Nations communities to adapt politically, survive, and prosper. Even more ironically, Miller (1996: 430) notes that while residential schools shaped students into political leaders, they became strong advocates of their traditional cultures. The missionaries certainly did not anticipate that the chiefs and the elite that emerged from the residential schools would instead serve First Nations interests by organizing themselves politically to denounce their situation of subjugation and fight for their rights. Mastering the dominant languages and writing, the First Nations people were able to reappropriate the power to speak in their own name, thus avoiding Euro-Canadian intermediaries (Morissette, 2004: 37, 41–42). But did the residential school experience and the multiple traumas the residents underwent cause some of them to become politically active as a result? This is what the story of Harold Cardinal (1969: 52–55, 85–87, in Miller 1996: 430), a former resident and Cree leader from Alberta, suggests. As Miller reports (1996: 430), "The school year experience scared him with its racism, hardened him with its severe treatment, and incited him to political action." Most former residents never really recovered from their experience. In 1990, revelations of sexual abuse at a residential school by Manitoba First Nations Chief Phil Fontaine led to a great awakening and the emergence of a counterpower that led to the Truth and Reconciliation Commission (Bousquet, 2012: 165, 188). Political action may have been the perfect vehicle for former residents to express themselves and to respond appropriately and in a life-saving way to the injustices suffered at Indian Residential Schools.

INDIAN AGENTS

Missionaries were not the only colonial actors who tried to influence the Anishinabe leadership and political climate at River Desert. The same is true of Indian Affairs agents. The memory of Indian Affairs agents is still alive among the Kitigan Zibi Anishinabeg. As for the Indian Affairs agents, the information available is scattered. They came to the reserves to "look after" Indian interests, and they have not been extensively researched, as Toby Morantz (2002a: 222) points out for the Cree and for Robin Brownlie (1994: 65) generally. Apart from a book by Brownlie (2003) on Indian agents in Ontario, the few articles about them include a portrait of an Indian agent (Brownlie, 1994) and discussions of their power of removal over chiefs and councillors (Satzewich and Mahood, 1994), their recruitment (Satzewich, 1996), their role within the residential school system (Satzewich and Mahood, 1995), their views on the "Indian problem" (Satzewich, 1997), and their view of Native fisheries (Schreiber, 2008). Politically, what impact have Indian agents had on reserves? Their presence has, in fact, contributed to the development of a local political identity in response to their way of doing First Nations politics. In concrete terms, what was the role of the Indian agent?

To be hired as an Indian agent, certain criteria had to be met; one had to be married, of good character, competent, honest, and physically fit (Satzewich, 1996: 226–32). Being married was essential since it prevented agents from taking Indian women as partners or marrying them (Satzewich, 1996: 227). Satzewich reports (1996: 226) that for the Department of Indian Affairs, the agents and their families were also examples of Euro-Canadian customs to be followed by First Nations people. Similarly, it expected the agents' wives to play a leading role in the socialization and "civilization" of Indian women (1996: 228). The mission of Indian Affairs agents was to integrate and as-similate First Nations people into Canadian society (Morantz, 2002a: 223). In addition to this cultural objective, they had a political, economic, and social agenda. It was clear that the agents were not working for the Indian commu-nity but for the benefit of the Department of Indian Affairs (Morantz, 2002a: 223). At River Desert, the first Indian agent, John White, was posted as early as 1860. Table 2.2 shows the chronology of Indian agents on the reserve.

Officially, Lorenzo Leclair was the last to hold the position of Indian agent, which ended in 1967. From 1964 to 1968, this Indian agent was also alder-man for the city of Maniwaki.[12] Being involved both in the town of Mani-waki and in the management of the Kitigan Zibi reserve does not appear to

Table 2.2. Indian Affairs Agents at River Desert

Indian Affairs Agents	Mandate (years)
John White	1860–1874 (July)
C. L. Baudin	1874 (July)–1875 (March)
Patrick Moore	1876 (May–-1879 (June or September[a])
Charles Logue	1879 (October)–1885 (January)
James Martin	1885 (July)–1896 (October)
William J. McCaffrey	1897 (March)–1913 (December)
Ernest S. Gauthier	1913 (December)–1939 (February)
Joe E. Gendron	c. 1939–1947 (December)
Russell Baker	1949 (January)–1953 (May)
Mlle M.C. Bertha Joanis[b]	1953 (November)
Lorenzo Leclair	c. 1954–c. 1967
Ernest McGregor[b]	c. 1967–c. 1970

[a] According to Holmes et al. (1999: 138), the agent would have completed his term in June 1879. According to McGregor (2004: 210), Agent Moore completed his term in September 1879.
[b] These individuals are not Indian agents but have assumed this responsibility during transitional periods.
Source: Table based on Joan Holmes et al. (1999: 138) and supplemented with information gathered from oral history interviews conducted for the Kitigan Zibi Anishinabeg Global Research Project.

be contradictory. It should be remembered that the creation of band councils by the *Indian Act* was intended to municipalize the First Nations chiefdoms. Ethically, however, holding a position of power within two neighboring local political structures raises serious questions about conflict of interest. According to Satzewich and Mahood (1995: 46), Indian agents had to look after the interests of other entities present at the local level, such as municipalities, agencies, and the church and missionary organizations, in their work. Attention to outside interests may have worked against the First Nations in some cases.[13]

Charles, a former elected official, summarizes the economic and political role of Indian agents at the River Desert as follows:

> Clearly, the process of dominance and control remained right to the end, the very end of Indian agent days until he was removed from office. You have the Indian agent, you have the local clergy, catholic priest, RCMP, who inserted a lot of control back in the 50s and 60s. Had a lot of influence on people by control on people's lives. The Indian agent decided every activity in the community. Where it had to do with roads, housing, income to basic needs or relief vouchers. The Indian agent called the shots. Most of the time, most people couldn't get anything from them. It was very, very conservative rule, as far as, what could be available and what couldn't be available. People had to pull their weight. The government, these agents, in my view, did not work very effectively for the benefit of the community. They were there for that but the community remained very poverty stricken. [. . .] The Indian agents often controlled a lot of the meetings because they said what was possible and not possible. They had the purse strings. It was not the Chief and Council that controlled the purse string (Charles, fifty-three years old, interview conducted in Kitigan Zibi on December 7, 1998, Kitigan Zibi Anishinabeg Global Research Project).

In fact, the Indian agent was the one who handled the band's finances. This economic authority was granted to him by the *Indian Act* (Brownlie, 1994: 67). Brownlie (1994: 67–68) recalls that the role of the Indian agent was to teach money management and responsibility for other resources (for example, natural resources to be exploited on the reserve, such as timber, or the management of rations allocated by the government). But this objective does not seem to have been a priority on the reserves. Moreover, the economic power of Indian agents had social repercussions because they were responsible for community development and the well-being of individuals in need. However, an Indian Affairs policy was that the Indian agent should, as often as possible, avoid providing financial assistance to families and keep band expenditures to a minimum (Brownlie, 1994: 81, 85–86). According to interviews conducted for the Global Research Project, River Desert band members went to the Indian agent for ration coupons, permits to cut and sell timber, farm animals, seed (especially for potatoes), seasonal equipment and farm materials (wire for fences, paint, lime, or a well). Former elected official Charles (fifty-three years old, interview conducted in Kitigan Zibi on December 7, 1998, Kitigan Zibi Anishinabeg Global Research Project) said that in most cases, money from band funds was used to pay for some of these amenities: "Funds, that have been generated from sales of wood at lumber barns [. . .]".

Control of the Band Meetings, but Not Necessarily Control of the Band

What was a band council like in the days of the Indian agents? As Brownlie (1994: 66) notes, at the political level, with the exception of not being able to vote at these political meetings, Indian agents were responsible for organizing, chairing, and exercising control over these sessions while setting out the thinking of the Department of Indian Affairs. It should also be recalled that the Indian agent had a veto power over decisions made at band council meetings (McGregor, 2004: 224). Thus, through his leadership, the Indian agent staged the band council assembly and thereby instructed the First Nations on the organization and rules to be followed at a political meeting in the formal image of Euro-Canadian political sessions. The words of the Elders and former chiefs on the band councils are very instructive in portraying these political meetings in Kitigan Zibi. According to Alexander, Elisabeth, and former Chief Charles,[14] the number of band council meetings increased from once a year to four times a year around 1920 and 1930—that is, on Saturdays every three months. In her book on the Algonquin chiefs of the River Desert, Jenny Tenasco (1986: 12) mentions that, during the mandate of Chief Patrick Brascoupé (1933–1936): "It was decided at a general band meeting that, in the future, meetings would be held on the first Saturday of each month instead of four times a year as previously." However, according to Alexander and Charles, it was not until the takeover in the late 1970s that the frequency of band councils was changed to a monthly basis.[15] Over the years, the gathering took place in different buildings: in a log house on Bitobi Road, at the first school on the reserve, or at the community hall where the chief, councillors, and Indian agent were present on a stage in front of the assembly.[16] This spatial arrangement of the band council actors certainly contributed to the theatricalization of the political spectacle where, as Abélès (2005: 158–59) notes, there is a gap between the protagonists and the spectators, the governors and the governed. The fact that the Indian agent was put on an equal footing with the chief, on the stage, also suggests a colonial staging.

What was the Indian agent doing at the River Desert band council? According to Victor (eighty-three years old, interview conducted in Kitigan Zibi on December 7, 1998, Kitigan Zibi Anishinabeg Global Research Project), the Indian agent was taking notes for a report to the office of the Department of Indian Affairs. But what is most evident from the oral history interviews is the control exercised by the Indian agent over both the decisions made and the opinions expressed by community members, as these excerpts show:

> But actually what I knew, as far as, when I was a kid to go into the meetings, it was the Indian agents and the Indian agents they use to call the shots, you know. Whatever the Indian agent says it goes, you know (Terry, sixty-two years old, interview conducted in Kitigan Zibi on November 20, 1998, Kitigan Zibi Anishinabeg Global Research Project).

> Nothing much went there because the Indian agent was in control. And a lot of our people were not able to read. [. . .] So, whatever passed there, even if they voted for it, how would they know what was written? (Elisabeth, seventy-four years old, interview conducted in Kitigan Zibi on November 20, 1998, Kitigan Zibi Anishinabeg Global Research Project).

> Well, the old timers they use to talk about him, they use to have a meeting at Ottawa Rd. [. . .] He's god, you know, when he talks there everybody shuts up, you know. No, no noise, nothing. Mr. Gauthier had spoken, that's it, that's the law [. . .] (Terry, sixty-two years old, interview conducted in Kitigan Zibi on November 20, 1998, Kitigan Zibi Anishinabeg Global Research Project).

> The Indian agent controlled everything. Although some individuals did take a very firm stand sometimes (Charles, fifty-three years old, interview conducted in Kitigan Zibi on December 7, 1998, Kitigan Zibi Anishinabeg Global Research Project).

> It's the same thing with the Indian agent. My father has been thrown out of band meetings because he dared, he dared to disagree with him (Elisabeth, seventy-four years old, interview conducted in Kitigan Zibi on November 20, 1998, Kitigan Zibi Anishinabeg Global Research Project).

Standing up to an Indian agent seems to have had consequences not only for band members, but also for elected officials. Referring to the 1930s, Morantz notes (2002a: 229): "The agents, not the chiefs, had the real power. . . . The chiefs and councillors helped maintain the status quo. They had no choice; to do otherwise would have meant dismissal." In a National Film Board documentary (Ouimet, 2000), former Chief William Commanda (1951–1970) also testifies to the great control exercised by Indian agents: "The Indian chiefs had no say. They made resolutions with the council. And the Indian agent, if he approved, it passed. If he didn't approve, well, often they were not renewed." In fact, as early as 1884, under the *Indian Act*, the superintendent general had the power to dismiss any chief and councillor deemed "incompetent, intemperate or immoral" according to the local Indian agent (Brownlie, 1994: 67). Vic Satzewich and Linda Mahood (1994) cite a fourth reason put forward in the *Indian Act*: dishonesty. As discussed in the previous chapter, one of the River Desert chiefs, John B. Chabot, paid the price for this policy when he was removed from office in the late 1920s.

An episode recounted by an Elder during oral history interviews demonstrates the ambition of Indian agents to further interfere in the affairs of the River Desert Band. In the mid-twentieth century, this Elder witnessed a meeting between three Indian Affairs agents and the then chief. The agents were trying to convince the chief "to put a white person as a chief and to keep the Indians people as the council" (Edward, seventy-eight years old, interview conducted in Kitigan Zibi on November 11, 1998, Kitigan Zibi Anishinabeg Global Research Project). The chief was not persuaded. What power of action was left to the Algonquins of River Desert in this context where the Indian agent had all the official powers? The following excerpt illustrates the difficulties of standing up against the Euro-Canadian political intrusion into River Desert:

> The fact that you have a very controlled system, the Indian agent being the supreme agent working with Ottawa. It was pretty difficult sometimes for the chief to think to sign a whole lot of power when it came up against that structure, at the time (Charles, fifty-three years old, interview conducted in Kitigan Zibi on December 7, 1998, Kitigan Zibi Anishinabeg Global Research Project).

McGregor (2004: 225) reports that some families on the reserve, who had had enough of the domination exercised by the Indian agent, either left the community for their trapline or permanently abandoned the band to settle among the Algonquins of Lac-Barrière. However, McGregor does not mention at what period this temporary or permanent exodus occurred or the motivations behind the choice of Lac-Barrière. While some families left the reserve because of the Indian agent, others were not impressed. This is the case of the family of Simon-John Makate-inini, better known as John Bull (McGregor, 2004: 207). In the late 1870s, John Bull wrote, through an intermediary, to Indian Affairs complaining about Indian Agent Patrick Moore (BAC, RG 10, vol. 2066, file 10, 270; McGregor, 2004: 210). In his letter, John Bull deplores, among other things, Agent Moore's uselessness and incompetence (McGregor, 2004: 210). John Bull's complaint against this agent was not the first of its kind to reach Indian Affairs. At the same time, the Chief and two sub-chiefs of the band had also requested the assignment of a new Indian agent to replace Agent Moore, who, among other things, lived too far from the reserve and did not provide information regarding band affairs and finances (BAC, RG 10, vol. 2066, file 10, 270). Although it is difficult to say whether John Bull's letter and that of the Chief and sub-chiefs of the band contributed to this, Agent Moore was replaced either in June, according to Holmes et al. (1999: 138) or in September 1879 according to McGregor (2004: 210).

From the late 1870s to 1895, John Bull, with the support of other families, also vigorously opposed the Euro-Canadian invasion of illegally surrendered lots of land belonging to his family, as well as the sale of half of the reserve land (Canada, 1883, 1884, 1885; Holmes et al., 1999: 81–85; McGregor, 2004: 212, 214–15). The Indian agent from 1879 to 1885, Charles Logue, in his correspondence with Indian Affairs, repeatedly mentioned the difficulties caused by this "stubborn" family, which frightened Euro-Canadian settlers, erected fences on the lots, and formed a faction against the sale of the reserve land (McGregor, 2004: 214). Nevertheless, the resistance and actions of John Bull and his family were successful. In 1885, Indian Affairs appointed the Indian agent for the reserve, James Martin, to resolve the situation (McGregor, 2004: 214). It was only after ten years of negotiations with Indian Affairs that John Bull and his family accepted financial compensation for their lost lots (2004: 215). According to McGregor (2004: 215), this victory against the authorities was short lived since the compensation ($7,950) was paid out of band funds.

Beginning in the early 1930s, it became more complex for individuals on reserves to make their voices heard by the authorities. At that time, a policy of the Department of Indian Affairs prohibited First Nations people from going directly to Ottawa to make requests or complaints. Everything had to be handled by the Indian agent (Brownlie 1994: 70; Morantz 2002a: 223). However, some First Nations persons defied this law. This is the case of Elisabeth's mother, who wrote to T. A. Crerar, Minister of Indian Affairs from October 1935 to November 1936, as well as to one of his predecessors (Elisabeth, seventy-four years old, interview conducted in Kitigan Zibi on November 20, 1998, Kitigan Zibi Anishinabeg Global Research Project; Holmes, 1999: 24–25). In her oral history interview, Elisabeth suggests that her mother, accompanied by another person, even traveled to Ottawa. Unfortunately, they were denied entry to the offices of the authorities concerned (Elisabeth, seventy-four years old, interview conducted in Kitigan Zibi on November 20, 1998, Kitigan Zibi Anishinabeg Global Research Project).

While the Indian agent controlled the affairs of the band, the examples of political stand and action at River Desert demonstrate that he was far from controlling individual band members. They had opinions about their own affairs and wanted to be heard. To achieve this, the Kitigan Zibi Anishinabeg dared to challenge the established order. In fact, Anishinabeg political actions and practices consisted of what James C. Scott (1989: 33) has described as daily forms of resistance by subordinate groups. In the analysis of conflict, these have generally not received the attention of scholars, who have focused more on open and direct confrontations, such as rebellion and riots, as they are less marginal practices (1989: 33–34, 50). Indirect, informal, and drawing little attention to perpetrators, everyday forms of resistance are silent tactics (1989: 34–35) that may nonetheless be successful in the long run. Because daily forms of resistance "imply in their intention or logic an accommodation with the structure of domination" (1989: 50–51), they are a good reflection of the situation of First Nations people in their power relations with the Canadian State. Sally Engle Merry (1995: 15) considers that micro acts of resistance can also be carried out within the legal framework. For Merry (1998: 101–2), acculturation is not the only outcome of a legal system on an *Other* cultural group. For these micro-acts to be understood, their cultural context must be taken into account, as a redefinition of identity and community may result, as well as a readjustment of power relations (Merry, 1995: 16, 23). Resistance and cultural appropriation of the law can create margins of power.

The Political Impact and Political Legacy of Indian Agents

As administrator, the Indian agent took charge of the political life of the reserve. He is not only the person in charge of elections but also the resource person with whom the First Nations people must deal. Morantz (2002a: 224) considers that these government agents had a considerable impact on the political leadership of the Crees: "Whether benevolent or autocratic, the Indian agents made most of the decisions for the Crees and undermined their traditional leadership, which was based on supernatural powers, wisdom, and age." The nonrecognition of traditional Cree leadership by government agents has necessarily weakened the Crees' confidence in their leaders and their values (Morantz, 2002b: 68). In fact, it may also have undermined, by extension, the Crees' confidence in their sociopolitical system. There is no doubt that this questioning of leadership by Indian Affairs officers may extend to other Algonquian communities. These agents may have dealt the final blow to a form of traditional leadership already in transition and transformation that was adapting to community life on reserves on an ongoing basis. By putting in place guidelines to govern the political and administrative functioning of the reserve, the agents have substituted the place of a chiefly style of traditional leadership in this new environment. Indeed, as Morantz (2002a: 229) notes, the Indian agent "had taken over many of the traditional duties of chiefs, such as helping people in difficulty." But the living conditions on reserved land made it difficult for the Algonquins to be completely self-sufficient. The use of the Indian agent by the Anishinabeg for various needs became systematic since he was the government representative responsible for welfare on the reserves. The same is true for a good number of Algonquian reserves where the population was dependent on the Indian agent at several levels to improve their daily lives. When the last River Desert Indian agent left his post in 1967, the community turned to the chief to meet all its needs (for example, housing, development, recreation, and social assistance). During the era of semi-nomadism, apart from exceptional circumstances, such as food shortages, recourse to the chief did not seem to be a characteristic of Algonquian groups in which individual autonomy prevailed. Regarding the Montagnais-Naskapi of Lac-Saint-Jean, Lips (1947: 401) reports: "On the other side, any Indian calling upon the chief for assistance would be regarded as unmanly, according to Tommy Moar. Upon my question in what case he would see fit to turn to the chieftain, he exclaimed with pronounced disdain: 'To go to a chief—what a dirty business!'"

Another of Lips's informants corroborates this (1947: 401). How can this turnaround be explained? While the Indian agents usurped some of the roles of the traditional chiefs, the band chiefs had to take over some of the duties of the Indian agents when they left to run the reserve under the direction of Indian Affairs. This in turn transformed Algonquian leadership once again and led to a new community response to this more bureaucratic form of political leadership, which will be discussed later.

Today, in the River Desert community, as on other Algonquin reserves, there is a lot of bitterness about Indian agents. Although the Indian Affairs representatives were different in personality, the characteristics that the Anishinabeg attributed to them are generally similar: they are seen as tyrannical, dictatorial, authoritarian, paternalistic. For the First Nations populations, it is no doubt difficult to present a more nuanced picture of their relations with Indian agents. Indeed, the consequences of reserve management and the political interference of Indian agents are still visible today. For example, it is difficult for the Kitigan Zibi Anishinabeg, but not impossible, to recover land ceded to the City of Maniwaki by Indian agents. The experience with the Indian agents has had a profound effect on the lives of all First Nations peoples in Canada: "Little wonder, then, that when Aboriginal leaders began to press for changes in the 1960s, one of their first and most successful campaigns was the elimination of the Indian agent system" (Brownlie, 1994: 86).

The end of the Indian agents at River Desert did not come abruptly, but rather followed a transitional period. In interviews on the oral history of the community, Elders[17] mentioned the appointment of a band member as the first successor to this position: "And after Leclair, let see a, I think Ernest McGregor took over. For a while. He's an Indian guy. he took over the Indian agent's job." He's an Indian guy. He took over the Indian agent's job." (Henri, seventy-eight years old, interview conducted in Kitigan Zibi,

November 20, 1998, Kitigan Zibi Anishinabeg Global Research Project). Ernest McGregor was not the first individual to assume some of the responsibilities usually attributed to Indian agents. According to Arthur (sixty-five years old, interview conducted in Kitigan Zibi on December 3, 1998, Kitigan Zibi Anishinabeg Global Research Project) and the firm that conducted the Global Research Project, Joan Holmes et al. (1999: 138), Miss M. C. Bertha Joanis had also been in charge of the Indian agent's activities in 1953 during a transitional period.[18] Miss Joanis appears to have been the daughter of the mayor of Maniwaki, Émile Joanis, in office from 1931 to 1933, then from January to July 1941 (Anonymous, 1943: 15; Comité des fêtes du 150ᵉ anniversaire de Maniwaki, 2001: 18). Once again there is a link between the Maniwaki town hall and the management of the Kitigan Zibi reserve. Why did this woman replace the Indian agent? Simply because she was already assisting the Indian agent in his duties. But this was not the case for Ernest McGregor. According to James (fifty-eight years old, interview conducted in Kitigan Zibi on November 20, 1998, Kitigan Zibi Anishinabeg Global Research Project), Ernest McGregor worked for Indian Affairs in Ottawa and was transferred to take over the Indian agent's duties. However, Ernest McGregor was not recognized as an Indian agent, but was no longer "a secretary or whatever, something like that [. . .]" (Arthur, sixty-five years old, interview conducted in Kitigan Zibi on December 3, 1998, Kitigan Zibi Anishinabeg Global Research Project). In this context, Ernest McGregor does not appear to have been negatively associated with the "tyrannical" and "dictatorial" role of Indian agent. Ernest McGregor certainly impressed the band as a successor to the Indian agent position, since he was elected chief in 1970. Has the office of chief and Indian agent been split since then? The words of Charles (fifty-three years old, interview conducted in Kitigan Zibi on December 7, 1998, Kitigan Zibi Anishinabeg Global Research Project) suggest that this transition has occurred:

> And then, we have Harold Vachon who works for Indian Affairs in the 70's before the band takes over, self administration, I think around 1972. Well, Vachon played the role of Indian agent manager at the time, because there's a transition period moving from Indian agent to self administration. Local government and administration. Harold was acting as an official of the government at the time. Which had decentralized services to Ottawa, to the region, the region to districts. They had a series of districts. Sometimes flow from the district of Montreal and other times from the district of Val d'Or.

However, the beginning of this "government" or local "administration" was headed by a chief who had previously worked for Indian Affairs, thus possessing new administrative skills for an Algonquin chief.

While Ernest McGregor assumed the responsibilities of an Indian agent and the management of the reserve, other Algonquins before him had been given a position of authority on the reserve to support the band council in the management of law and order by joining the police force.

ALGONQUIN CONSTABLES AND
STATE OVERSIGHT: THE DOMINION POLICE
AND THE ROYAL CANADIAN MOUNTED POLICE (RCMP)

The colonization of a population proceeds on the basis of law, order, and force. Indian missionaries and agents were not the only Euro-Canadian protagonists responsible for maintaining order in reserve areas (Sawaya, 2012: 36). The *Police Act* of 1868 set the Dominion Police in motion to ensure the protection of the newly formed Canada (McGregor, 2004: 249). As early as 1880, Canadian authorities included First Nations persons in the police force in order to maximize the effectiveness of their interventions (Sawaya, 2012: 36). This inclusion did not aim at equitable access to employment for First Nations people, as they did not have the same prerogatives as their off-reserve Canadian counterparts who enjoyed better pay and full-time duties, whereas the work was seasonal or casual for First Nations constables (ibid.: 156). As Sawaya (2012: 156) points out, they did not have the same prerogatives as their off-reserve Canadian counterparts, who enjoyed better pay and full-time duties; the work was seasonal or casual for First Nations constables. The inclusion of First Nations was practical, symbolic, and strategic: a cheap local workforce that smoothly embodied the state in a familiar face, spoke the language, and knew the actions of other band members (2012: 39–42). In 1889, Algonquin John Hays was to become a constable of the Dominion Police in Maniwaki, where he had "promised to be an efficient peace officer" (ARDIA 1889: 35, in Sawaya, 2012: 41). Between 1880 and 1920, another Algonquin from Maniwaki, Leo Bernard, was appointed constable and served the River Desert Reserve (Sawaya, 2012: 60). With their uniforms and their "instruments of power" (handcuffs, truncheons, revolvers), the constables embodied authority (the *Police Act* and the *Indian Act*) and were responsible for ensuring safety, respect for the laws, and protection of other First Nations persons, including the fight against trafficking and the consumption of alcohol[19] through constant surveillance of the reserve (Sawaya, 2012: 38, 82, 95, 98). This involvement of band members in the Dominion police force does not appear to have left a mark on the memory of the Kitigan Zibi Anishinabeg, as this fact is not reflected in their discourse on policing and is not mentioned in the history of the community (McGregor, 2004). However, their discourses changed when a Royal Canadian

Mounted Police (RCMP) detachment was established on the reserve in 1942, the Dominion Police having been incorporated into the RCMP since 1920 (McGregor, 2004: 250), and "taking over pan-Canadian policing" (Sawaya, 2012: 156). In our work on Algonquian alcohol culture, Marie-Pierre Bousquet and I (2009: 149) noted: "Stories abound, among informants and in the literature, of interference by the Royal Canadian Mounted Police (RCMP), whose representatives would enter communities and homes without a warrant and who would attend weddings as a matter of course to control the consumption of guests." McGregor (2004: 250) makes the same observation about Kitigan Zibi:

> Some Algonquin Elders compared the RCMP [Royal Canadian Mounted Police] presence to that of living in a police state, in that their activities were monitored, especially if the RCMP suspected these activities were connected to boot-legged liquor or home-brewed wine. The RCMP [. . .] could invade Algonquin homes to search the premises for illegal liquor. They did not need permission or warrant. They simply walked in, or burst in, at their own discretion. [. . .] The River Desert would be subjected to nearly five decades of RCMP aggression.

The territory, in the forest, then became the place par excellence for illicit practices where alcohol manufacturing and trafficking were prevalent (Bousquet and Morissette, 2009: 149–50; Sawaya, 2012: 105). The omnipresence of the RCMP and the cavalier manner of their constables created a regime of fear in Kitigan Zibi. McGregor (2004: 259–60) recounts several RCMP interventions that traumatized children on the reserve. As the children grew up and aged, they adopted behaviors to ensure that they did not attract the attention of the RCMP, even after the end of the RCMP's mandate on the reserve[20] (2004: 259–60). Some Algonquins dared to retaliate and challenge RCMP constables. and inevitably ended up in prison (2004: 259–60). Unlike the Euro-Canadians, a stay in prison for a First Nations person was so commonplace that it was ordinary and part of an individual's usual journey. Acts of passive resistance were also perpetrated by the Algonquins against the RCMP (2004: 260). Among them, McGregor (2004: 260) mentions the perpetuation of outings to the village of Maniwaki after repeated imprisonment, misinformation about illegal activities on the reserve in order to deflect constables on false leads, and the habit of some offenders of being given a real manhunt instead of complying with their arrest. Algonquin underground practices to counter the RCMP and Canadian authorities have also been organized with the help of an allied nation. Fearing the seizure of their wampum belts by the RCMP, as was the case on the Six Nations Reserve in Ontario in 1924, the River Desert Algonquins entrusted their political documents to the Iroquois Nation of the Tuscarora Reserve in the United States (Graymont, 1973: 73–74; Einhorn, 1974: 76; McGregor, 2004: 250–51). In 1926, Chief

Chabot headed the delegation that went to New York to temporarily hand over the wampum keeper's position to Chief Clinton Rickard (Einhorn, 1974: 76). The wampum returned to the Kitigan Zibi Anishinabeg on July 9, 1970 after an exile of forty-four years (Einhorn, 1974: 73; Kitigan Zibi Anishinabeg's 150th Commemoration, 2003). Although RCMP officers attempted to legally, physically, and judicially control the Indians on the reserve, the chief still had some control over his band and its internal affairs, as evidenced by the episode of the wampum hiding. In this context, it was not surprising that the authorities were so eager to have a chief who would better represent the interests of the state.

TRAINING INDIAN LEADERS
FOR TRIBE SOCIAL ADVANCEMENT

It was on the initiative of a social worker employed by Indian Affairs, Miss Berthe Fortin, that the first course on Indian leadership was held in Quebec City in 1954[21] (Résumé du cours de formation de responsables sociales "Leadership," 1960: 1).[22] As noted in Rapport des cours de formation de leaders sociaux (1959: 39),[23] the 1959 and 1960 Indian leadership courses attracted much interest and publicity in the local, provincial, and missionary press, as well as on television (Le Droit, 1959 and La Gatineau, 1959) (Anonymous, 1959b: 3, 1960b: 7; RRSL, 1960: 5). These training courses were major events surrounded by decorum, where the Indians wore their ceremonial costumes and feathered headdresses for the occasion. Opening ceremonies, cultural shows, and the signing of the guest book at the Maniwaki town hall in 1959 were among the protocolary activities surrounding these formations. This type of course was not unique to Quebec. Noel Dyck (1991: 103) notes that for the federal government, the period around the 1960s was a good time for the community development program and the development of local government on reserves: "For adults a series of leadership training courses were organized to prepare reserve communities to take greater part in managing their own affairs." Two reports and summaries of these courses[24] that were offered in Quebec provide an overview of these week-long courses, which were designed to "train Indian social 'leaders' who would be able to participate actively in the community organization of their reserve" (RLS, 1959: 5). The goal seems ethnocentric, since it denied that leadership could exist among the original inhabitants. Also, it obscures the fact that First Nations people's leadership may be different from a Euro-Canadian form of leadership. First Nation leadership was undoubtedly more diffuse and less visible to Euro-Canadians, who did not necessarily have the keys to deciphering Algonquian cultural subtleties in terms of authority. By offering leadership training, did government authorities consider that First Nations were incapable of governing themselves?

An article on the 1959 formation at Maniwaki, published in the Oblate journal *Vie indienne*, reports: "From November 16 to 21, representatives of eight Indian reserves met at Maniwaki to study the problem of Indian leaders" (Anonymous, 1959b: 3). It is not known what the problem was, but these words suggest that the missionaries had a poor opinion of First Nation leadership. In his article published in two newspapers (*Oblate News*, n.d., *The Dilemma for Our Indian People*, n.d.) and also reproduced in *Vie indienne* in 1964, missionary J. P. Mulvihill, OMI, is even more scathing and contemptuous of First Nation leadership, judged incompetent, and of the First Nations people:

> The Indian has been isolated and overprotected for so long that he has forgotten or lost his own democratic traditions and sense of leadership [. . .] The government wants to become a counsellor rather than the guardian and protector it has always been. However, it does not want to give up all control until the Indians have their own competence [. . .] It is not enough to plan certain improvements if the talents, attitudes and leadership among them [the Indians] are absent [. . .] The Indians need a good nucleus of chiefs with at least average intelligence if they are to raise their standard of living. This will take years, but training of these future leaders should begin immediately (Mulvihill, 1964: 6–7).

The imposition and political control of band affairs by Canadian authorities does not attest to the fact that the Indian has forgotten or lost his democratic traditions. It is quite possible that Indian democracy and leadership may exist in other spheres, for example, within the territory. Mulvihill (1964: 6) also sees undesirable types of First Nation leadership: the chief invited to a gathering of "Whites" who begins his speech with, "When are you going to hand over our country?"; the chief who always suspects the worst and who accuses the government of bad faith without proof; the old Indian whose hobby, "after fishing," is to blame the government and especially the superintendent of the Indian agency. It does not seem to have occurred to the missionary that his words could reflect a certain First Nation reality. The grievances about the Canadian authorities expressed by First Nations were based on their life experience where the dispossession of their territory and the subjugation and domination of the state had consequences on their daily lives. In a guardianship system that completely managed the First Nation experience on the reserve, how could First Nations have obtained official documents that could serve as evidence for their allegations? In order to train "adequate" leaders according to the missionary's vision, the need for "very simple" leadership courses was suggested by Mulvihill (1964: 6), when these already existed. Who attended the leadership courses offered in 1959 and 1960?

Indian participants, known as delegates, were selected exclusively by local First Nations organizations on reserves, the band council, and the Indian Homemaker's Club (RRSL, 1960: 2).[25] But the 1959 report suggests that the organizers made a selection from among the chosen participants (RLS, 1959: 42). The comments made at the welcome address of the 1954 leadership course by Laval Fortier, then Deputy Minister of Citizenship, confirmed the elitist nature of the Indian delegates: "Your group is the first in this province to participate in a leadership development course. In the eyes of the Ministry, you represent a kind of elite, since you were chosen for your abilities and your understanding of social problems" (Anonymous, 1954a: 8).

In 1959, seventeen delegates attended the training in Maniwaki, including two *tribal*[26] chiefs and their wives (Village-Huron, Hunter's Point). In 1960, twenty-eight delegates were present at Village-Huron, including a tribal chief and nine councillors. In addition to occupation and their role in community life, the course reports portrayed the delegates according to the reserve inhabited, age, and level of education. Algonquins (Maniwaki, Témiscaming, Rapid Lake), Mohawks (Oka), Montagnais (Pointe-Bleue, Sept-Îles, Bersimis), Huron (Lorette) and Abenaki (Odanak) participated in the Indian leadership training. At the course in Maniwaki, the majority of the delegates were between thirty and forty years of age, while the following year they were between twenty and thirty years of age at Village-Huron. The level of education of the participants was higher at the Village-Huron where a majority had reached grade seven and eight delegates had more than grade ten. In Maniwaki, the majority of the delegates had between a grade three and five and only two participants had attained a grade ten or higher.

The delegates were convinced of the merits of the formation of social leaders, as this excerpt from an article that appeared in the Oblate journal *The Indian Missionary Record* after the first course on Indian leadership that took place in Quebec City from May 3 to 8, 1954, shows:

> Mr. Charles Courtois, a 22-year-old Montagnais from Pointe-Bleue, says that these courses "are instructive because they help Indians to be self-sufficient, earn a living and establish themselves honourably." Mrs. Ernest Cree, Iroquois, whose husband is the chief of the town of Oka, said that the courses would "enable us to learn about our rights" (Anonymous, 1954b: 7).

Mrs. Ernest Cree's commentary attests that, in reality, the situation of domination was not so internalized by the First Nations people. Indeed, it shows that the First Nations perceived themselves as having distinct rights. The Euro-Canadian hegemony over the First Peoples does not seem to act on all levels. Did the formations of subsequent years meet the same expectations?

Teaching Organizational Structures and Leadership Techniques to First Nations Peoples

The objectives of the leadership courses were as follows (RLS, 1959: 5):

1. To initiate the Indian to become aware of the social problems[27] in his or her community;
2. To help them find ways to remedy these problems;
3. Sources of information in the areas of work, education, health, and recreation;
4. Stimulate the Indian to participate in any outside social organizations that could improve his living conditions.

At the heart of these training sessions were round tables, group studies (particularly on the "problems" of Quebec Indians, such as alcoholism, low economic status, and health and hygiene deficiencies); discussions; films; lectures; sociology courses; sessions on leisure activities; recreational evenings; demonstrations and exhibitions of crafts; and industrial, school, and recreational visits (for example, to the Zoological Garden), along with attending church services (RLS, 1959: 1–2; RRSL, 1960: 1). Among the facilitators and panelists were representatives of various community organizations, such as the Rotary Club, the Richelieu Club, the Knights of Columbus, Alcoholics Anonymous, the Lacordaire Circle, the Cercle de Fermières, and the 4-H Club.[28] These organizations are primarily parish or municipal creations. At that time, they were part of community life in Quebec villages. The inclusion of these organizations in the course on Indian leadership and the encouragement to participate in their activities were also part of the goal of municipalizing First Nations reserves.

Specialists in employment (representatives of the National Employment Service, the Chamber of Commerce and the Conseil de la Coopérative du Québec), health (doctor and nurse from the Indian Health Service), education (Indian school inspectors, adult education specialist) and "Indian culture" (a missionary, director of the Oblate Indian and Eskimo works, and a representative of the centre for popular culture) were also collaborators and speakers in these trainings and led sessions on their respective fields. Without a doubt, these multidisciplinary demonstrations served to educate the people of the reserves to develop a community life with services, recreation, and social agencies. The presence of community or municipal organizations and trainers from the neighboring town shows the extent of Maniwaki's involvement in the life of Kitigan Zibi. In contrast, Algonquin leaders had never really sought alliances with White leaders. A master-apprentice relationship seems to have eventually linked the town and the reserve. This omnipresence also reinforces the idea that Kitigan Zibi should be made to reflect the image of the municipality of Maniwaki. To guide the delegates, the speakers presented steps to follow, sometimes step by step, to carry out community projects (for example, the development of a recreation committee). In doing so, the facilitators and specialists taught the basics of an organizational structure to the First Nations peoples. It seems obvious that the Euro-Canadian specialists thought about what a community or reserve should be and how it should be technically organized.[29]

Providing delegates with leadership skills (e.g., analyzing community needs, organizing projects, preparing for an assembly, etc.) was central to the training. In these courses, the notion of leadership was said to consist of "influencing a group—large or small—in the pursuit of certain goals. Example: the organization of a collection, bazaar, social evening, credit union, etc." (RRSL, 1960: 17). Moreover, leadership was seen as effective when it was shared—that is, when it used "the talents and resources of some of our neighbours and also of agencies in our community that are already established and that can contribute to the social action project" (RRSL, 1960: 17). It is interesting to note that this explanation, given by a non-Indigenous person, has as its narrative perspective that of a First Nations person. Was the message more likely to be successful if it was conveyed through a game of mimicry? This way of communicating seems to infantilize the First Nations delegates. What is certain is that the comments made suggest that it was believed First Nation leadership cannot be independent, that it necessarily requires the help of "White" people to function properly. Although the organizers' wish was to equip First Nations people to depend less on civil and religious societies, the various directives issued during the courses show that the Euro-Canadian authorities still wanted to keep a certain control over the development of the reserves and the social actions that could emerge there. Thus, at the end of these leadership courses, the "Indian leader" was called to serve as "a liaison between the social worker and his own people," to work "in close collaboration with the superintendent of his reserve, the missionary, the nurse, the educator, and finally, with all those who were in a position to give directives" (RLS, 1959: 5). Throughout the reports, emphasis is placed on the good relations that the First Nations had to maintain with these various actors. It must be noted that an implicit goal of these courses seemed to be better cooperation on the part of First Nations with the non-Indigenous stakeholders present on the reserve in order to set up various community services similar to those in Quebec villages. Since the courses were developed by a social worker, they were guided by the vision of this profession. In social work, leadership has a special definition: the leader is a trusted person who can make decisions. Social workers study those with leadership to determine who has influence, who is capable of leadership, but from a social development perspective, not a political one. In an organizational structure, the goal is to provide services and to perform well. Thus, it seems that Indian leaders were expected to be more knowledgeable about how to design a community among non-Indigenous people in order to achieve this goal of "municipalization" of their reserves. Leadership therefore seems crucial for the development of reserves. What skills and competencies did an individual need to demonstrate leadership?

The Chief: The Exemplary Man of the Reserve

According to the trainers, the qualities associated with a leader include: having a social sense, having the good sense to call on experts at the right time, being discreet, being courageous, having knowledge of human weaknesses, having an acceptable conduct, being farsighted, and knowing how to analyze what is essential or not (RRSL, 1960: 18–19). Formulas such as "calling on experts" and "analyzing what is essential or not" implied a vision of the leader as a manager within a well-structured organization. This may not have been consistent with the qualities and understanding of a leader from the First Nation perspective at the same period. I would like to be able to say what the qualities of a leader were from the Algonquin perspective in the late 1950s and early 1960s, but there is no precise data on the subject. I have often questioned the Anishinabeg to find out why a leader was chosen at that time. "Because it was him" is the kind of answer that is often given, as if leadership naturally falls on one leader rather than another. It was probably an obvious choice since the individual had to be the most competent in the eyes of all. As discussed in chapter 1, for the people of River Desert, at that time it was William Commanda, who was the chief of the reserve, a leader with traditional skills. Did these skills go hand in hand with the qualities outlined in the social leadership courses? Did William Commanda have qualities that were valued as a leader from an Indian Affairs perspective? Possibly he did, because he did not complain against Indian Affairs; he was also sober and was respected by his people. In the report of the training that took place in Maniwaki, a positive portrait of Chief Commanda was drawn. He is presented as a man committed to his community since he was a member of the Knights of Columbus, the Lacordaire Circle, and the Maniwaki Chamber of Commerce (RLS, 1959: 11–12, 29). Armand Benard, president of the Lacordaire Circle of Maniwaki, a Catholic temperance movement, states: "All Indians should follow this good example set by the chief" (RLS, 1959: 29). At that time, the chief was expected to serve as a role model on the reserve, and this was also encouraged among social leaders through leadership courses. But what did Indian Affairs expect from an Indian leader?

The Indian Affairs Vision of an Indian Social Leader

According to Ms. Fortin, a social worker, and Regional Supervisor of Indian Affairs R. L. Boulanger, the role of an Indian social leader was:

- To convince the members of his Tribe of the importance of teamwork for the improvement of the social conditions of the group.
- Create an atmosphere of cooperation.
- To interest people in activities that are enjoyable, pleasing and accepted by them.
- To ensure order and discipline.
- Teaching people to share and to be good losers.
- Convincing people of the importance of taking care of their own affairs, giving them a sense of responsibility. Stimulate the aspirations of the group. E.g.: Presenting new and attractive activities. Promote community organizations. Ex. Domestic Circles, 4-H Club, Guiding and Scouting.
- Encourage the development of constructive programmes for the general welfare of their community, discuss these programmes with the Chief, Councillors, Domestic Circle Members, former Leaders.
- Offer assistance to the Social Worker, the Missionary, the Superintendent, to help them to solve the social problems of the reserve (RLS, 1959: 33).

In analyzing this description of the responsibilities of an Indian leader, these two Indian Affairs workers seemed to suggest that First Nations people did not work in teams, did not share, were bad losers, and had no sense of responsibility. This negative portrayal of First Nations people and their cultures by government authorities was commonplace. It reflected not only the Euro-Canadians' lack of knowledge of the First Peoples, but also the colonizing spirit that distorted the First Nations person, who was seen as inferior. Speaking of the Algonquin ideological system, Jacques Frenette (1988: 48) notes that "morality insisted on generosity and mutual aid." Autonomy was also a value conveyed within the Algonquin bands prior to sedentarization. It is possible that reserve settlement may have altered the forms of cooperation and independence of the Anishinabeg. Since support networks of allied families still exist today in Kitigan Zibi, it is likely that the same was true in the 1950s and 1960s. No doubt, the authorities did not understand the forms of First Nations cooperation in action (such as mutual aid and sharing) since they were most often a matter of private life for First Nations peoples. Moreover, several elements mentioned in the two reports on the leadership courses suggest that civil and religious authorities, as well as other non-Indigenous stakeholders, sometimes did not understand the Algonquian rules of good manners. For example, they criticized the First Nations peoples for not being loquacious about their desires and lacking confidence in front of an audience. Highly respectful of everyone's autonomy, the Algonquians did not directly verbalize a request to another individual so as not to oblige him or her. Since Algonquian culture is based on an egalitarian ideology, an individual does not put himself in front of others in public or, if he has to do so, it is because he is recognized as having the competence or legitimacy to do so. The organizers of the leadership courses also asked delegates to introduce themselves to the assembly at the beginning of the courses. This is further evidence of Euro-Canadians' ignorance of Algonquian rules of etiquette. Within Algonquian cultures, one does not introduce oneself. This is why the delegates suggested that in the future, their colleagues should present them at the assembly (RRSL, 1960: 4).

The Political Culture of a Reserve

In the 1959 social leadership training course in Maniwaki, in addition to the attention paid to the notions of leadership, emphasis is placed on explaining a "Community Structure of an Indian Reserve based on 'the family.'" Figure 2.2, taken from the report, presents this organizational chart. It shows that all the services offered on the reserve were the responsibility of the civil and religious societies. The *Tribal* Council had no formal community role other than that of rapporteur, as indicated in this excerpt from the presentation on the structure: "Special attention was given to the importance of electing Tribal Council chiefs and councillors capable of interpreting the needs and rights of Indian families to Civil Society on the one hand, and informing Indians of their duties to Civil and Religious Society on the other hand" (RLS, 1959: 7). Delegating more authority and responsibility to band councils was, however, an Indian Affairs policy, as stated by R. L. Boulanger, the regional supervisor (RLS, 1959: 28).

Politically, the Indian leadership courses also featured demonstrations of a *Tribal* Council election as well as a *Tribal* Council meeting. These demonstrations were followed by explanations, discussions, and the distribution of pamphlets on rules and procedures (RRSL, 1960: 39). By teaching how to vote and hold a political assembly, the Canadian authorities attempted, on the one hand, to explain the implementation of Euro-Canadian democracy as applied to the First Nations. For Marc Abélès (1992: 17, 23) political culture—that is, "a set of ways of doing and thinking politics shared by a human community"—is embodied in symbolism and rituals. Thus, Canadian authorities have, on the other hand, attempted to radically change First Nations political cultures by introducing procedures, symbolism, and rituals.

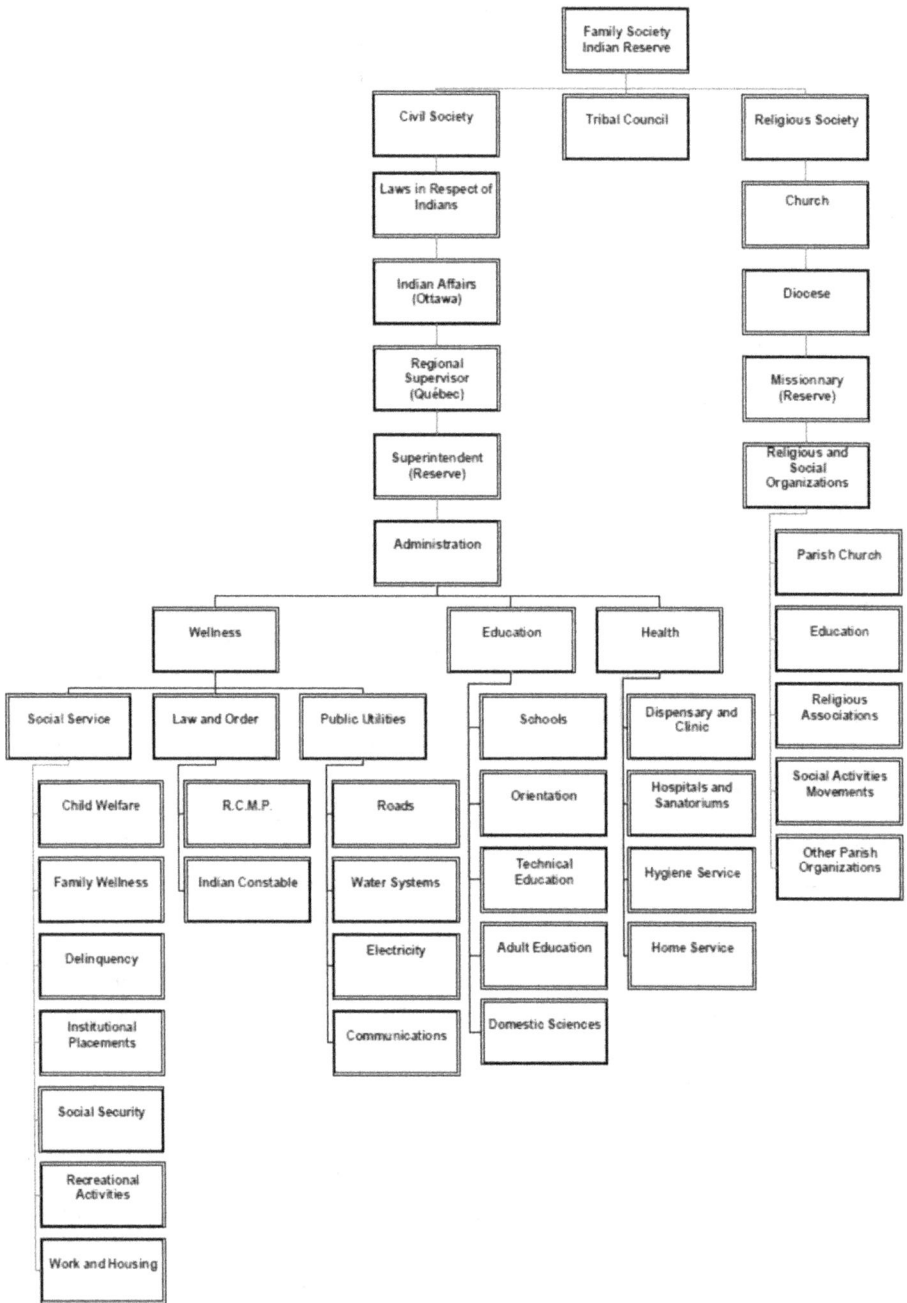

Figure 2.2. Community Structure of an Indian Reserve based on 'the family'"

CONCLUSION

Although today Indian Affairs agents, missionaries, and RCMP constables are often viewed negatively in the communities because they were colonizing actors, the fact remains that challenging these power figures allowed the Anishinabeg to develop a political identity and leadership in response to them. These actors also contributed to First Nations political behavior, the ritualization of politics, the acquisition of new symbolic power, and community attachment. Actors from outside Algonquin culture may thus be part of the political legacy of the Kitigan Zibi Anishinabeg. Indian leadership courses have attempted to equip First Nations leaders with new technical skills to deal with the imposed reserve political system, its organization, administration, and bureaucracy. Indian Affairs and religious authorities were thus attempting to train a chief who represented the standards of the State. However, it is difficult to assess the political impact of these leadership trainings on First Nations reserves. Only a detailed portrait of the individuals who took these courses would be able to draw up the effects. The fact of having taken this training does not necessarily imply that First Nations leaders have applied to the letter the ways of doing things advocated by the State. In a context of social and political change, the main protagonists at the heart of the transformation make choices, adopt behaviors and rely on references at the expense of other criteria. In their attempts to transform First Nation leadership, the authorities may have underestimated the power of free will of chiefs and leaders that resides in the "cracks" of their control. Thus, the residential schools' ambition to train future leaders has had mixed success because the former residents have perpetuated the powers of Euro-Canadian political leaders to some extent but have mostly been instigators of counterpowers. The Euro-Canadianized First Nation leadership envisioned and desired by the government and religious authorities did not rigidly set itself up as a single, unilateral form of leadership and did not provide a standard model of a homogenous First Nation chief on reserves. The perpetuation of the chiefs' control over their band and its internal political dynamics allowed them to maintain local power and freedom of action. Finally, a new style of First Nations leadership is emerging from the interstices of Euro-Canadian reshaping and the continuation of the chief's influence over his people.

NOTES

1. Expression often used in missionary writings. See especially Carrière (1958: 24).

2. Letter from J.-M. Nédélec to Superior General Fabre, February 15, 1864, in *Missions de la Congrégation des Missionnaires Oblats de Marie-Immaculée*, vol. 4, 1865: 167, in Bédard, 1988: 107.

3. Interviews conducted in Kitigan Zibi with Mark (forty-seven years old), July 4, 2007, February 5, 2008.

4. On this subject, see, for example, the letter from Father Étienne Babin, OMI, written in 1922 to the Department of Indian Affairs, denouncing the contempt and ill-treatment of the Algonquins of Abitibi-Témiscamingue in Leroux et al. (2004: 56, 59–66). See also the account of Father Joseph-Étienne Guinard, OMI (1945: 131–34, in Clermont, 1982: 117–20), of a meeting in the 1920s between a delegation of Indians (from the Saint-Maurice, Gatineau, La Lièvre, La Rouge, Migiskan Rivers), led by the missionary, and Minister Taschereau.

5. In 1988, the Kitigan Zibi Anishinabeg Band received financial compensation for the loss of this territory.

6. These are the residential schools in Amos, Fort George, Pointe-Bleue, and Sept-Îles (Bousquet, 2006: 1). Two other residential schools of the Anglican faith were in operation in the province: the residential school in La Tuque and another also located in Fort George (Bousquet, 2012: 169).

7. The residential school experience was emotionally, psychologically, ideologically, behaviorally, relationally, family-wise, identity-wise, culturally, spiritually, physically, and sexually traumatic for the Kitigan Zibi Anishinabeg and all First Nations children in Canada. In addition to being uprooted from their way of life, from their parents, being forced into "White" ways, and growing up with the feeling that what was Indian was wrong, the residents also experienced punishment, public humiliation, and physical and sexual abuse. The painful aftermath of this period is still part of the daily lives of the former residents and their families. Since the consequences of residential schools continue today, they are, according to Milloy (1999: xiv), one of the most damaging elements of the colonization of Canada's first inhabitants. For a history of residential schools in Canada, see in particular Miller (1996) and Milloy (1999). For writings on the consequences of residential schooling, see, among others, Furniss (1995), Dion Stout and Kipling (2003), Wesley-Esquimaux and Smolewski (2004) and Bousquet (2006).

8. In fact, an amendment to the *Indian Act* in this regard had been in effect since 1920, and Quebec authorities should have applied the federal law beforehand but did not (Bousquet, 2006: 5). It should be noted that Indian agents were already involved in schooling First Nations children to some extent, but especially those from settled families.

9. On the history of classical colleges and convents in Quebec, see among others Galarneau (1978), Dumont and Fahmy-Eid (1986).

10. The contradictions between the Euro-Canadian and Algonquian rules of good manners were mostly a source of punishment. For example, looking the other person in the eye for Algonquians is considered disrespectful, whereas it is de rigueur for Euro-Canadians to do so.

11. The election of student councils was not unique to Pointe-Bleue residential school. The same was true at other residential schools. In 1962, the Journal *Vie indienne* even made headlines for the student council elections at the Sept-Îles residential

school (Anonymous, 1962: 3). Unlike the Pointe-Bleue student council, the Sept-Îles student council was composed solely of boys (Anonymous, 1962: 3). Thus, each residential school had its own political colors.

12. Retrieved from the Répertoire des élus municipaux en Outaouais de 1845 à 1975 website, http://craoutaouais.ca/repertoire/Web/maniwaki.html, accessed March 1, 2013. Charles (sixty-eight years old, Kitigan Zibi, telephone interview conducted on March 6, 2013 by a band member) also confirms Lorenzo Leclair's double employment because, to his knowledge, there was only one man with that name and political profile in the Maniwaki region at that time.

13. Notably in the transfer of land from the River Desert Reserve. See McGregor (2004: 210, 215, 225).

14. Alexander (seventy years old), interview conducted in Kitigan Zibi on December 3, 1998; Elisabeth (seventy-four years old), interview conducted in Kitigan Zibi November 20, 1998; Charles (fifty-three years old), interview conducted in Kitigan Zibi on December 7, 1998, Kitigan Zibi Anishinabeg Global Research Project.

15. Alexander (seventy years old), interview conducted in Kitigan Zibi on December 3, 1998; Elisabeth (seventy-four years old), interview conducted in Kitigan Zibi November 20, 1998; Charles (fifty-three years old), interview conducted in Kitigan Zibi on December 7, 1998, Kitigan Zibi Anishinabeg Global Research Project.

16. Adam, sixty-five years old, interview conducted in Kitigan Zibi on December 3, 1998; Elisabeth (seventy-four years old), interview conducted in Kitigan Zibi November 20, 1998; Victor, eighty-three years old, interview conducted in Kitigan Zibi on December 7, 1998, Kitigan Zibi Anishinabeg Global Research Project.

17. They are Henri, seventy-eight years old, interview conducted in Kitigan Zibi on November 20, 1998; James, fifty-eight years old, interview conducted in Kitigan Zibi on November 20, 1998; and Arthur, six-ty-five years old, interview conducted in Kitigan Zibi on December 3, 1998, Kitigan Zibi Anishinabeg Global Research Project.

18. See table 2.2.

19. Upon its coming into force, the *Indian Act* prohibited the sale, production, and consumption of alcohol by First Nations (Sawaya, 2012: 18–19). It was only after the Drybones decision in 1971 that First Nations peoples were able to enjoy full freedom in terms of alcohol consumption (Bousquet and Morissette, 2009: 149).

20. The RCMP's mandate ended in Maniwaki in 1967 (McGregor, 2004: 260). The Sûreté du Québec provincial police took over. The River Desert police force was created in 1981 with the first three police officers from the reserve: Leonard Odjick, Francis McDougall and Michael Twenish (McGregor, 2004: 321). For a history of the development of Indigenous policing in Quebec and the development of the Service de la police amérindienne see, among others, Sûreté du Québec (1979), Monique Michaud (1986), Aubert and Jaccoud (2009), and Jean-Pierre Sawaya (2012).

21. The "social advancement of the tribe" is a common formulation in reports on Indian leadership courses. Other such phrases include "to promote the social evolution of the tribe" (see, for example, le rapport des cours de formation de leaders sociaux, 1959: 6, 37). Résumé du cours de formation de responsables sociales "Leadership"; hereinafter RRSL.

22. Rapport des cours de formation de leaders sociaux; hereinafter RLS.

23. *Le Droit*, 1959 and *La Gatineau*, 1959, in Rapport des cours de formation de leaders sociaux, 1959: 39; *Vie indienne*, Anonyme, 1959b: 3, 1960b: 7; RRSL, 1960: 5.

24. These course reports were found in the Archives Deschâtelets, see reference HR901.

25. The Homemaker's Clubs of the Maniwaki Reserve and the Village-Huron actively participated in the event. This will be discussed further in chapter 4 on women's empowerment.

26. The term *tribe* is used in the reports. It refers to the band.

27. Among the problems existing on reserves at the time, R. L. Boulanger, Regional Supervisor, Indian Affairs Division, noted alcohol abuse, low economic, health and hygiene standards (RLS, 1959: 2). According to him, these problems were the result "of the disadvantageous situation in which most Quebec Indians find themselves, both economically and socially, culturally and politically" (RRSL, 1960: 1).

28. These community organizations provided, and still provide, opportunities for members to fraternize with each other through a variety of activities, while accomplishing various social goals. The Rotary Club, the Knights of Columbus, the Lacordaire Circle, Alcoholics Anonymous, and the 4-H Club were born in the United States in the early twentieth century and soon crossed Canadian borders (RLS, 1959: 12–13; http://www.aa.org; http://4-h.org). Of these organizations, only the 4-H Club is aimed at young people and aims to promote their environmental interests and skills (see http://www.clubs4h.qc.ca/). Alcoholics Anonymous is an organization that provides men and women with a problem of alcohol abuse with support to end their addiction. A women's association, the Cercle de Fermières aims to improve the living conditions of women and their families by sharing knowledge and know-how (see http://www.cfq.qc.ca). The Rotary Club and the Richelieu Club have been accepting women into their ranks since the 1980s, while the Knights of Columbus and the Lacordaire Circle have remained male (http://www.richelieu.org, http://www.rotary. org). However, the Order of the Daughters of Isabella and the Cercle Sainte-Jeanne-D'Arc can be considered the feminine variants of these associations.

29. For the Algonquians, the community existed without "living together" before the settlement. There was a sense of community because everyone came together at summer gatherings. The community rites practiced at these gatherings (for example, the shaking tent rite) helped to cement the community. However, First Nations rites considered "pagan" by the missionaries had no place on the reserves. Per contra, settlement in villages did not eradicate Algonquian ritual practices that took place in the forest (see Armitage, 1992).

Chapter Three

"Bottom-Up" Governance

The Implications of the Overlap of the First Nation and Euro-Canadian Political Universes on the Role of Chief

Since the 1960s, Indian Affairs agents have not been present on reserves. Initiated in 1965, the gradual takeover by Indian bands allowed for greater local political freedom and openness to First Nations. Has it also introduced new political dynamics or sources of power within bands? In fact, this gradual takeover coincides with what could be described as the beginning of "bottom-up" governance. Speaking of the contemporary situation of Indigenous peoples' political autonomy, Martin Papillon (2006: 472) summarizes governance "from the top" and "from the bottom" as follows: "The challenge these governments [Indigenous governments] face is considerable, given that it involves breaking away from the model of governance 'from above' associated with the colonial regime and the *Indian Act*, and (re)creating within communities a genuine democratic life allying traditional practices with the requirements of modern government."

Papillon's use of the verb *recreate* implies the prior existence of democracy on the reserves. The idea of an open system was not unfamiliar to the Anishinabeg and Algonquians in general, as in their traditional system all had a voice. The right to vote in band council elections under the *Indian Act* however does not guarantee democracy. The political interference of Indian agents discussed in the previous chapter demonstrated the absence of local participation in decision-making in the formal framework on reserves. Before democratic life on reserves can be "recreated," it must first be created. Has "bottom-up" governance led to an opening up of the political process and social mixing, or has it led to a new decision-making monopoly through the chiefs' takeover? Certainly, the beginning of "bottom-up" governance implies a new personification of power, a metamorphosis of leadership. How does this transition to formal Indian-style leadership take place? This chapter

is devoted to governance "from below," to the process of openness and negotiation between the Algonquin and Euro-Canadian political worlds accom-
plished by the chief. Compared to the past and the aim of openness, several
paradoxes emerge from the new local power structures and the broadening of
the chief's field of action. These paradoxes should not be seen as anomalies,
but rather as the result of a cultural experience of their own arising from a
structural change that ultimately gives meaning to everyday Anishinabe politics and its power relations.

By governance, I mean the set of rules, practices, ways of doing things, and
mechanisms by which a society is directed, governed, controlled, managed,
and administered. The political analysis of a First Nation reserve is complex
because its current governance is a dynamic endogenous process that is renewed daily through the chief in order to deal with two opposing worlds of
reference: one Indigenous and the other Western. To speak of governance
"from below" in a context where the band council is a local structure whose
forms and ideology derive from elsewhere may seem contradictory. Some
might argue that "bottom-up" governance would only be possible if the local
level consists solely of recognized First Nation institutions incorporated into
a postcolonial Canadian state and federalism. The outcome of "bottom-up"
governance—that is, the creation of an autonomous postcolonial First Nation
political entity—is not a spontaneous process. It is possible to observe the
beginning of "bottom-up" governance even in its most embryonic practices.
The incorporation of First Nations leadership within the imposed Euro-
Canadian structure, the acquisition of decision-making power—even partial—regarding reserve affairs, the original appropriation of certain practices
by the political actors involved, and the attachment of traditional functions
and dynamics to the formal structure constitute the beginning of governance
"from below." The latter does not have the power to modify the imposed
structure of governance "from above," but it renews from within, through the
establishment of a dialogue, the relationship between First Nations leaders
and representatives of the State, which gives local actors room for maneuver.

Combining Indigenous references and Euro-Canadian political demands
is not a simple process; rather, it is the result of reflection and a selection
of elements or behaviors to the detriment of others. Christiane Guay and
Thibault Martin (2008: 640–41), in their article on Indigenous governance
and the territory, put forward the "reflexive work of Aboriginal societies on
themselves"—that is, the process of reflection in their choice of traditional
non-state normative elements or Western normative systems that has governed and still guides the Indigenous present. Is it fair to believe that this
reflexive work is the product of a whole society, as Guay and Martin suggest?
Is Algonquian politics conceptualized, analyzed, and conscientized only by

those who practice it? It is relevant to ask what place the population occupies in this reflexive societal work. Thus, we must distinguish between formal institutions, rhetoric, cultural values, and the interests of the population. The latter may not be as homogeneous as one might think.

This chapter will first discuss the transformation of the role of band chief brought about by the administrative takeover of the Kitigan Zibi community. New skills and new political behaviors are now required for this function. The role of the Anishinabe chief is changing: he is no longer equal to all.[1] A portrait of the contemporary eligible candidates of Kitigan Zibi will then be presented in order to illustrate the characteristics and qualities of the current elected officials as well as the limits of participation in power. The exploration of a First Nation political campaign will make it possible to grasp the articulation of the formal system, but also the stakes of a political position in a reserve environment. The last part will focus on the dynamic evolution of the band's political universe by studying the draft electoral code of the Kitigan Zibi Anishinabeg, which constitutes another step toward their political autonomy.

INSTRUMENTAL USE OF STATE'S REQUIREMENTS

It was during the 1970s that being a band chief once again changed dramatically at River Desert. The same was true in other Algonquian communities at the same time (see in particular La Rusic, 1979, about the Crees). Wishing to encourage the development of local government, the devolution of power program of the Department of Indian Affairs gave responsibility for the administration of local services to the bands (La Rusic, 1979: 125). Local services included education, health, social services, and reserve maintenance. As a result, the role of the band chief was transferred to an institutionalized, full-time employment role. Being a band chief was not a profession in Algonquian societies. Rather, this position of authority was a "moral" role in community life. This was still the case at River Desert during the nineteen years of William Commanda's mandate (1951–1970). Henri and Charles, former members of the band council, testify to Chief Commanda's obligation to have a paid job to support himself:

> Of course, them days the chiefs have to go out and work. Some day he goes to place around here, then you have to out and you have no choice. And Willy him he had a job there he was gone far as New Brunswick. (In editable) [*sic*]. He needed his bread and butter him to right. Didn't have no choice but he made it (Henri, seventy-eight years old, interview conducted in Kitigan Zibi, November 20, 1998, Kitigan Zibi Anishinabeg Global Research Project).

[. . .] when there was times when they were away to maintain their livelihood because there were no form of government subsidisation. Everybody had to fend for himself, one way or another. So, the chief was often not here. Actually, it reached the 50's, I guess, when the chief would be away often, in the 50's, he'd be working elsewhere (Charles, fifty-three years old, interview conducted in Kitigan Zibi on December 7, 1998, Kitigan Zibi Anishinabeg Global Research Project).

Faced with the new administrative challenges of taking charge of a community, a new kind of chief was needed. Being educated and fluent in the official languages were now imperatives to lead the band's institutional structure. These new skills required a different generation than that of previous leaders, that of Elders with traditional knowledge (Indigenous language, knowledge of the territory, etc.). The skills required for the position of chief were held by a younger generation that could translate the values of its group into a clear political demand to Euro-Canadians. This younger generation would change the generational dynamics of First Nations political leadership by taking the place of the Elders at the head of the band (Morissette, 2007: 132).

Because he worked off the reserve, experienced and saw what was being done elsewhere, had a perspective that was different from that of other band members (Charles, sixty-three years old, Kitigan Zibi, May 1, 2008), and had an education in the academic sense, Jean-Guy Whiteduck was elected chief of River Desert in 1976 when he was only thirty-one years old. It is a political revolution for the Algonquins to have had such a young individual at the helm. But this does not imply that this election went against Anishinabeg principles and values. As discussed earlier, it was traditionally the individual with the most experience in hunting, knowledge of the land, and relationships with the spirits of nature and the masters of the animals who was recognized as the chief. The new skills required for band council operations changed the areas in which an Algonquin chief needed to have experience. Speaking the Algonquin language was not useful with Indian Affairs administrators, but technocratic language was now indispensable. For example, being educated had become an essential asset in the administrative management of a reserve.

In politics, Jean-Guy Whiteduck had no experience, and he was not familiar with the functioning of reserve authorities, as the other members of his band council were (Charles, sixty-three years old, Kitigan Zibi, May 1, 2008). However, the new chief and his councillors were eager to learn, as evidenced by the comments of a front-line informant at that time:

And from there we have a vision to develop the community, improve services and take charge. Taking charge of our own business. We've had meetings with Indian Affairs, which is the main government body for the operation of the reserve. In those years we had district offices and regional offices and we dealt with the Montreal district office with the communities of Caughnawaga, Oka, there were 4–5 communities. So we called the regional leaders of the district office and told them that we want to have a meeting with your employees from the different services, we want to know how things are going. And we had with us a list with essential things to do in the coming years. These people were not used to it, they were used to working with people who asked almost nothing, who said almost nothing. So, they were faced with people who were much more aggressive. Listen to us, we don't accept the way things are going anymore. Because we knew that other communities were receiving a lot more than we were. And we thought it's time for it to stop. When Caughnawaga was near the district office and the Huron village in Quebec City, for example, they had more things. Why is that the case? Then we put our demands on the table and we said this is what we want: we want to have more houses, we want to improve our communities. People were still taking water from the streams. There were a few wells but not many. We put, as we say, our wish list on the table. And from there they said "you are aggressive." We said we want to have services and we are entitled to them. And that's how it started, we took charge (Charles, sixty-three years old, Kitigan Zibi, May 1, 2008).

In this new rapport with Euro-Canadian institutions, Algonquin leaders adopted a proactive behavior that demonstrated their willingness to equip themselves to orchestrate and build their community. Verbalizing their demands to Indian Affairs representatives was unusual for the Algonquins, since this way of doing things went against their rules of good manners, as mentioned in the previous chapter. In carrying out their requests, the Kitigan Zibi Anishinabeg set aside certain cultural behaviors to play the bureaucratic game in order to advance community interests and perhaps their own status. The Algonquins had to change their behavior because, as La Rusic (1979: 172) explains, "Band councils now had to take the initiative in asking Indian Affairs to introduce each program into the community and provide the necessary funds for its operation." Indigenous peoples did not have Western-style organizational traditions (Robichaud, 1992: 42) such as a bureaucratic infrastructure or public administration. The chief and band council members in Kitigan Zibi, as elsewhere, acquired their administrative skills over time. They have been "trained on the job" as Robichaud (1992: 42) mentions with respect to band managers.[2] Because of the abilities of First Nations political actors, which differed from one reserve to another, each community took its own path to empowerment. The personality, capacity for action, and social and political commitment of a band chief played a key role in the development of a community and influenced its political evolution. Dealing with institutional parameters and formal requirements was instrumental to success within a bureaucracy. It was a strategy of action in which Euro-Canadian institutions represented a structure of political opportunity for Algonquins in which they could finally participate.

Being part of a political structure is advantageous for a participant who wants to question, redefine, or operate the system. According to Charest (1992: 70), the devolution of administrative power did not give real power to First Nations, but a margin of maneuver. This margin of maneuver nevertheless constitutes the beginning of bottom-up governance of First Nations local politics. Indeed, with a First Nations leader at its head representing local interests, local politics was becoming more democratic. The Indian agent who represented the department's interests, as discussed earlier, would no longer run the reserve or control band council meetings. By obtaining formal executive authority, some Kitigan Zibi Anishinabeg would no longer just be administrative and political witnesses to their affairs, but participants. Community needs as they were experienced could theoretically be expressed and taken into consideration. Decisions affecting the band would be compatible with local realities, since the chief was a member of the band. One would think that in the absence of a departmental representative at band council meetings, the population would immediately exercise freedom of speech and henceforth express itself without constraint at political meetings. Despite the shift of certain powers to local structures managed by locals, public participation did not immediately increase. Joseph (sixty years old, Montreal, May 29, 2012) explains that it took several years before the older people on the reserve trusted the new chief and understood that he was not an Indian agent. The Elders used to distrust the Indian agent and not speak up. At that time, Joseph continued, there were four politically active family "clans" that made decisions without going through council (for example, with the mayor of the neighboring community of Maniwaki), using their influence in other ways without ever becoming chief. Beyond this political practice "in the cracks" and on the margins of official power exercised by these four clans, band members were not interested in politics, confirms Joseph. According to him, it was only after almost ten years of the takeover that the younger members became more interested in politics and began to speak at band council meetings.

On the other hand, as soon as the devolution of administrative power began, the chief became a key administrative contact with the various players in the Ministry of Indian Affairs. The Kitigan Zibi band had a local voice that was officially heard and transmitted. A dialogue was finally beginning to be established between local Algonquin leaders and government authorities. From an anthropological point of view, this dialogue is part of what can be described as a patronage relationship,[3] the links between Indian Affairs, the chief, and the band members being those of "patron intermediary, and client," respectively. Thus, the role of band chief has become that of an "intermediary" (broker) with Euro-Canadians. Robert Paine (1971: 6), who has studied patrons and intermediaries in the Eastern Arctic, defines the role of the broker as follows:

> A broker is a typical middleman role; however, it should be distinguished, in analysis, from another: the go-between. The distinction relates to the manner in which the task of intermediary is performed: where messages or instructions are handled faithfully, we recognize the role of go-between, but where they are manipulated and "processed," we recognize the role of broker.

The band chief is not a go-between because he does not strictly transmit or faithfully follow all instructions from Indian Affairs. It is in this manipulation of messages or instructions by the chief, this power of interpretation of the role of intermediary, that the room for maneuver of the First Nations and the beginning of a bottom-up governance lies. Even if the assumption of responsibility was a government initiative and once again the First Nations had to follow this resolution, the fact remains that they would benefit from entering more deeply into the political game with the State through administrative channels. The chief's administrative position provided him with visibility and political legitimacy with the authorities. In fact, he really fulfilled his function as the political representative of the band. Certainly, the chief had already been a representative for the people of the River Desert. However, by not participating in the routine official affairs of the band, he had not necessarily been seen in this light by the actors of Indian Affairs. Now, his bureaucratic participation would open up political space for him, as Martin Papillon (2009: 420) suggests: "Administrative intergovernmental relations can become political spaces in which aboriginal governing institutions can assert their authority and legitimacy, and transform administrative dynamics into political ones." The day-to-day exercise of executive administrative power and relations with Indian Affairs would strengthen the political capacities of the First Nations chiefs.

A band chief could gain political power from administrative power. La Rusic (1979: 160–61) notes: "For Quebec bureaucracies, as for any other government, there is always power behind the most powerful civil servants." It should be noted that the band council is part of the civil service. It is a "branch," to use the term of La Rusic (1979: 126), of the Department of Indian Affairs. The chief is, therefore, a bureaucrat of the state. According to La Rusic (1979: 161), in the long run Cree bureaucrats would have power. At River Desert, from 1976 to 2006, the band council grew from 1 to 110 full-time and 100 part-time employees, from a budget of $200,000 per year to $25,000,000 (Charles, sixty-three years old, Kitigan Zibi, May 1, 2008). At the local level, the chief has gained considerable power as a major employer and project administrator. The autonomy, expertise in the routine administration of the band, and mastery of the bureaucratic system acquired by the chief have enabled him to develop not only external credibility, but also political strength—that is, the ability to exercise formal power and/or counterpower vis-à-vis the government. Denis Robichaud (1992: 22), who has studied the administration of First Nations bands, notes that "several authors recognize the importance of having a competent and effective Aboriginal administration to support political action." Taking charge of the communities' own affairs was much more than the appropriation of an exogenous system. First Nations peoples did not simply gain control of an existing system, but they attached certain functions normally managed by "hidden" and "traditional" dynamics to the formal structure. There is no doubt that there is some ambiguity about the contemporary role of First Nation chief. Once again, the role of chief has many facets and dimensions. In order to understand its subtleties, it is important to distinguish between the formal function of chief in a bureaucratic system and its cultural role and status. Even though he is an official of the State and the official representative of the band, for the Algonquins, the chief remains an Indigenous symbol and still has Indigenous significance, despite the evolution of his activities. He is the past symbol of semi-nomadism, of the political survival[4] of the group, and he is linked to the future politics of self-government. This plural dimension of the role of band chief has been completely overshadowed by Taiaiake Alfred, an ultra-activist Indigenous academic. Alfred unabashedly considers that only traditional leaders are true leaders and that individuals in positions of authority within the current colonial political system "are less leaders (with apologies to the rare exceptions) than tools of the state" (Alfred, 1999: 30). Not only does Alfred make a homogenous value judgment about Indigenous societies as a whole by distinguishing between "true" and "false" leaders, but he denies the possibility that traditional and formal roles can coexist within the office of chief. From the traditional perspective, the chief was an authority figure. With the gradual takeover, he also became a formal power figure. Thus, a First Nation chief can be said to embody the three types of authority documented by Weber (1965): legal, charismatic, and traditional. However, it should be noted that chiefs do not necessarily combine all three qualities: some are not charismatic at all.

For Alfred (1999: 32), it is clear that individuals within the imposed Euro-Canadian political system are working against their own people. It is true that some chiefs have little leadership, function like bureaucrats, and seem to represent only the State. But the reality has more nuances than Alfred's generalization suggests. In addition to the chief who acts as an intermediary between the State and his locality, there is also the anti-state chief. Indeed, some First Nations have given the band council a different vocation: that of political lobbying. As Raymond Hudon and Stéphanie Yates (2008: 380) note, lobbying is "a legitimate means of action in a democratic society." It allows interest groups to express their grievances to political institutions (2008: 381). Like patronage, lobbying is a practice of "mediation between members of society and the formal political decision-making bodies" (2008: 380). This mediation exists both within the band and in its external relations with the authorities. Internally within the band, lobbying may mean that power is now centralized, and therefore access to power is more restricted for the majority. By claiming access to the same services as those of the Caughnawaga reserve and the Huron Village from the very beginning of the takeover, the Algonquins of the River Desert were already putting pressure on the government authorities. Over time, the band council became the central organization for local, land and comprehensive claims. From a legal point of view, this is self-evident since the band council is the only political apparatus recognized by Canadian authorities as being able to represent First Nations. If there is pressure to be brought to bear against a local project that could harm the environment, for example, it is inevitably to the band council that members turn. The band council was and is the ideal body to intervene, since it is a legitimate grouping; it has bureaucratic tools, contacts, knowledge of the system, and experience with the authorities; and it masters Euro-Canadian conventions, concepts, and technocratic language. But not all bands can rely on the experience of people already on the council. Expertise sometimes needs to be completely rebuilt when newly elected officials take over.

For the population of River Desert, as elsewhere, administration and bureaucratization have become normal within local indigenous politics. Why is this so? For the Anishinabeg, there are already several generations living with an administration whose modern structure derives from Euro-Canadian institutions. Administration and bureaucratization seem to them to be the way in which everything is granted by government authorities. They are the means of communication with the Euro-Canadian authorities. The Algonquins do not question a system, or even a strategy, that has proven to be effective in making their voices heard. The more the population uses administration and bureaucracy, the more necessary they become. In doing so, the population emphasizes and reproduces the hierarchy of the system (patron-intermediate) even while attempting to repatriate certain local administrative functions. In the absence of another valid substitute, an alternative structure to manage their realities, bureaucracy has become a "habitus" rooted in the daily life of the reserve. This "naturalization" of band bureaucracy is reinforced by the fact that with the takeover the band chief has acquired a new form of authority and legitimacy based on the control of the administrative and bureaucratic bases recognized by the Euro-Canadian-dominated structure.

The Chief, a King on the Reserve?

In the past, the sense of leadership was based on the territory. Now, leadership is embodied in one person in particular, the chief. The mythical and spiritual structure behind the "charismatic" power of the "Indian chief" is no longer relevant in a context of formalizing politics. Charisma is no longer the basis of power but simply a useful personal attribute. Weber (1965: 389), who, among other things, described the transformation from a charismatic leader to an elected leader, notes: "The introduction of elected officials always involves a radical alteration in the position of the charismatic leader. He becomes the servant of those under his authority." Nowadays, if things go wrong on a reserve, people often blame the chief. Cora J. Voyageur (2008: 12) notes: "As chiefs, they are the highest-ranking decision makers in the community. This means that all decisions whether deemed good or bad by the community government, or industry, fall back on them." While the expectations of the population are no longer met, we return to Frazer's (1890) argument on the role of the scapegoat king. Does it seem that the chief sometimes acts as "king" on the reserve? The comments of Max (forty-two years old), a band member whom I met in April 2008, point in this direction (Kitigan Zibi, April 27, 2008). Max considers that, nowadays, band council members do not do anything anymore because it is the chief who decides and has the last word (Kitigan Zibi, April 27, 2008). This lack of democracy felt by Max resembles a dictatorship in its most extreme form. According to Max, the councillors no longer take into account the needs of the population: "Before, it was quite the opposite." He recalls that First Nations peoples made their decisions together as a community and that the chief would inform the authorities: "The chief was the emissary." According to Max, since the chief was the one who gave the results of community decisions, the consequences of those decisions were felt by the entire community and not just the chief. Sometimes, he says, the chief would make the decisions, but it was all borne by the group. There is a process, a progression to consensus building, as Alfred (1999: 93) points out:

> In indigenous traditions, consensus decision-making is a group process in which the common will is determined through patient listening to all points of view. Leadership takes the form of guidance and persuasion within the larger respectful debate. In cases where individual interests must be balanced against those of the community, there should be a considered evaluation of the individual's needs (as opposed to wants); these needs should be balanced with those of the community; and the entire debate must be carried out on firm ground of agreed-

upon values and principles. If any one of these elements is missing, consensus decision-making cannot happen; processes that purport to be consensual become mere exercises in power-wielding, manipulation, and enticement simply to gain the assent majority.

Alfred's words are idealistic. Far from the consensual process, Max says that "now the chief decides." He explains that the population not only feels that they are not informed of what is going on, but also that they are not involved in the decisions. It also seems difficult to go to the other extreme and consult the population in a consensual manner in everything. The bureaucratic system depends, according to Weber, on a narrow and impersonal rationality. This system and its democratic decision-making process has created a relational distance between the chief and band members, even a hierarchy. The chief is no longer the equal of all but is accountable for his actions. Discussing the sense of accountability between the First Nation leader and the community, Alfred (1999: 91) notes: "Accountability in the indigenous sense needs to be understood not just as a set of processes but as a relationship." This means that accountability goes beyond impeccable accounting to include maintaining a link between decision-makers and those affected by decisions (Alfred, 1999: 91). One of the chiefs' challenges is therefore to maintain a relationship with the population by keeping them informed of the many ongoing files concerning the band in order to demonstrate that they are working in the interest of all.

CONTEMPORARY ELIGIBLE CANDIDATES

How and why does one individual become and remain a chief more than another? Chief Jean-Guy Whiteduck held the position from 1976 to 2006. Being a band chief for thirty years, fourteen consecutive mandates, is exceptional among First Nations in the contemporary era. It has allowed for stability and continuity in the management of the community's affairs, in the development of various projects and the advancement of political issues. It should be noted that political stability is not only ensured by a formal system of leadership, but also by informal arrangements around power. The kinship networks of a chief who remains in office have become more important. These are used to support and implement the chief's policies, thereby initiating a spiral of strengthening the power of the chief. The sustainability of a chief in office leads to political stability. Robichaud (1992: 95) remarks: "It is also noted that the stability of the political system has a direct effect on band administration. In cases where the band is politically unstable, the administration also shows symptoms of instability and inefficiency. Frequent changes in political leadership lead to chronic insecurity and fragmentation of administrative units."

A change of band chief implies a period of adaptation for him before he can offer his full potential in the management of the community and take the political actions necessary for the advancement of the band. Indeed, a new elected chief must, among other things, understand the structure, master the files, learn the daily tasks, be initiated into band council procedures, and know the *Indian Act*. To help new chiefs and councillors, the Department of Indian Affairs even produced in 2003 the *Guide sur la gouvernance des Premières Nations: Une source d'information pour rehausser l'efficacité des conseils* (First Nations Governance Handbook: A Resource Guide for Effective Councils). The general information described, although useful,[5] does not provide knowledge of the specific affairs of a band. This suggests that, ultimately, the formal system has nothing to do with the "real" local system. However, producing documentation for First Nations does not imply that the people take it into consideration. My findings indicate that there are a considerable number of pamphlets on the reserve and in every home that explain various aspects of life in First Nations communities (diabetes among First Peoples, the *Indian Act*, residential school resolutions, gambling and smoking addiction). Finally, this production of documentation trivializes information that might prove useful if it were consulted. After all, mastery of rhetoric is at the heart of the intermediary position of the chief who, for example, must be familiar with all the codes (First Nations and non-Indigenous) in order to advance their various claims through negotiations with authorities. However, not consulting official documentation can be a form of laziness, forgetfulness, lack of interest, protest, resistance, or indifference on the part of newly elected First Nations chief—a way of boycotting the Euro-Canadian colonizing methods, of making one's own experience of the structure according to one's principles and visions. It is possible that the newly elected chief may consult this documentation while declaring the opposite. The heavy daily workload of a band office[6] also often takes its toll on the time that could be devoted to the reading of informative documents by newly elected.

Who Becomes Chief Nowadays?

In his study of the traditional and contemporary process of selecting First Nations leaders, J. Anthony Long (1990: 763) presents statistics on the numbers of candidates running for election on the Blood and Peigan Nations reserves in the Prairies over two decades (1965–1989). Unfortunately, Long does not portray the elected officials and their supporters, thus obscuring the human experience and process of this selection. Long's study remains mechanical and dual because it does not delve deeply into the possibility of an overlap of criteria from the First Nations and Euro-Canadian political worlds regarding the choice of leaders. The analysis of a candidate's past and his or her attributes allows us to understand the societal and cultural transition brought about by the change in the elective system and the assumption of local governance by First Nations peoples.

It is no coincidence that since 2006 in Kitigan Zibi, elected chiefs have been related to former chiefs. On a reserve, some ties are more important than others and become the basis of power. This is the case with kinship ties. On the subject of the Algonquins, Marie-Pierre Bousquet (2001: 386) notes: "The chiefs have genealogical links with their predecessors, but this is hardly surprising in villages where all the people are more or less related to each other. It is therefore tricky to speak of family dynasties, although the reputation of the candidates' families seems to play a role in their election or eviction." The activation of the kinship network for the election of one of their relatives is certainly a decisive electoral vector, but the eligible candidate must have a certain legitimacy. In his research in Saint-Germain, France, Marc Abélès (1989: 28) stressed the importance of the legitimacy of those eligible in a kinship network:

> Legitimacy is transmitted here as a heritage within a lineage. Everything happens as if the name was enough to "authorize," to confer on its holder the capacity to assume local responsibilities. From local roots, belonging to a lineage that has historically "distinguished" itself, in the double sense of the term. Here, it seems, are the indispensable conditions to accede to the status of elected official. Similar situations can be found in many local authorities where the same continuity of notables can be found.

What about the Kitigan Zibi Anishinabeg? Upon the political retirement of Chief Jean-Guy Whiteduck in 2006, Stephen McGregor was elected chief at the age of forty-five. He is the son of the late Chief Ernest McGregor. The fact that he spent his childhood (his father was a councillor before he was elected chief) and adolescence in a house where politics was the order of the day (Kitigan Zibi, July 4, 2007) may have given Stephen McGregor political capital. From a learning perspective, he was able to benefit from his father's experience. Stephen McGregor is also knowledgeable about the local history of the band. He is the author of the book *Since Time Immemorial: "Our Story,"* which I quoted earlier. Today, First Nations production of their band's history involves not only identity, but also political and legal issues, as Bousquet (2001: 109) points out. It is an asset in land claims cases and courts of law because it serves as evidence in their defense (2001: 109). Stephen McGregor was able to gain the support of a certain electorate in the community that could be described as traditional and another part of the electorate that wanted a competent administrator. Indeed, prior to his election, he held the position of assistant band manager. Thus, he possessed administrative skills in the management of the reserve. According to one informant (forty-six years old, Kitigan Zibi July 4, 2007), Stephen McGregor was elected "because people wanted stability, to keep the status quo and people working hard. To run the community." Chief McGregor has served a single term as band chief. Taking over the reins from a band chief who served for thirty years was certainly not an easy thing to do. From a political and administrative point of view, the band has undergone a significant transition in the ways of doing things by a new kind of leader to whom it was not accustomed.

In 2008, Gilbert Whiteduck, brother of former chief Jean-Guy Whiteduck, was elected chief of Kitigan Zibi. Once again, there is a genealogical link with a past chief. The networks that ensured the election of Jean-Guy for three decades have reactivated to elect Gilbert. Other elements contributed to the election of this man. First, Gilbert Whiteduck had political experience. He was a band councillor for twelve years.[7] He is also what is called a social personality in the community, that is, "an individual who holds a key position, outside of political life, who has a certain prestige and notoriety." (Morissette, 2004: 101). Gilbert Whiteduck, a teacher, school principal, and director of the Kitigan Zibi Education Council, has worked in the field of education for more than thirty years.[8] His involvement in education extends beyond the community.[9] Gilbert Whiteduck also has a higher education: "He holds an Honors Bachelor Degree in Social Science, a Bachelor of Education Degree, a Masters of Education Degree and an Honorary Doctorate Degree in the field of Education."[10] A respected man, having held a key position, dedicated to community and cultural preservation, Gilbert Whiteduck had many assets to be elected chief. He is the typical personification of contemporary First Nation power, as he is proficient in the rhetoric and other "non-Indigenous" technologies and the cultural references of his people. In 2010, no candidate ran against him in the elections. Perhaps this is a testament to the caliber of authority of this man and his networks.

Family and Allies: Vectors of Success or Setbacks in a First Nation Political Campaign

Political campaigning is a relatively recent phenomenon in First Nations communities. This Euro-Canadian way of doing things, this democratic tradition, has been introduced at different times on reserves according to their own paths. Generally speaking, First Nation political campaigning seems to be a practice that intensified in the second half of the twentieth century. The birth of political campaigning among First Nations goes hand in hand with their takeover of the band council system. Since local power was no longer in the hands of Indian agents, it became within the reach of a band member. From then on, the stakes of a political position were higher because it gave access to certain privileges that will be discussed later. As more power was now at stake, competition for election was fiercer and would gradually create the need for campaigning. Campaigning was an opportunity for candidates to take the time to explain new political issues to the population and, more importantly, to show that they had original ideas for dealing with them. For an individual, campaigning is about publicly and voluntarily putting oneself in the forefront by displaying one's qualities. As discussed above, this type of behavior was contrary to Algonquian rules of good manners and was condemned by the group. This has partially changed as Algonquians have embraced village-style politics. Euro-Canadian political practices did not necessarily contrast with the sedentary life on the reserve. The First Nations undoubtedly brought nuances to these exogenous political practices.

In Quebec, a First Nation political campaign is more discreet than its Euro-Canadian equivalent: no election signs posted on the reserve, no buttons or slogans. While candidates do not normally go door-to-door,[10] family members and friends in Kitigan Zibi significantly increase their courtesy visits to the reserve several weeks before the election. People move back and forth from one house to another and conversations about fishing, or any other subject, inevitably lead to discussions about the qualities and shortcomings of the candidates for election. In the workplace, at the grocery store, wherever you are, family and allies also promote their candidate's candidacy to the detriment of another, but in a subtle way, without ever directly formulating "you should vote for so-and-so." One should not believe that the approach of supporting the family and allies is disinterested, as this River Desert informant testifies: "And often it is because it is family regroupings that will bring the most to families if that person is elected. It's always that concept" (Charles, sixty-three years old, Kitigan Zibi, May 2, 2008). This statement is consistent with José Mailhot's (1999: 78–79) remarks about the Sheshashit Innu politics in the mid-1970s:

Candidates for the positions of chiefs and councillors are elected with the support of their respective groups, although alliances occur between groups through marriage and adoption. In return, elected candidates distribute privileges of all kinds to members of their own group. This may be a new house that will be given to them on their next housing project, or a used truck that can be bought back from the band council at a low cost, or home repairs—all of these things are free of charge since the costs will have been charged to the band council's account. It may also include employment in one of the programs administered by the council or the privilege of participating in a caribou hunt by charter plane. This system of distributing favours (which at first glance could be likened to patronage) is today the fundamental feature of Innu politics in Sheshashit. The challenge is therefore for each faction to get as many candidates elected as possible and, above all, to get one of their own elected to the position of chief.

Father Jean Fortin, OMI (1992), an Oblate missionary who was present in Natashquan in the 1960s, confirms a similar situation within this Innu band of the North Shore. According to the data I have collected from several Algonquian communities since 2003, this "system of distribution of favors" is still in place. However, beyond the immediate and extended family mentioned by Mailhot, elected candidates are also elected through other social networks with diverse bases. For example, social networks based on friendships, religious or spiritual beliefs, shared experiences (including the residential school experience), and shared community engagement. Is this system the result of the *Indian Act*, of village-style political practice on the reserve, of an Algonquian tradition of redistribution of amenities by the chief? A political system, even when imposed, cannot be held responsible for the behavior of the elected officials who participate in it. The band council system is not the instigator of the system of distribution of favors by the chief. However, it has provided the chief with privileged access to resources in an environment where resources are limited or controlled by exogenous power. On a reserve, economic development and employment opportunities are almost nonexistent and housing is often overcrowded and inadequate to serve a growing population. As Vincent Lemieux (1971: 235) noted in his study of kinship and politics on Île d'Orléans in the 1960s, "[Patronage] is the only hope of getting out of a difficult economic situation." This observation is valid and still relevant in First Nations reserves. Patronage is probably not the only hope for improvement in an economic situation, but is the most immediate avenue available to band members because it involves networking rather than more formal and complex processes. Because he controls resources, the chief has become the boss over community members. As Freeman (1971: 35) summarizes, "The power of the patron lies mainly in his control of a scarce resource valued and desired by the client." Hidden issues of redistribution of favors are not part of election campaigns [. . .] Nevertheless, access to a position of power brings obligations.

In his article on Chief Jean-Baptiste Boucher, Gélinas (1998: 33) reminds us that "in 'egalitarian societies,' power is generally accompanied by debt." Gélinas (1998: 33) continues his explanation by drawing on the work of Marshall Sahlins (1976: 181–82): "The chief must be grateful for the prestige he is given, and this gratitude was usually manifested through acts of generosity." The time has passed for the feast offered by the chief, as was the case with the Atikamekw chiefs (Petiguay and Neweashish) in the second half of the nineteenth century, as reported by Gélinas (1998: 33). Collective sharing seems more difficult on reserves where the band's population has increased considerably. For example, the River Desert Band numbered 469 individuals in 1923 (Speck, 1929: 108), while it had 3,370 members in 2018.[11] In the context of a populous community, it is not surprising that the privileges granted by an Algonquian chief serve first and foremost to repay the "electoral debt" he contracted with the various networks that elected him. If he fails to adequately repay his allies, the chief will not receive a second term in office. The family and allies of an elected candidate implicitly expect preferential treatment or a greater voice on the band council. It is possible that the Algonquian "family"[12] may still be perceived as a unit of production, as was the case with hunting groups in the days of semi-nomadism. One thing is certain: the Algonquian family is a network of solidarity and cooperation that is always active and serves to improve the quality of life of its members. The system of distribution of favors to the family and its allies is more discreet in some communities. Its presence nevertheless testifies to the control of resources exercised by the band chief. From my observations, the system of distribution of favors seems to contribute to the internal division of Algonquian bands. For Larsen (1983: 109), who has studied the Mi'kmaq of Nova Scotia, "conflicts are symptomatic of the manner in which resources circulate on reserves."

According to Susan (forty-seven years old) and Louise (forty-six years old) (Kitigan Zibi, February 10, 2008), two members of the Kitigan Zibi Band, "everyone in the community is trying to pull the rug out from under their feet." They feel it is time for everyone to come together on the reserve. There is often talk of division at River Desert. However, the reasons behind this division are never clearly explained. It seems that the criticisms are not new. The privileged access to goods, jobs, and services; the influential role of certain families; the lack of participation of individuals; and aborted projects seem to me to be grievances of some against others at the heart of the band's split. Competition for access to resources on the reserve inevitably leads to social fragmentation. Redistributive power in politics does not seem to be restricted to the position of chief.

Being a Councillor: A Coveted Position

In recent years, the trend of having an impressive number of candidates vying for the position of councillor has demonstrated a definite attraction to this political office. There are a number of reasons for this interest. For example, the desire to make a difference on the reserve through access to the decision structure, hidden benefits, and the acquisition of a job for an unemployed person. In the 2008 elections, twenty-three candidates ran for one of the six mandates of councillor at River Desert.[13] According to Andrew (twenty-six years old, Kitigan Zibi, June 3, 2006), the number of candidates in the 2006 election was thirteen. In two years, the number of candidates nearly doubled. By 2008 almost all families on the reserve were represented. However, this does not mean that the position was open to all. The fact that there were so many individuals from different families may have meant, among other things, that at that time in the community there was not one family that held more authority than another. What is the actual function of a band councillor? For Bernard (fifty-five years old, Kitigan Zibi, February 6, 2008), who worked at the band council, a councillor provides support to the chief and knows all the files. Susan (forty-seven years old, Kitigan Zibi, April 27, 2008), who had already applied for the position of councillor, explained that each of the six councillors has a file from a sector of the community, such as health, public works, education, and so on, and that each of them was responsible for a specific file. She mentioned that it is the councillors who decide at council meetings, including the participation of the chief, on the directives that will be pursued in these fields of action. Thereafter, she said, the decisions taken will be carried out by the directors of these various sectors. Max (forty-two years old, Kitigan Zibi, April 27, 2008) specified that the chief receives a salary for his position, but that the councillors receive an honorarium. According to Bernard (fifty-five years old, Kitigan Zibi, February 6, 2008), these are paid once a month. Thus, being a councillor does not appear to be a full-time permanent job at River Desert. For some, it is a step toward becoming chief.

For the Kitigan Zibi Anishinabeg, the presence of many candidates for the position of councillor is not viewed favorably. According to them, this divides the vote of the population and the elected person is not necessarily unanimous. How do the Kitigan Zibi Anishinabeg choose who to vote for as a councillor? When asked, Louise (forty-six years old, Kitigan Zibi, April 27, 2008) simply replied, "Well, we know them." In a community where there were 1,549[14] band members living on the reserve in 2008, you can't hide anything from anyone; you obviously know everyone's experience. In profiling the candidates, I noticed that Louise referred not only to their own actions, but also to those of their relatives. As Bousquet (2001: 386) foresaw, I found that the family's reputation is in some cases beneficial and in others a negative factor. A person's capacity for judgment—that is, whether that person can "keep his or her pants on and stand on his or her own two feet"—is also a sought-after attribute and one that my informant would take into account. The friends of the candidate also influence the impression the candidate makes. If a candidate stands with "drug addicts" or "people who drink," it can be detrimental. A candidate's state of health is also a factor that can be negative. Louise cites as an example the candidacy of an individual prone to burnout.

This condition casts doubt on the candidate's ability to cope with the burden of future duties and obligations of a councillor. School education is also taken into consideration in the selection of a band councillor. Parenting skills (being a good or bad parent) are also taken into account. It is conceivable that the criteria for the selection of a councillor cited by my informant could be applied by extension to the selection of a chief. Another band member summarized the electoral choice of voters as follows:

> Today we are back with a parliamentary, democratic system, where people can appoint and support someone who thinks he or she can make a good leader or who will bring about things as they wish. Often people have needand we say, "Who's the best?" It's like normal non-Aboriginal politics, it's who's going to be in the best position, better articulated to bring stability to the community and bring the resources to develop. [. . .] There is especially the leadership aspect that plays an important role; is it someone who is going to protect our interests when it comes to Aboriginal rights? Is it someone who will negotiate well with the government authorities around us? It's all these aspects that come into play (Charles, sixty-three years old, Kitigan Zibi, May 2, 2008).

Elections in Kitigan Zibi follow the rules set out in the *Indian Act*. After the selection of an electoral officer, the nomination of candidates is the first step in the electoral process. As mentioned in this excerpt, to be valid, a nomination must be supported by two band members. The nomination may be made by means of a form sent by mail to the electoral officer or orally at the meeting of electors of the Kitigan Zibi Anishinabeg, also known as the *Nomination meeting* (flyer, Kitigan Zibi March 2008). This meeting is held six weeks before the election date (Kitigan Zibi, April 25, 2008). It sometimes happens that an individual's nomination is made by band members without his or her knowledge. According to Charles (sixty-three years old, Kitigan Zibi, April 30, 2008), the individual must then fill out a form to have his candidacy withdrawn from the electoral list. The nomination meeting is a critical moment in the election campaign when candidates have the opportunity to speak publicly to band members. Economic development and the fight against the social scourges that afflict the reserve are among the issues at stake. For some candidates, this public presentation will work in their favor and additional votes will result. For others, orally inept and less experienced, it will have the opposite effect. Speaking up is not a requirement for candidates for councillor. Some prefer to abstain.

The reserve nomination meeting is also an opportunity to legally inform band members through the distribution of the *Indian Act* and the Department of Justice *Indian Band Election Regulations* document, as was the case at the April 26, 2008, meeting. In fact, the election process remains unclear to many band members. Euro-Canadian legal jargon does not facilitate understanding. The distribution of legal documents is also a demonstration of the official character of the community meeting among familiars, a way to give a serious and protocol tone to the assembly, a way to give credibility to the band members in charge of the elections, a way to make the Euro-Canadian electoral process legitimate. After the nomination meeting, the election campaign gained momentum as the assembly was an opportunity for voters to make a first selection.

Election Statement

To get elected, some candidates for councillor and chief ran their political campaign by writing to the community in the weekly newsletter, commonly known as the "flyer." This form of speech is a demonstration of the mastery of "non-Indigenous" and formal rhetoric. For the 2008 elections, the candidates had their message published a month and a half before the elections. Their messages were varied: projects for band development; improving community life; preservation of Aboriginal rights; promotion of language, culture, and education; and leadership and political assemblies. In addition to promoting a candidacy, the publication of a statement by a candidate in the flyer sometimes serves to scotch rumors about him or her circulating in the community. According to a former member of the band council (Charles, sixty-three years old, Kitigan Zibi, April 25, 2008), tittle-tattle and election "gossip" lasts from the nomination to the election: six weeks. He characterized this period as "very painful." In the reserves, as elsewhere, the "smearing" campaigns at election time are part of the backdrop of the race for power. These are often based on the shortcomings of the candidate or former elected official (e.g., lack of leadership, candidate X does not live on the reserve) and the history of the official's actions (e.g., lack of accessibility when in office, X's administration cutting budgets for cultural and community activities). With two months to go before the election, the subject of the election is on everyone's lips. No matter where one goes on the reserve, to the supermarket, the health center, the hardware store, the bingo game, in every home, lively discussions about the candidates are inevitable. But even in normal times, there is a great deal of interest in local politics. This seems obvious in an environment where every aspect of life is managed by the band council. According to Charles (sixty-three years old, Kitigan Zibi, April 25, 2008), there is year-round talk of politics on the reserve. It's an inexhaustible subject. According to Susan (Kitigan Zibi, April 28, 2008), candidate for councillor, it is two to three months after the election before everything goes back to normal for a candidate. For Charles, the election is not the end of election gossip. These gossip practices are a form of outlet and in fact reveal tensions within the community. These tensions help to manage passions (e.g., jealousy, resentment, suffering, animosity, antipathy, etc.) and internal situations suffered: contrasting economic realities from one household to another, demoralizing social conditions, weakening of solidarity and cooperation.

As noted by Regina Flanerry (1934) and Ronald Niezen (1993: 244) for the Cree, Edward Rogers (1965: 264) for the Cree and Ojibway of Eastern Canada, and Armin Geertz (2011: 383) for the Hopi Indians, among others, gossip is a mechanism of ethics, morality, and conformity that serves, among other functions, to control social relations. Electoral gossip among the Anishinabeg is undoubtedly a form of popular control of elected representatives, even a powerful political tool. Elected representatives and dissatisfaction with them are endless topics of conversation in Kitigan Zibi. Is this a legacy of traditional politics? Alfred's (1999: 92) explanation of disagreement within the traditional Indigenous political system suggests so:

> Thus active and fractious disagreement is a sign of health in a traditional system: it means the people are engaging their leaders and challenging them to prove the righteousness of their position. It means they are making them accountable. [. . .] Consider the words of an Elder from the Fort Yuma Indian Reservation in California: "We Quechans try to get somebody to do better by tearing him down—criticizing him. You whites, you try to get somebody to do better by making him feel good, by praising him."

While the practice of criticizing leadership and eligible candidates is still current, the positive vision of it does not resonate in the reserves. The proximity of individuals in this environment means that what is said in elections directly affects the private lives of individuals. Those who are eligible and those who are elected are not immune to criticism and slander and to the resulting distressing atmosphere for them and their immediate family members. All their gestures, or lack thereof, are analyzed and scrutinized. The written publication of an electoral speech does not escape criticism and judgment by members of the community, nor does its absence.

Are there generational differences in the electoral discourse in Kitigan Zibi? In their written statement to the population, the younger generations displayed their degrees and various educational backgrounds. The older generation, on the other hand, put forward their life experience, while not hiding their primary schooling. This is a perfect illustration of the gap between past and present Algonquian political realities. As discussed earlier, life experience was an essential quality for a leader in the era of semi-nomadism. With the bureaucratization and administration of the reserve, schooling—and therefore youth—became a necessity for its leaders. Today, the two schools of political thought still exist side by side. The last generation of Elders who experienced semi-nomadism is dying out. It is difficult to assess whether life experience will continue to be valued as a quality in an Algonquian leader and will be sufficient to get an individual with no formal education elected.

One thing is certain, the life experience of Elders is still valued in everyday life since band members do not hesitate to consult them. During the 2006 elections, a young candidate for the position of councillor went to question Elders to find out how he would proceed with his election campaign (Andrew, twenty-six years old, Kitigan Zibi, June 3, 2006). Their advice was as follows: "You hide for six weeks." The Elders seemed to advise the young candidate to protect himself by hiding. This response also demonstrates that, for the older generation on the reserve, an election campaign may seem unnecessary. In the end, for them, an individual's reputation still seems to be enough for their election. Perhaps it is to avoid damaging that reputation that it is best for a candidate to "hide" from band members on the eve of an election. It is conceivable that the Elders' advice reflects another reality: the campaign is already settled before it is officially launched. Along with the formal politics that defines power and its policies, informal arrangements between networks remain.

From my observations, over the past few years in Kitigan Zibi, there is a desire among band members to regain political power from the imposed official apparatus. This is evidenced by the following excerpts from the election campaign published in the flyer: "The people must be the driving force in the control of our reserve"; "Community members to regain power, theirs is the final say." Doesn't bottom-up governance start with band members? Within the Abitibiwinni First Nation, the political organization chart for the reserve does not have the chief heading the branches of the administrative areas of the reserve but rather the band members (see appendix 2). If electoral rhetoric focuses on the empowerment of the reserve population, it is probably because the reserve population feels powerless at the end of the day. The campaign speech of one candidate, an Elder, published in the flyer (Kitigan Zibi, April 29, 2008), offers a clue to understanding this sense of loss of power: "The chief and council don't have the full power, it is the majority of the community members who have the final say." The chief and councillors may be perceived as the holders of power at the expense of the rest of the population who have become subordinate and voiceless.

Elections are not the preferred method in Kitigan Zibi, given the low voter turnout. In 2008, 805 ballots were counted for the position of chief and 802 ballots for the positions of councillors out of 2,122 eligible voters (flyer, Kitigan Zibi April 14, 2008). Less than half of the electors exercised their right to vote. The 2010 elections attracted even less interest. Of a possible 2,171 voters, only 518 ballots were counted (flyer, Kitigan Zibi, June 20, 2010). Less than one-quarter of voters turned out at the polls or voted in advance by mail.

The acclaimed election of the chief and a smaller number of candidates running for council (eleven in 2010 compared to twenty-three in 2008) may have contributed to the low voter turnout in the 2010 elections (flyer, Kitigan Zibi, June 14, 2008; flyer, Kitigan Zibi, June 20, 2010). Overall, why do Anishinabeg not vote? Several reasons can be given for this, including indifference, lack of civic culture,[15] and the belief that candidates are already "elected" before the election. Non-participation in elections is not a new phenomenon in Kitigan Zibi, as this excerpt from the report by Hawthorn and Tremblay (1967: 206) shows:

> A high degree of continuity combined with low voting and number of candidates per post could signify minimal interest in running for office and in elections. This would appear to be the case in Cheam and Maniwaki. However, the same pattern (high continuity combined with low voting and candidates per post) could signify the survival of an hereditary system behind the front of an elective one, with the band council still playing a significant role in the eyes of band members, despite the superficial indices of low voting and candidature.

The hypothesis of the presence of a traditional regime seems possible at the time of data collection for this report in the 1960s, when William Commanda was the band chief. Is this hypothesis valid today? It is not a traditional system that seems to have persisted, but rather a traditional attitude of leaving the decision to the most competent, capable people in the band to decide by voting to select the chief and councillors. One informant even confessed to feeling politically incompetent as a voter (fifty years old, Montreal, June 28, 2012). In various informal conversations, band members indicated that not participating in elections is also a way to challenge the imposed political system. Some band members do not recognize contemporary elections as Algonquin and therefore legitimate. Disillusioned with the system and Euro-Canadian guardianship, other band members do not see any concrete change to their situation, whether it is an individual serving on the band council or another. The Kitigan Zibi Band's low voter turnout in local elections is also reflected in provincial and federal elections. This is evidenced by the following comments taken from Beatrice Fantoni's[16] (2010) article "First Nations franchise: Buying in or selling out?"

> The nation of Kitigan Zibi in the riding of Pontiac, Que., has one of the lowest on-reserve voter turnout rates in Canada.

> "Our community has rarely voted in federal or provincial elections," says Kitigan Zibi's chief, Gilbert Whiteduck. "We view those levels of government as not being ours. . . . First of all, we're Anishinabe."

In the last federal election, only 54 people out of 877 eligible voters turned up to vote at the Kitigan Zibi poll—about 6 per cent. The overall turnout in Pontiac was 55 per cent.

Whiteduck says a big part of peoples' decisions not to vote in federal elections has to do with maintaining the sovereignty of their nation, and not assimilating into Canadian society. But individuals on the reserve are always free to participate in federal elections or not, he says.

Chief Whiteduck's comments may also explain why band members do not vote for the band council: they do not recognize the band council as their own and do not want to be assimilated into the Euro-Canadian system by voting. Fantoni (2010) considers that "many First Nations today still feel voting is equivalent to participating in a colonial institution and giving up their identity." The Kitigan Zibi Band does not vote massively in order to preserve its identity. But how can Anishinabeg manage to insert their identity within the official political mechanisms imposed?

THE DYNAMIC EVOLUTION
OF THE BAND'S POLITICAL UNIVERSE

Since the takeover, there has been a restructuring of the band's political organization. Although it has been a local driving force, the takeover is of course not the only thing responsible for the reshaping of the Algonquian political universe. Several events have contributed to the political development of Indigenous societies, including the emergence of modern Indigenous movements and associations following the challenge to the White Paper (Canada, 1969), the mobilization of the Cree and Inuit (1970) against the first hydroelectric dams in Northern Quebec, the comprehensive and specific land claims policy (1973)[17] and the Oka crisis (1990).

In Kitigan Zibi, a political restructuring, even a dynamic evolution, is still in progress today. For example, in July 2008, the band council consulted with the community to establish guidelines for the conduct of band council meetings. To this effect, a questionnaire was distributed to band members in the weekly newsletter, the flyer, issued by the band council. The consultation of band members, as a process, is reminiscent of the Algonquian consensus decision-making process. The questions were cultural, behavioral, and technical in nature. On the cultural level, the desire to begin and end the meeting with a prayer and the circular arrangement of the assembly were invoked. At the behavioral level, questions focused on what to do if inappropriate language was used or there was threatening behavior toward those present. From a technical point of view, the chairmanship and frequency of band council meetings, its agenda, and the number of interventions by the audience were among the issues addressed in the questionnaire. The need to issue guidelines during public band council meetings is a testament to the climate of tension that prevails there. The dissatisfaction and frustrations of band members are expressed at these meetings. Debates concerning band affairs are heated, as one would expect in a transitional situation.

It would be wrong to think that expressing discontent to leaders is a new phenomenon among First Nations. They did not live in peace and serenity, as some clichés about them suggest. Quarrels existed, otherwise the chief would not have been a judge. However, the public challenge to the chief in the Euro-Canadian media seems to be a recent phenomenon. The legitimacy of elected chiefs is openly questioned beyond the reserve space. If band members go beyond the local level to criticize their chief, the chiefs in turn use the national, and even international level but with the opposite goal: to strengthen their local power and the power of the band.

The Indian Act: A Well-Established and Embedded Daily Habitus

The development of Anishinabe politics goes hand in hand with a reappropriation of official politics. Indeed, the band is in the process of developing its own electoral code. However, in 2008, the River Desert Band did not seem prepared for this political transformation. The words of a former member of the band council bear witness to this:

> Yes, I think that here we will find to develop our own rules, a customary way for us. But people are reluctant for one reason or another. They are used to the *Indian Act*. It's going to be difficult to change. [. . .] People are afraid. But change is going to be necessary, that's all. The system we have for two years doesn't work. We have to change everything, that's for sure (Charles, sixty-three years old, Kitigan Zibi, May 2, 2008).

This excerpt refers to the habit of band members to be governed by the *Indian Act*. Despite the imposition and numerous repercussions of this exogenous law on their way of life, this law is well anchored and incorporated by First Nations peoples because it is part of their daily life. In Algonquian communities that have experienced a great deal of upheaval in a short period of time, the possibility of profound and permanent change is looked upon with apprehension. Any transformation on the reserve over which Algonquians can have some form of control seems to proceed quietly. If the two-year election system "doesn't work," the implementation of the Kitigan Zibi Anishinabeg electoral code will allow the Kitigan Zibi Anishinabeg to introduce their own operating logic, including their norms, within an imposed political mechanism.

The Kitigan Zibi Anishinabeg Election Code:
A Democratic Step in Self-Government

The elaboration of the electoral code of Kitigan Zibi is a real political revolution in the community. Indeed, since the implementation of the *Indian Act*, the River Desert Anishinabeg have always followed the regulations governing elections developed by the Act. In 1971, among all First Nations in Canada, the percentage of bands following the electoral provisions of the *Indian Act* was 71 percent (Canada, 2010: 6).[18] Today, 32 percent of bands continue to use the election rules of the *Indian Act*.[19] Just as First Nations are heterogeneous, the electoral codes developed by First Nations are not similar (Canada, 2010: 11). Some Bands partially modify the election provisions of the *Indian Act*, while others change them radically (Canada, 2010: 11). For some First Nations communities, such as the Manawan Atikamekw Band,[20] the creation of an electoral code was an opportunity to introduce traditional aspects of their governance and culture. The Electoral Code of the Atikamekw Council of Manawan, implemented in 2002, "includes, among other things, the obligation of elected officials (chief and councillors) to master the Atikamekw language (oral and written) and the participation of the Council of Elders in order to resolve an election challenge or impeachment procedure" (Morissette, 2004: 99).

The Council of Elders was not a grouping of the Atikamekw political universe before the Euro-Canadian presence but, calling upon the most experienced individuals of the band, was part of the Algonquian tradition. The mastery of the Atikamekw language also suggests a link with tradition while ensuring Atikamekw control of politics (Morissette, 2004: 99). Finally, the Atikamekw electoral code gives great importance to oral rather than written form. For example, it is possible for an elected official to resign from his or her position orally, without a letter of resignation.

Frequently discussed at Kitigan Zibi band council meetings, the importance of establishing the community's electoral code had been part of the objectives of the Community Strategic Plan (2000–2005) since the early 2000s, and at the end of 2008, the development of an electoral code was increasingly the subject of band council meetings, with research work for a first draft initiated in 2009 (Kitigan Zibi Anishinabeg Band Council, 2010: i). In February 2010, this first draft of the Community Election Code was submitted to the members of the Kitigan Zibi community. It was essential for the band council that the population be able to give its comments, ask questions, make recommendations, and suggest changes throughout the process leading to the approval of the code through an upcoming referendum (Kitigan Zibi Anishinabeg Band Council, 2010: i). It should be noted that an electoral code must not only be approved by a majority of the members of the issuing band, but must also receive the acceptance of the Department of Indian Affairs and Northern Development Canada—now Indigenous Services Canada (Morissette, 2004: 99; Canada, 2010: 10). Once the code is approved by the minister, the supervision of its evolution is entirely the responsibility of the band (Canada, 2010: 12). Two Canadian court judgments have allowed bands to no longer depend on delegated authority for custom elections: *Bone v. Sioux* (1996) and *Campbell et al. v. British Columbia* (2000) (Canada, 2010: 12).[21] According to these cases, a band has an inherent power, an Aboriginal right, to elect its leaders and choose its method of designation, as well as the power to make changes to its rules (Canada, 2010: 12). In order to receive the acceptance of the Minister, any electoral code[22] developed by a band must provide: "consistency with the Canadian *Charter of Rights and Freedoms*; provision for the settlement of election appeals; participation of offreserve members; and community approval of the custom code" (Canada, 2010: 9). In addition to these requirements, what is unique about the first draft of the Kitigan Zibi Anishinabeg Election Code? In Kitigan Zibi, the focus of the electoral code is not clearly culturally oriented. The absence of an Elders Council in the draft electoral code indicates that involving Elders is no longer relevant or is completely separate from official reserve policy. However, the need for interpreters (clause 10.15) is a reminder that this is an Algonquin community where the Algonquin language is still spoken among the Elders.

One of the particularities of the Kitigan Zibi Anishinabeg electoral code is the detailed elaboration of a code of ethics. The code of ethics appears to be intended to prevent corruption in electoral practices, to hinder the freedom and tarnish the reputation of the candidates during their campaigns, allow access to information, and avoid disputes within the community. Thus, it responds to a good number of concerns, dissatisfactions, accusations, opinions, rumors, and favoritism discussed by band members in discussions I have witnessed. According to testimony gathered during the public hearings (May to October 2009) of the Standing Senate Committee on Aboriginal Peoples on the issue of elections under the *Indian Act*: "Many First Nations witnesses spoke of how the *Indian Act* system of governance has fostered divisions within their communities and eroded systems of accountability" (Canada, 2010: 17). Kitigan Zibi's draft electoral code fills gaps in *Indian Act* elections. First, the electoral process is detailed and seems to address any unforeseen circumstances. For example, it explains, among other things, the voting process from the moment a person arrives at the polling station.[23] In addition to establishing a form of standardization, this explanation is necessary because, as I have found, the procedure was not clear to voters, as several informants told me that they did not know what to do when they had to go to vote. This great formalization of the electoral process also suggests that more bureaucracy and supervision was needed. This seems paradoxical when attempting to indigenize a system of governance. But the formality of the procedures draws a line between public and private, legal and illegal, formal and informal.

In my opinion, the draft electoral code for Kitigan Zibi aims for greater accountability and political transparency, with the goal of collective cohesion. Testifying in October 2009 before the Senate Committee on First Nations Elections, Chief Gilbert Whiteduck stated: "On the day we signed our audit report this year, it was on our website within an hour for Canadians and community members to see. I believe we are one of the few communities to have done so. We have nothing to hide [. . .] Why would we? That is transparency and accountability" (Ottawa, 2009). The Kitigan Zibi band council also demonstrated its transparency by posting its draft electoral code on the community's website. Having access to a First Nation's electoral code is very difficult. In Quebec, band councils generally consider it to be an internal matter of the band and do not wish to disclose it. But transparency may have its limits. In Kitigan Zibi, it seems easier to publicly display the result of a deliberation than to show the process leading up to it.

In Quebec municipalities, city council meetings are public. Clause 7.14 of the draft Kitigan Zibi electoral code specifies the exclusive participation of band members in the nomination meeting, thus excluding any foreigner. Legislating the exclusion of outsiders from this meeting appears to contradict the broad principles previously stated by the chief regarding the political transparency of the band council. The exercise of political transparency is not disinterested. Its absence, in this case, is indicative of a form of protectionism. Several postulates may explain the private nature of the electoral process in Kitigan Zibi. The candidacy assembly is perhaps a public means for candidates to denounce the political behavior of former elected officials and to expose the social problems to be countered. The Kitigan Zibi Anishinabeg may not be ready for Euro-Canadians to witness a political session that reveals the dark side of their reality on the reserve. With the prejudices and stereotypes about them in Euro-Canadian society, perhaps the Anishinabeg want to preserve their reputation, save face, by keeping outsiders away from witnessing certain publicly denounced deviant behaviors. It is possible that the private nature of this event stems from a fear that publicly disclosed information will be turned against them. However, nothing prevents this from being done by a member of the band itself. This exclusion of outsiders may be a way of not recognizing non-Algonquins as part of their society. Is this exclusion a manifestation of the *them/us* dichotomy that would be perpetually updated? In the past, Euro-Canadian interference (e.g., missionaries and Indian agents) has undermined band governance by its members. It is conceivable that this privatization of political meetings is a demonstration of the ability to manage internal affairs on their own, an assertion of the *us* Kitigan Zibi Anishinabeg. Is it an expression of self-government? According to Williamson J., who sat in *Campbell et al. v. British Columbia*, "The choice of how one's political leaders are to be selected is an exercise in self-government" (Canada, 2010: 12). Thus, the development of the electoral code by the Kitigan Zibi Band is an affirmation of their self-government. Developed by band members, the code provides a responsive system that responds to the community and political realities of Kitigan Zibi. However, the years pass and the Kitigan Zibi Anishinabeg electoral code has not yet come into force. This reflects both the complexity of establishing a new electoral system within a band and the changing priorities of elected band councils over time.

CONCLUSION

When it comes to reserve politics, it is not a concrete thing, but rather a dynamic in a given time and place where there is a redefinition of the authority and legitimacy of politics. The chief is at the heart of the development and political emancipation of a band. His leadership is exercised through a variety of traditions, values, and legitimacies. Over time, the cultural role of the band chief has been supplemented by the bureaucratic function of reserve administrator, the position of band political representative, and the advocacy role of the chief of a lobby group. "Bottom-up" governance has not led to the opening up of the political process for the band as a whole, since access to the chief's position of power is limited to a few. "Bottom-up" governance imposes forms of silent hierarchy that did not exist before and that tradition cannot recognize because it lacks the conceptual means. "Bottom-up" governance is not simply a local adaptation of a non-Indigenous system that "sells" itself to the locals because it gives some people opportunities that the old system did not give them. This governance has brought about a change in the way we think about Algonquin society, as its leadership is intruding at the interstice between the formal system and the cultural limits of the leadership role, creating a new dynamic. If Algonquian politics was previously dictated by a form of authority naturally recognized by the band, it is now conceptualized, analyzed, and conscientized by those who practice it. In the past, band politics allowed for social cohesion. But this is no longer the case today because politics contributes to the division of the band. The transfer of power to the local level has created new opportunities that define a new Algonquin political dynamic that is much more oriented toward individual choice. We are witnessing the creation of "secret" networks that make it possible to evacuate traditional dynamics of sharing that have become "clandestine." The Algonquians' reflexive work about their political universe allows them to include more and more of their ways of doing things at the heart of the official politics imposed in order to have a more satisfying system that resembles them and brings them together. The situation of each reserve is in continuous movement, and the same goes for its politics. The chief's vision ensures that each community develops its own political colors.

NOTES

1. Arthur Mason (2002) had also noted this transformation about Alutiiq leaders in Alaska and Marybelle Mitchell (1996) among Canadian Inuit.

2. The position of band manager (also known as general manager or band council manager) appeared in the communities at the same time as the takeover, around 1965 (Robichaud, 1992: 41, 61), with a strictly administrative function (1992: 67). His tasks vary from one band to another. Generally speaking, the Department of Indian Affairs summarizes the band manager's duties as follows: He supervises the band's affairs, programs, finances, and workforce; makes recommendations; and guides the band council so that everything is in accordance with the Department of Indian Affairs guidelines (MAINC, n.d., procedure 12.1, in Robichaud, 1992: 69–70).

3. On patronage and client relationships, see among others Boissevain (1962, 1966, 1973), Silvermann (1965), Balandier (1969), Blok (1969), Paine (1971), Kaufman (1974), Eisenstadt and Roniger (1984).

4. By *political survival*, I mean the continuation of an organization (formal, informal, even symbolic), ensuring social cohesion, collective interests, and unification (identity, territorial) in the face of external groups.

5. This guide includes a description of the roles and responsibilities of chief and councillors to their band council, band members, the band council director or manager, Indian and Northern Affairs Canada, and other stakeholders, such as Indigenous organizations and federal or provincial government agencies, as well as private sector service providers on reserve.

6. According to Bernard (fifty-five years old, Kitigan Zibi, February 6, 2008), who holds a senior position on the band council, the band council had ninety-five employees in 2008 in various departments: finance, job creation, human resources, Indian registration, economic development, land claims, forestry, public works, and others. Bernard feels that the band council is understaffed and that all staff are overwhelmed by the tasks at hand. Band members are also unanimous in pointing out that band council employees and elected officials constantly lack the time to deal with their respective demands.

7. Based on the *Proceedings of the Standing Senate Committee on Aboriginal Peoples*, Issue 15—Evidence, November 24, retrieved from the Senate of Canada website https://sencanada.ca, accessed February 5, 2018.

8. Based on the *Proceedings of the Standing Senate Committee on Aboriginal Peoples*, Issue 15—Evidence, November 24, retrieved from the Senate of Canada website https://sencanada.ca, accessed February 5, 2018.

9. Based on the *Proceedings of the Standing Senate Committee on Aboriginal Peoples*, Issue 15—Evidence—November 24, retrieved from the Senate of Canada website https://sencanada.ca, accessed February 5, 2018.

10. Based on the *Proceedings of the Standing Senate Committee on Aboriginal Peoples*, Issue 15—Evidence—November 24, retrieved from the Senate of Canada website https://sencanada.ca, accessed February 5, 2018.

11. It should be noted that in the 2020 band elections campaign, one candidate to the chief position used door-to-door as a campaign strategy. The same year, campaigning using social media gained in popularity.

12. Based on the Indian Register data as of December 31, 2018, retrieved from Indian and Northern Affairs Canada, http://www.ainc-inac.gc.ca, accessed November 3, 2020.

13. Semantically, the use of the Western term "family" leads to ambiguities when applied to an *Other* culture. I borrow Bousquet's definition of the Algonquins of Pikogan: "I understand family to mean the circle of close relatives, which includes those who have been adopted or cared for" (Bousquet, 2001: 421). According to Joseph (fifty-nine years old, Montreal, September 26, 2011), in Kitigan Zibi, having the same surname does not guarantee a family relationship: "It is not the same so-and-so." The task of identifying kinship networks is all the more complex in this context.

14. The situation of multiple candidates is not unique to Kitigan Zibi. During the August 9, 2010, elections in the Atikamekw community of Manawan, twenty-four candidates ran for the six available councillor positions (retrieved from the website of the Atikamekw community of Manawan www.manawan.com, accessed on September 7, 2010).

15. Based on the Indian Register data as of December 31, 2008, retrieved from Affaires indiennes et du Nord Canada, http://www.ainc-inac.gc.ca, accessed July 20, 2009.

16. Citizen culture refers to "a certain number of effective practices by citizens to actively participate in the animation of collective life in the City. Values, norms and effective social behaviours: these are the elements of a culture in the sociological sense of the term, which is not 'natural', but on the contrary varies according to place and time, and thus appears as a historical 'construct' that must consequently be acquired and transmitted in order to survive and develop" (Chanel, 1999).

17. Retrieved from *Capital News Online*, http://www.capitalnews.ca, accessed February 17, 2011.

18. This policy, developed following the Calder decision, allows Aboriginal groups that have never ceded their Aboriginal rights to negotiate with Canadian authorities. Renée Dupuis (1995b: 4) summarizes the Calder case as follows: "Indians in British Columbia [the Nisga'a] applied to the Canadian courts for a declaration

that their aboriginal or ancestral rights still existed in 1973 because they had not been surrendered or extinguished. The Supreme Court issued a judgment (*Calder v. British Columbia* (AG), 1973, S.C.R. 313) that was unsuccessful, but a minority of the judges stated that they still had rights in that province. Even if they disagreed on the merits of the question, six judges of the Court still concluded that the Indians have rights to the traditional lands they have occupied and used in Canada solely because they were the original inhabitants of this country, even if the laws of this country did not recognize it."

19. For a history of the *Indian Act* electoral system, see W. Daugherty and D. Madill (1980).

20. Retrieved from Indigenous Services Canada, https://www.sac-isc.gc.ca/, accessed November 3, 2020. The *First Nations Election Act* took effect in 2015 and established a new official and optional way to select a chief and councillors. Among other things, the Act expands the term of office to four years, it offers the opportunity for band council to reduce the number of councillors, it reduces the election period (Retrieved from Indigenous Services Canada, https://www.sac-isc.gc.ca/, accessed November 3, 2020.). Today, only 12 percent of bands hold elections under this Act. To find out more about the *First Nations Election Act* consult Indigenous Services Canada at the website above.

21. In the absence of having access to an electoral code from another Algonquin community in Quebec, I would like to compare the code of the Atikamekw of Manawan to that of Kitigan Zibi.

22. Bands governed by custom encompass two categories. The first is those bands that have retained their customary mode of election (Canada, 2010: 9, hereditary, clan, or consensus based) and have never been subject to the *Indian Act* election system (Canada, 2010: 9). The second includes those bands that followed the *Indian Act*'s electoral provisions but subsequently abandoned this approach to establish their own electoral codes (Canada, 2010: 9). The term *custom* here refers to the second category.

23. See Department of Indian Affairs and Northern Development, *Conversion to Community Election System Policy*.

24. A polling station is the place where voting takes place during an election.

Chapter Four

At the Interstice of Power; or, How to Regain Lost Power

Reengaging and Empowering Anishinabeg Women

The upheaval brought about by colonization has changed the social organization of Algonquian societies, diminishing women's status and power at all levels, leading to the loss of political action by First Nations women. How do you regain lost power and regain your place in a community? Is there interstitial female leadership on reserves? In Quebec, the literature on the political and influencing role of First Nations women is devoted mainly to the history of women's organizations and to the statutory question of Indian women (Séguin, 1981; Morissette, 1982; Lévesque, 1990). There is also an asymmetry in the treatment given to Indigenous women in social science research in Quebec.[1] In general, they are included in the data relating to men. The anthropological literature on First Nations women in Quebec is limited (Labrecque, 1984a, 1984b; Vincent, 1983; Craig, 1987; Lévesque, 1990; Desmarais et al., 1994). Moreover, the rare anthropological research on the role of First Nations women in their society (Routhier, 1984; Beaudet, 1987; Fecteau and Roy, 2005) often confines these social actors to typically female domains (for example, an interest in midwifery and childbirth, the domestic and household universe). The rare portraits of politically active First Nations women and influential Indigenous women in general are mainly due to their participation at the national level.[2] The exceptions are the in-house survey conducted by the journal *Rencontre*[3] (Séguin, 1991: 5–7) and a component of the social survey conducted by the Conseil des Atikamekw et des Montagnais[4] (CAM, 1992: 38–40) on the place of women in reserve politics, as well as an interview with Bernadette Bacon, elected councillor in the Innu community of Betsiamites in 1954, published in the first issue of *Recherches amérindiennes au Québec* devoted on Indigenous women (Saint-Onge, 1983: 269–72) and a few articles from daily newspapers and regional media on the election of women chiefs (Radio-Canada, 2007, 2009; Ducas, 2011). Only the recent book by Andrée Lajoie (2009), *Le rôle des femmes et des aînés dans la gouvernance autochtone au Québec*, provided an overview of the involvement of First Nations women in the political life (whether formal or informal) of their communities, tribal councils and contemporary organizations.[5] She does not, however, provide a portrait of women elected chiefs in the province. A report published in 2010 by the Conseil du statut de la femme on the realities of elected First Nations women in Quebec and Labrador fills the gap by offering a collection of the words of elected women. Documentation on women chiefs is also scarce in the rest of Canada (Fiske, 1990; Miller, 1992; Maracle, 2003; Voyageur, 2003, 2005, 2008, 2011a, 2011b; Anderson, 2009). The emergence of this field of research is slow. Lack of visibility is not synonymous with the inactivity and passivity of First Nations women in their society.

Traditionally, Algonquian women did not hold the role of band chief, but they were not left out of collective decision-making (Mailhot, 1983: 296). Elder women possessed knowledge, as did their alter egos, and were consulted (Leacock, 1978; Ezzo, 1988). Some women possessed shamanic powers and could even perform the shaking tent ritual (Leacock, 1958: 204). They were figures of authority because of their knowledge, and respect for them increased as they grew older. As reported by Father Le Jeune in the seventeenth century *Jesuit Relations*: "Women had 'great power'" within the Montagnais-Naskapi bands (Leacock, 1978: 249). They had equal status with men (Mailhot, 1983: 296) and this may have been perceived as a great power indeed by the Euro-Canadian missionaries who came to civilize and Christianize the First Nations. This equality of the sexes was not unique to the Montagnais-Naskapi: it characterized precolonial societies organized in bands (Leacock, 1981; Mailhot, 1983: 296).

The political role, power, and status of Algonquian women gradually declined in part due to the introduction by missionaries of disciplinary measures that reinforced male authority (Leacock, 1978: 249);[6] the decline of shamanic practices; the participation of First Nations societies in the capitalist economy (Leacock, 1981; Fiske, 1991); the establishment of Western medical services and discourse marking, among other things, the end of midwifery and the abandonment of traditional medicinal practices (Routhier, 1984; Leroux, 1995: 56); the spread of patriarchy among First Nations men (Labrecque, 1984b: 83; Turpel, 1993: 181–82); and the integration of men into a colonial normative order (Smandych and Lee, 1995; Mailhot, 1983). The imposition of Euro-Canadian laws discriminating against First Nations women has reinforced and formalized their marginalization. The *Indian Act* limited women's rights more than those of First Nations men: patrilineally determined Indian status, the political system, the right to vote and to participate in political meetings reserved for men (until 1951), and the restriction of property inheritance for women (Fiske, 1990: 121). The leaders who formed the Grand General Indian Council of Ontario and Quebec had opposed the first application of these 1869 legislative measures (Canada, 1934: 3541, in Jamieson, 1984: 66; Séguin, 1981: 254; Jamieson, 1984: 66). Until very recently, the implementation of this legislation has had the effect of keeping women out of public policy. The decline in the political role and loss of power of women in Algonquian societies has had disastrous repercussions and aftereffects on them.

Nowadays, the assessment of the Indigenous women conditions is shocking: they are the most vulnerable population in Canada according to several international organizations, including Amnesty International. Discrimination, socioeconomic marginality (unemployment, poverty), poor health status (diabetes, smoking, substance abuse), victimization (violence, abuse, violent death), criminalization, overrepresentation in prison (LaPrairie, 1987; Jaccoud, 1992) are more prevalent among Indigenous women.[7] In general, the struggle to change their living conditions is central to First Nations women's leadership. How has the most oppressed social faction gradually organized itself at the local level? What are the results of women's mobilization on a reserve?

This chapter focuses on the trajectory and reengagement of Algonquian women in their communities. Beyond their participation in informal networks, First Nations women are active in the public arena and are now elected to the band council. Public figures appear and leaders stand out. First Nations women's leadership emerges from a situation "in the cracks" alongside that of First Nations men, parallel to the formal structure. As summarized by Carole Mailloux (2004: 46) in her doctoral dissertation *La position et l'engagement des femmes de deux communautés innues*, the concept of engagement is generally defined by the authors[8] as "taking action"—that is, taking action to change the situation. By reengagement, I mean reentering the public scene. I borrow the definition of the public scene from Jacques Leroux (1995: 66), who refers to it as "debates about social affairs, future prospects and collective strategies." The public scene is distinct from the political and community scenes. The political scene refers to the official system in place, its ritualization, the corridors of power and counterpower. The community scene, on the other hand, boils down to local participation in the daily life of the collectivity. Reengagement on the public scene emerges from women's empowerment and entails women's participation in power relations. Taken from psychology,[9] the notion of empowerment in anthropology is currently ambiguous in its definition and its French translation. The expressions *prise de pouvoir, pouvoir d'agir,* and *pouvoir d'action* are French equivalents of *empowerment.* The use of this terminology in anthropology is often associated with the study of gender, international development, the postcolonial world, and globalization. In the 1970s, empowerment mainly referred to access to the development of economic activities by the weakest (Wright, 1994: 163, in Cheater, 1999: 5). In the 1990s, the notion of empowerment "seems above all to be about vocal, having a right to 'voice'" (Cheater, 1999: 4). How have First Nations women regained a voice in their society?

To understand the articulation of the different areas of the process of political reengagement of Algonquian women, the methodology developed by Sophie Charlier (2006) is useful. In her work on women in fair trade organizations, she takes stock of the debates surrounding the notion of empowerment and offers a typology of the powers included in this concept. Among these, she distinguishes between "power over," "power to" and "power with" (2006: 93). "Power over" refers to relations of domination or subordination (2006: 93). The "power to" is based on capabilities (authority, creativity, knowledge, and know-how) and "access to and control over the means of production and benefits" (2006: 93). "Power with," on the other hand, refers to political and social power—that is, manifestations of solidarity, mobilization for a common purpose (2006: 94). Applied to Anishinabeg women, the acquisition of empowerment should imply: (1) a questioning of relationships of domination and subordination; (2) the capacity for action; and (3) a willingness to organize. This approach stands out from certain writings on Indigenous women that put forth a notion of empowerment that sometimes reduces them to their maternal capacities (for example, Lavell-Harvard and Corbière Lavell, 2006; Sunseri, 2009). The power to transmit First Nations cultures to one's children is a powerful tool to combat the colonial alienation experienced by First Nations mothers. However, it is problematic to reduce women's power to their biological capacity to bear children. I have known many Anishinabeg women who did not give birth, but who still contributed greatly culturally, socially, and politically to their communities. The function of motherhood is not only biological; it is largely social. Nevertheless, women exist as individuals beyond this role. Rather, my approach is consistent with the classic definition of women's empowerment: "[It] signifies increase in women's power to achieve equality with men" (Sharma, 2000: 22).

The women of Kitigan Zibi are of course not a homogenous group. I have selected a few groups that have imposed themselves over the course of my ethnographic fieldwork, either because of the women's discourse on them (the Waseya[10] House, a shelter for First Nations women victims of family violence, informal networks), because of their community outreach (the Miss Algonquin Nation contest), or because of their public presence (display case at the Cultural Centre of the River Desert Homemaker's Club history and archival photos). These groups, present in the informal, public, and formal worlds, offer a sampling of the various female realities on the reserve. The groups that I have not selected are not "anti-cases" that would invalidate the conclusions of this book.

This chapter is divided into five parts. The first part deals with the Kitigan Zibi Indian Homemaker's Club and how the community's well-being is taken care of by its members. As a new meeting place and place of power, this organization has contributed to valuing and defining the contemporary role of women on the reserve, including that of leader. The informal organization of the women of the River Desert is at the heart of the second part. It reflects the parallel courses of action favored by various sub-groups of women in reserve life. Thirdly, this chapter focuses on mobilization against domestic violence, which has the effect of countering women's political alienation by bringing their concerns into the public arena. The fourth part deals with women's exclusion and participation in formal band politics. Despite the growing number of women chiefs in Algonquin societies and the egalitarian discourse of women candidates in community elections, no women have yet gained access to chieftaincy in Kitigan Zibi. The final section focuses on the roles of ambassador, role model, and leader played by young women elected as Princesses and Miss Algonquin. Through their community involvement and activism, these young women are contributing to the growth of their gender in the public scene and to women's political renewal. The rise of an Indigenous feminist wave—which began in 1968 with the political and legal battle over the right of First Nations women to retain their Indian status after marrying non-Indigenous men[11]—cannot explain by itself the increasingly important place of women in politics.

INDIAN HOMEMAKER'S CLUB

The emergence of women's groups on reserves has enabled First Nations women to regain lost power and has helped to improve their status. It would be wrong to underestimate the role of women's groups, no matter how trivial they may seem at first glance. For Diane Morissette (1982: 88), Indigenous women's voluntary associations are new venues for women's meetings and cooperation, different from those based on hunting, fishing, and trapping. A sedentary lifestyle, changes in production methods, the need to attend residential schools, and economic dependence on government benefits have, among other things, disrupted the social structures of women's groupings and collaboration.[12] In an article on the sacred role of women published in the journal *Rencontre*, author Thérèse Niquay (1991: 5), an Atikamekw from

Manawan, notes: "The value system has undergone major changes over the last few generations. Mutual aid, cooperation, courage and a sense of responsibility have given way somewhat to individualism, indifference and social disengagement." Filial solidarity on reserve has been transformed, but the collective village context has also led to a redefinition of mutual aid. In the absence of family mutual aid, band members were able to count on mutual aid that was now community based. This became institutionalized in an organization, with a name and structure. This institutionalization of mutual aid was going to alleviate the pressure of the gift/counter-gift traditional obligation, which was working less and less.

Indian Homemaker's Clubs were voluntary associations established in 1937 in Saskatchewan under the aegis of Indian Affairs with the purpose of improving the domestic conditions of First Nations women (Morissette, 1982: 89). In fact, the authorities considered that First Nations women were partly responsible for the poor living conditions on reserves and the resulting social problems (Magee, 2009: 27; Carter, 1997: 107, in Magee, 2009: 27). In 1958, 157 Indian Homemaker's Clubs were found throughout Canada (Canada, 1958: 58). At that time, Indian and Northern Affairs Canada believed that Homemaker's Clubs, as well as Indian leadership courses, 4-H clubs, and sports associations, were to be used for community development on reserves (Canada, 1958: 41). Community development for the government consisted of organizing reserves not only through the development of local education, health, and labor infrastructure, but also through recreation (RLS, 1959: 5). To achieve this, the activities and programs of the Homemaker's Club included: "monthly meetings, picnics, elementary housekeeping classes, lectures and educational films on hygiene, recreational evenings, courses in first aid for the wounded and housekeeping, and discussions on topics related to family budgeting, education and other social problems" (Canada, 1958: 41). These instructions in home economics, homemaking, and family health were typical of the education provided to young Canadian women in the 1950s. "Really taking care of your business" and "the well-being of your family" was however a goal that was reinforced by INAC through various initiatives at that time (RLS, 1959: 6). The Homemaker's Club was formed in 1942 at River Desert to help the most disadvantaged families in the community "and to promote an atmosphere of well being" (McGregor, 2004: 311). The women of the club met on the first and third Wednesdays of the month in the church basement and then at the Algonquin Centre in the 1950s (2004: 311). On these occasions, they used to engage in sewing, including quilting, which gave them the nickname "Quilting bees." The quilts were given to families in need or sold to raise funds for community activities (2004: 311). In addition to sewing, knitting, canning, gardening, helping the elderly, and assisting pregnant women, women in the club took part in picnics, dinners, and trips (McGregor, 2004: 311). According to Debbie (fifty-five years old, Kitigan Zibi, 12 February 2008), money was also distributed by the women to disadvantaged families during the holiday season. Participating in self-help activities is not a new phenomenon for women in the community. They were involved long before they came together in quasi-formal organizations. But the Homemaker's Club seems at first glance to be nothing more than a system reminiscent of religious patronage. Nevertheless, a leadership was to emerge from this structure because women held a "power to"—that is, capacities and control over benefits that they redistributed.

To subsidize their activities and the aid given to the most in need, the members of the club organized dances and sold various items. The band council sometimes contributed financially to the activities of the club and the women could administer this money themselves. This gave them independence from the formal structure of local power controlled by men. Through this funding, they also obtained recognition and support from the band council in the achievement of their objectives (Magee, 2009: 39). The club also benefited from local autonomy from the management of the Indian Homemaker's Clubs at Indian Affairs. Indeed, the initiatives and organization of the association on the reserve were primarily the responsibility of the women of the community.

Indigenous women's voluntary associations were not only new places of encounter and cooperation, as Morissette (1982: 88) noted, they were also new places of power. Indeed, the creation of Indian Women's Homemaker's Clubs in Canada would serve First Nations women far beyond the objectives of Indian Affairs:

> Little did the department know that these seemingly harmless women's meetings served as a means for Indian women to organize dissent and create strategies for change in their condition both on the reserve and in the wider Canadian society. [. . .] Political activity that began as part of community-sanctioned "home economics" gatherings occurring on Indian reserves throughout Canada spawned a plethora of First Nations women's rights organizations (Voyageur, 2008: 10–11).

The River Desert Indian Homemaker's Club did not develop into a political organization. What conditions were required for this political evolution? Jo-Anne Fiske (1990) documented the transformation of a women's voluntary organization into a political organization in British Columbia in the 1960s. In the case observed by Fiske (1990: 128), the band council had failed to negotiate well with the authorities to obtain essential services for the community. It was the women of the "Mother Guild," a fictitious name given by the author, who lobbied the band council and government authorities. The women's association emerged as a political organization because of the shortcomings of the leadership of the formal political structure on the reserve.

By taking charge of the social well-being of the community at a time when the formal and institutional infrastructure of the reserves was not yet developed, the women of the River Desert Homemaker's Club participated in the social governance of their band. In fact, the government had left some of the community programs usually managed by Indian Affairs officers in the areas of education and health to the women of these organizations (Magee, 2009: 41). By gaining "power over" these areas, women were challenging their subordinate status. Thus, these women did not simply play the game of the Homemaker's Clubs program launched in the 1940s by the government for First Nations peoples, as this one aimed to integrate First Nations women into Canadian society (Bohaker and Iacovetta, 2009: 445). For Kathryn Magee (2009: 30), who examined the operation of Alberta's Native Homemaker's Clubs from 1942 to 1970, these clubs were "a vehicle for women's education, activism and empowerment." But the early 1970s at River Desert marked the beginning of services to the community through the chief and the band council now in charge of the reserve (Charles, sixty-three years old, Kitigan Zibi, May 1, 2008). From then on, the band council and the Homemaker's Clubs competed to meet community needs in the same areas. It is likely that, as the resources obtained by the band council were more substantial, there was no longer any reason for the women's organization to exist. In his autohistory book on the community of Kitigan Zibi, band member Stephen McGregor (2004: 311) notes: "With the changing times and noticeable improvement in the standard of living at River Desert, the Homemaker's Club found their role had gradually diminished. The Homemaker's Club disbanded in 1977." The River Desert Homemaker's Club was nevertheless recognized as one of the most active Indian Homemaker's Clubs in Quebec (Morissette, 1982: 89). This means that women's participation and organized activities were more numerous there than on other reserves. To run such an active club, it must surely have had strong leadership. Why then did the Homemaker's Club cease to exist? As McGregor noted, times were changing for women in the 1970s. Indeed, women's liberation was taking place. The rise of an Indigenous feminist wave in the late 1960s and the declining interest of young women in the homemaking activities offered by the Homemaker's Club contributed to the end of this club. According to Debbie (fifty-five years old), the daughter of a former president of the community's Homemaker's Club, the club ended in the 1970s because "women were getting older" (Kitigan Zibi, February 12, 2008). This testimony confirms that there was no succession to ensure the continuity of the club's activities. Even if the River Desert club did not develop into a lobby group for First Nations women's law and justice, as is the case with the Homemaker's Club of British Columbia,[13] it nevertheless helped to stimulate women's community involvement and to value their contemporary role. As Kathryn Magee (2009: 37) noted, the biannual conventions that included club delegates from various communities were opportunities for First Nations women to define themselves. This definition went beyond the role of housewife and also included the role of mother (2009: 37). Defining oneself as a First Nation mother is a source of power in the Canadian context where Indigenous women were victims of forced sterilization[14] and legally stripped of their right to transmit Indian status to their children when they married non-Indigenous people. The Canadian authorities' goal of assimilation is also countered when the role of the First Nation mother is defined and valued, as it includes the transmission and survival of Indigenous cultures. The conventions were also opportunities for First Nations women to travel and meet other women with other realities. For example, in the summer of 1953 the Maritime and Quebec Indian Homemaker's Club Convention was held on the Huron reserve of Loretteville, Quebec, while the second semiannual convention in 1954, in July, was held in a Maritime Mi'kmaq community (Anonymous, 1954c: 1; Anonymous, 1954d: 12). The conventions also offered great visibility to First Nations women through exhibitions open to the public where they could show off their skills (Anonymous, 1953: 3). Each local meeting of the Indian Homemaker's Club was in fact an opportunity for First Nations women to gain power by defining themselves as women, housewives, or mothers and to discover leaders. In terms of leadership, this gathering confirmed some of the female authority figures present in the community and, to some extent, formed new female leaders who have been political leaders in hindsight. Valuing the natural authority and know-how of certain women and the skills and abilities of emerging female leaders would give these women the "power to" make a difference on the reserve.

From an organizational point of view, the Homemaker's Club was very structured and formal: a president, a vice president, a secretary, a treasurer, monthly reports, correspondence with Indian Affairs (Magee, 2009: 34). This organizational formality had an explicit purpose, as Magee explains: "The structured leadership of the clubs enhanced their legitimacy as a legitimate organization recognized by both their community and the Canadian government" (2009: 34). Mary Smith Commanda, wife of Chief William Commanda, was among the women who served as president of the Club. There are several reasons for this choice, foremost being the prestige and influence she held because of her husband's social role and function. Her marital status gave her power and made her a public figure. Mary Commanda, who was raised in the bush, was also an experienced woman with traditional skills (trapping, skinning game, canoe building, etc.) (Assiniwi, 1972; Gidmark, 1980). Her abilities were valued among women as well. Recognized and highly visible socially, possessing cultural qualities valued by her peers, Mary Smith Commanda had the legitimacy to be appointed to this position because she was already an authority figure. In other contexts, club presidents were chosen because they were the most culturally competent. The power of these women may be due to their leadership qualities, their style, or their behavior, but not necessarily. As has often been the case during my Algonquin fieldwork, it is difficult to highlight the selection criteria of an individual because that person appears to be the logical choice by his or her peers.

For her part, Carmen, who held the position of secretary, subsequently distinguished herself in several areas, including the preservation of the Algonquin language, education, and cultural revitalization. She was also the second woman from the reserve to be elected as a councillor. Today, she is recognized as one of the community's leading figures according to all the informants. Joining a voluntary association seems to be part of the journey for women who subsequently decide to become more politically involved, either within the formal political structure of the band council or within the local chapter of the Native Women's Association. For example, Evelyne O'Bomsawin, an Abenaki of Odanak, president of the Quebec Native Women's Association (QNW) from 1977 to 1983, was previously very active in her community Homemaker's Club before joining QNW (Morissette, 1983: 273). Violet Pachanos (former chief of the Cree community of Chisasibi) and Carol McBride (former chief of the Algonquin community of Témiscamingue) were also involved in voluntary or local organizations before being elected chiefs (Séguin, 1991: 5).

The women of the Homemaker's Club of Kitigan Zibi have contributed to the improvement of living conditions on the reserve. To some extent, they have taken on the role of "consciousness-raising agents" and "social animators" associated by Simard (1983: 64) with government officials working on the reserve and missionaries, as discussed in chapter 2. In doing so, their community involvement has given women visibility in the public scene, an area usually reserved for men. The Homemaker's Club has undoubtedly contributed to improving the status of First Nations women in Quebec, just as it did for women in Alberta, which Magee (2009: 44) refers to: "The clubs created new images of Native women, depicting them as symbols of guidance, respect, and social progress, rather than sources of social problems and low standards of living." The dismantling of the Kitigan Zibi Homemaker's Club in 1977 marked the end of organizations representing women in the community. However, this does not imply that women on the reserve did not remain active and publicly visible.

KITIGAN ZIBI WOMEN'S INFORMAL ORGANIZATION

At the provincial level, the 1970s were marked by the establishment of as-sertion and recognition movements, including that of the Quebec Native Women's Association (QNW) founded in 1974 (Lévesque, 1990: 74). The purpose of this organization was to defend the interests of First Nations women (Morissette, 1982: 113). In an article devoted to the status of Indian women in Canada, Claire Séguin (1981: 258) describes the task of QNW as follows: "A large part of their work consists in disseminating as much infor-mation as possible in order to create a power relationship with band councils and the government which will eventually allow women to have a voice." We are then witnessing a multiplication of local QNW centers (Séguin, 1981: 260). Although the women of Kitigan Zibi did not mention any development of a chapter of the association in the community, in the 1981 study conducted by Diane Morissette (1982: 110) on women's participation in the organiza-tion, she indicates on a map a QNW location in Maniwaki. The report of the *Itinéraires d'égalité* symposium (Montreal, February 22, 23, and 24, 2005), organized by the DIALOG Network and the QNW, also highlights the contri-bution of one of the members of the River Desert Band to the creation of the QNW: "In 1974, she [Sylvia Watso] joined Shirley Tooly [Tolley] of Mani-waki and Margaret Horn of Kahnawake to organize the founding meeting of the Quebec Native Women's Association at the Sir George William campus of Concordia University" (Goyette et al., 2005: 63). Shirley Tolley's involve-ment in the development of a politically active organization is not surprising since she was a pioneer in this field in Kitigan Zibi. In 1972, Shirley Tolley was the first woman councillor elected to the band council (Tenasco, 1986: 18). If it did exist, the local chapter of the QNW in Maniwaki seems to have been short-lived and did not make a lasting impression on the memories of the women interviewed. Why did the QNW not develop in Kitigan Zibi?

Andrea (forty years old, Kitigan Zibi, January 17, 2008) heard a former chief question the representativeness and goals of such an organization in the following terms: "Who does women Native represent?" "If there is a Na-tive women's group what is their purpose?" So, Andrea continues, he didn't send women to the meetings of this association. The chief's questioning of the organization may have been a means he used to discourage women from joining QNW. There is resistance to the formation of women's groups on reserves by men and some band councils (Morissette, 1982: 122). Morissette found that in the early 1980s there was fear, embarrassment, and even a kind of ban on women participating in local QNW activities. Morissette (1982: 123) puts forward the following hypothesis to explain this situation: "This fear is not due solely to the reaction or resistance of fragments of the male population, but rather is the result of a historical process in which women have had some of their decision-making power taken away." This hypothesis becomes relevant when we note that in the community it seems to have been the prerogative of the band chief to send a woman as an emissary to QNW meetings. This demonstrates a certain form of decision-making dependence on the chief and the machismo's hold on Anishinabeg women.

In Kitigan Zibi, there is also no women's committee or council as there is in other communities (e.g., Manawan). According to a former band council member, "I often told women, 'listen if you want you can have a women's council only if you all get together.' It's the same situation in Canada. Women don't seem to be able to mobilize their people" (Charles, sixty-three years old, Kitigan Zibi, May 1, 2008). In a speech delivered after a provincial tour, Monik Sioui, QNW president in 1977, also noted the "disunity" of Indigenous women in Quebec (Morissette, 1982: 113). Based on my observations, this is not an inability to mobilize that prevents women from coming together in a formal structure in Kitigan Zibi. It is, in part, a question of representativeness. It is essential to remember that the "women" of the community do not represent a uniform cohort, a homogenous "whole." Cultural origin (member of another Canadian or American Indigenous nation), Indian status, religion or spirituality, education, whether or not they are employed, cultural practices, being in a couple or single-parent relationship, languages spoken (French, English, Anishinabe) are elements that not only bring women together, but are sometimes also sources of division among them on the reserve.[15] This creates an informal mosaic of subgroups of women connected by family ties, places of origin, affinities, hobbies, and shared experiences. Some women are also unwilling to take the lead in a formal reunion. In recent years, Gabrielle (sixty years old, Kitigan Zibi, January 21, 2008) and her daughter attended a QNW meeting in the region. The women of the association wanted them to become presidents of a local chapter, thus enabling the creation of this infrastructure in Kitigan Zibi. They came to meet them as observers and declined QNW's offer. Gabrielle and her daughter do not seem to have participated again in the activities of this association. Furthermore, it is possible that the women of the River Desert do not need a formal structure to represent them and make their voices heard.

Women's involvement at the community level, therefore, did not end with the dismantling of the Homemaker's Club. After the Homemaker's Club ceased to exist in Kitigan Zibi, daughters of former members, including Carmen's daughter, were in turn involved in voluntary activities (e.g., community and cultural celebrations) in the community and are still involved. Women's social commitment seems to be perpetuated in some families more than others. Volunteer involvement from mother to daughter is not unique to the River Desert Band. In the profile of QNW members, Diane Morissette (1982: 112) notes that some of the women in charge or presidents of this organization on reserves had mothers who were part of Indian Homemaker's Clubs. Carole Mailloux (2004: 177) also noted in her interviews that the Innu women of Uashat and Maliotenam followed the example of their mothers' and grandmothers' involvement. According to Andrea (forty years old, Kitigan Zibi, January 17, 2008), a very committed volunteer like her mother was, it is the same core group of women who participate collectively on the reserve: "It is more the women from certain family units that come together." In fact, Andrea points out that the women from families in the community, which she lists, are very "authoritarian." Andrea (forty years old) and Diane (forty-three years old) (Kitigan Zibi, January 17, 2008) do not perceive women as a political clan. For Andrea, women's power in the community is not organized. She explains that when a problem arises, they will support each other; when people threaten their lives, they will come together and do something to change the situation. For example, Andrea recounts how these women organized two marches in the community to protest against drug cultivation and organized crime. The theme of the marches was healthy living. The mobilization that followed the disappearance in September 2008 of two teenage girls from the band, Maisy Odjick (sixteen years old) and Shannon Alexander (seventeen years old), is another example. Unfortunately, as is often the case with the disappearance of Indigenous women and girls in Canada,[16] the unexplained absence of Maisy Odjick and Shannon Alexander did not attract the immediate attention of authorities and the media, hence the need for Maisy's mother Laurie Odjick to rally family and community members to search for them (Orfali, 2012; Talaga, 2012). The death of Gladys Tolley, who was struck in 2001 in Kitigan Zibi by a Sûreté du Québec police patrol, also prompted the mobilization of her daughter Bridget and other women in her family (Duffault, 2009). The women denounced a conflict of interest at the heart of the investigation, since the police officer in charge of the investigation was the brother of the patroller involved in the accident (Duffault, 2009).[17] Several other irregularities surround the investigation and the treatment of the victim (NWAC, 2009: 82). Vigils, marches, and petitions have been organized to draw the attention of authorities to the hope of an independent investigation into the accidental death of Gladys Tolley (Duffault, 2009; Justice for Missing and Murdered Indigenous Women, 2009; Justice pour les bavures policières, 2012).

Thus, "power with" is flexible because there is a spontaneous nature to women's mobilization in Kitigan Zibi as well as organizational flexibility in leadership from one event to another. It is possible that the use of informality stems from the fact that First Nations women in Canada were legally excluded from the formal local political structure, the band council, until 1951. In this context, the women of River Desert may have been accustomed to making other arrangements. Éric Gagnon (1995: 62), who has been interested in the social involvement of women in Quebec, offers some hypotheses to consider about First Nations women who prefer not to pursue the political route: "Politics is often seen as divisive and threatening to values. It seems to require knowledge. Community action, notes Godbout (1987), rather gives a sense of solidarity, social cohesion, and builds on people's experience. For these reasons, political action does not always appear to be the most interesting or the most effective." This reflects the dichotomy already discussed between the political structure of the band council, which requires knowledge and causes dissension, and the traditional band structure based on experience and often idealized today for its cohesive power. According to Claire Séguin (1981: 257), "the contribution of women is then situated in various movements not related to direct power but fulfilling an essential function of awakening to fundamental problems." Community action promoted by women is therefore a form of indirect power. Women thus possess an authority whose scope of action is the community. In a research note on women in the Canadian North, Peggy Martin Brizinski (1981: 264) suggested that a more detailed analysis of women political leaders, and more specifically their political and cultural "place" (Barth, 1963: 9–10, in Brizinski, 1981: 264), be undertaken. Community space manifests itself as the political locus of First Nations women. For First Nations women, it is in this reality that they were active on their reserve, even though they were officially made invisible. Their struggle against political alienation goes hand in hand with their struggle against social ills.

COMBATING POLITICAL ALIENATION THROUGH MOBILIZATION AGAINST VIOLENCE: THE WASEYA HOUSE

The contemporary choices of the women of the River Desert are also based on their experiences of a more informal world. The words of Gabrielle (sixty years old, Kitigan Zibi, January 21, 2008), on the absence of formal women's committees in the community, lead us to consider another avenue to explain this fact: "We don't have that here, but we have Waseya." It was in 1985–1986 that the River Desert Band took over the health and social services sector. According to a 1988 study conducted by these services, "nearly 35% of the population was experiencing problems related to family violence" (Decontie, 1991: 17). Founded in 1991 by the women's initiative on the reserve, Waseya House is a shelter for First Nations women who are victims of family violence, offering professional consulting services (health, legal) and training and employment programs (Decontie, 1991: 17). These programs are economic tools that enable women to physically escape from an abusive situation and become financially independent. Waseya House also conducts awareness-raising activities on domestic violence (Pharand, 2008: 37) and organizes commemorative days, notably on the anniversary of the École polytechnique de Montréal massacre[18] and International Women's Day (Diane, forty-three years old, Kitigan Zibi, January 17, 2008). The shelter's clientele is first from Rapid Lake, then from Kitigan Zibi, then from Lac-Simon, and finally from Pikogan, Diane, who works in the health sector on the reserve, explains. She recounts the reaction of the men of the band to the establishment of Waseya: "At first, the men of the community felt threatened. They were afraid that the police and people from the centre would come knocking on their door." By establishing Waseya House, the women of the River Desert provided a major solution to the problems of abuse and violence on the reserve and, in so doing, empowered themselves by bringing their concerns to the community scene. Focusing on bodily, psychological, identity, and spiritual processes, social science researchers have generally paid little attention to the sociopolitical effects of this mobilization against violence by women on First Nations reserves. From one reserve to another, mobilization leads to different solutions. While in Kitigan Zibi a safe house (also called a "crisis shelter") was set up, in Manawan the Atikamekw formed the Women's Council in 1992 (Chaumel, 1993–1994: 11). Délima Niquay, the instigator of the grouping, testifies to the creation of the Manawan Women's Council: "It was one of the first topics [violence] that women talked about," recalls Délima. "We realized that most of us had been sexually abused, violently abused, from childhood. But each one of us had hidden her pain out of shame until that day. So, we thought we had to do something about it" (Chaumel, 1993–1994: 11). By institutionalizing the fight against abuse and violence, the development of local women's committees was not necessary at the River Desert. Speaking of social problems and more specifically of family violence, Mylène Jaccoud (1999: 82) states that Indigenous peoples: "have developed the habit of 'entrusting' the management of their disorders to state institutions. This attitude is partly a result of the historical socio-political reduction of First Nations communities, but it also contributes to a heightened sense of alienation and powerlessness in these communities."

The establishment of a shelter to manage crisis situations involving domestic violence demonstrates that the habit of an institutional framework may have proven more effective than the lack of a community-based framework in addressing this serious and ongoing problem on the Kitigan Zibi reserve. On the other hand, the creation and ownership by community members of such an infrastructure demonstrates the opposite of what Jaccoud said, namely the sociopolitical growth of the community, which participates in strengthening a sense of community development and community power through the reappropriation of the management of their disorders.

The model of pathogenesis developed by Scott and Conn (1987) for the Naskapi of Davis Inlet, Labrador, suggests that political alienation is one of the factors contributing to manifestations of violence, suicide, alcohol and drug abuse, child neglect, abuse, and delinquency. On the other hand, it is possible to believe that the emergence of women's committees or crisis centers can contribute to breaking not only the cycle of violence, but also the political alienation of these women. This is reflected in the approach favored by Waseya House: "For such a facility to function, the approach must be holistic, that is it must involve the family if not the entire community" (McDougall-Whiteduck, 1991: 15). The emergence of women's concerns about domestic violence in the public arena and this societal integration of support for women's issues counter the political alienation of Anishinabeg women. This is an empowerment of women victims within their society.

Through their struggles and the creation of committees and institutions for women, the Algonquin and Atikamekw women have led to a renegotiation of the internal relational dynamic by redefining their role at the political level. Marie-Pierre Bousquet (2005: 134) argues that an individual's detoxification sometimes calls into question kinship ties. According to this author, committees were created to compensate for the fact that family networks no longer responded to the management of social disorder. Following this line of thought, the mobilization of women victims of abuse and violence challenges the Algonquian sociopolitical world. Délima Niquay, herself a victim of abuse and violence, is an example not only of women's empowerment through her mobilization but also of leadership. Her overcome past gives her power (she is no longer a victim) and legitimacy as a leader to carry out an action plan in Manawan. First Nations peoples often say that one must have gone through the problems that the majority of them experience to be a good leader. These leaders have personal knowledge of the problems in question and have shown that they are capable of coping with them. Through the establishment of the Manawan Women's Council, Délima Niquay has entered the public scene by creating a parallel path to the structures and institutions in place. Many First Nations women who are leaders of national groups, chiefs and councillors, or informal leaders in their communities have experienced episodes of domestic violence and are making this scourge a political battleground.

Order management and politics were traditionally linked among Algonquians. The chief was responsible not only for ensuring that the bands collaborated with each other, but also for intervening in inter-band family disputes involving the neglect of women by their husbands (Leroux, 1995: 60). In the era of semi-nomadism, inter-band alliances were necessary because of the rule of exogamy, which prevented marriage within the same unit (Leroux, 1995: 60.). As Leroux (1995: 60–61) argues, a symbolic pact existed in Algonquin society and it conferred respect on women:

> It then appears that the system of reciprocal duties and obligations which prevailed in relations between the bands was to condition the husband's behaviour, since the husband's behaviour was not only binding on his own reputation but also that of his band, and this constraint was to oblige him to maintain the consideration that had been signified by the customs of marriage [. . .] If the old networks provided the basis for an order that ensured, to some extent, respect and security for women, it is conceivable that the historical retreat of the bands into themselves may have contributed to weakening their position by depriving them of the bonds that allowed them to escape the grip of the violent.

According to Leroux (1995: 60), the dismantling of networks, including the creation of administrative bands and reserves, has put an end to the interventionist role of the chief in family conflicts related to domestic violence. In this case, it is not surprising to find in the literature and in the various field surveys conducted in First Nations communities, discourses along these lines: "Madeleine Bellefleur, Montagnaise, points out that conjugal violence is rarely taken in hand by the band council" (Séguin, 1991: 6). This is why electing a woman to the band council often seems beneficial to make such concerns heard and to set up concrete action plans to improve the status of women. For Leroux (1995: 66), the increased representation of women on the Kitcisakik band council "testifies to the advancement of the cause and the dynamism that animates the activity of the most oppressed social fraction of the community." The same seems to be true in other Algonquin and Indigenous communities in general.

THE EXCLUSION AND PARTICIPATION OF WOMEN IN THE OFFICIAL POLITICAL LIFE OF THE BAND

The participation of First Nations women in the political life of their reserve is a recent phenomenon. Not everyone was allowed to go to the band council meetings at River Desert in the 1930s. Elisabeth (seventy-four years old, interview conducted in Kitigan Zibi on November 20, 1998, Kitigan Zibi Anishinabeg Global Research Project) recalls: "And people used to sit, the women used to sit on the hill, in the summertime 'cause I remember seeing this. They were not allowed in the band meeting, they were not allowed, only men and boys. That was about in 19, my goodness, I born in 24, could be in 1934." McGregor (2004: 224) points out that the Indian agent formally prohibited women from entering political sessions because the *Indian Act* discriminated against women. For his part, Thomas (eighty-five years old) mentions that, in the 1940s, although women attended band meetings, they did not have the right to speak (interview conducted in Kitigan Zibi on November 20, 1998, Kitigan Zibi Anishinabeg Global Research Project), and recalls an incident when the Indian agent at the time told a woman to be quiet, that she was forbidden to speak. Asked whether the exclusion of women was a matter of tradition or of the Indian agent, Elisabeth (seventy-four years old) testifies: "I have no idea. Well, you have to remember, women were not considered people till 1929. [. . .] So you had no rights; you had no say in anything, but of course on the reserve, I would imagine they had something to say to their husbands or, you know, their chief and Indians [. . .]" (interview conducted in Kitigan Zibi on November 20, 1998, Kitigan Zibi Anishinabeg Global Research Project). When asked whether the women knew what was going on during these meetings, Elisabeth answers that when their husbands returned home, they were informed. Elisabeth's testimony suggests that the Algonquin women of River Desert were not so politically passive. Their direct access to information and their right to express themselves were officially limited, but this does not imply that they did not express themselves on the reserve.

The 1951 amendments to the *Indian Act* would bring political progress for First Nations women. Not only were women now able to participate in band council meetings and vote in elections, but they were also able to run for chief and councillor (Voyageur, 2008: xvi, in Voyageur, 2011a: 221). Access to formal power was no longer going to be exclusive to men. As early as 1952, the first woman was elected band chief: Elsie Marie Knott,[19] an Ojibway from the Curve Lake Band in Ontario (Canada, 1975: 100). The election of women to band councils was to be gradual, as Claire Séguin (1981: 257) notes: "In 1964, for all of Canada, there were barely 7 women chiefs and 107 women councillors out of 557 bands." In Quebec, Alice Mowatt[20] was appointed acting chief at Pikogan in 1985 for a few months. It wasn't until the late 1980s that a woman was elected band chief. In 1989, Violet Pachanos, a Cree from Chisasibi, was elected chief by defeating four other male candidates, including two former chiefs (TSA, 2003). In 1981, women's participation in Algonquin band councils was still minimal: out of nine chiefs, all were men, and out of a possible twenty-nine councillor positions, only three were held by women, including Pauline Decontie at River Desert (Morissette, 1982: 81; Tenasco, 1986: 20). In 1990, Carol McBride of the Timiskaming First Nation became the first Anishinabe to become band chief, a position she held for ten consecutive years.[21] It was during the 2000s that more and more First Nations women in the province broke the gender barrier in local politics not only by becoming chief but also by holding more councillor positions. This trend has also been noticeable in Algonquin communities, where more than half of them have already had female band chiefs at the head of their communities: Carol McBride (1990–2000, Timiskaming First Nation),[22] Sacha Wabie (2019, Timiskaming First Nation), Alice Jérôme (2007–2015, Pikogan), Catherine Anichinapéo (1992–1995, Kitcisakik),[23] Adrienne Anichinapéo (2009–2017, Kitcisakik), Madeleine Paul (2011–2015, Eagle village First Nation Kipawa), Salomée McKenzie (2011–2016, Lac-Simon), Adrienne Jérôme (2016–present, Lac-Simon), Lisa Robinson (2018–present, Wolf Lake). The political involvement of Algonquin women is also increasing at the tribal council level. According to Andrée Lajoie's (2009: 105) study on the role of women in Indigenous governance, "the Algonquin Nation Programs and Services Secretariat and the Algonquin Nation of Anishinabe Tribal Council [. . .] have 83% and 58% women respectively." The growing number of women in First Nations politics has not only led to a reflection on parity, but also to the creation of certain structures. Since 2007, a working group of elected women has existed within the Assembly of First Nations of Quebec and Labrador, which aims to improve the representation of women in the decision-making apparatus of this organization and to create a support structure for elected women (Conseil du statut de la femme, 2010: 3). The need for such a structure suggests that there are additional challenges to being an elected First Nations woman. As has been the case for men, First Nations women in politics have also had to learn "on the job" (Séguin, 1991: 5). In the collective portrait of First Nations women elected officials, the Conseil du statut de la femme (2010: 19–21) highlighted the underlying motives for a support structure: providing solutions, affording political affirmation, managing confrontation, acquiring knowledge, transmitting information, and filling the need for training (law, politics, negotiation, management, communication). In his portrait of the emergence of women in politics at River Desert, Charles also relates the difficulties of reconciling work and family for an elected official:

Initially until 1976 it was rare that we had women. We had a woman before and after that in my council there were no women. And later we invited women to come forward every time and quietly there was one woman and then 3–4. Then there was a woman almost every time after that. In my last term I think we had two women. My council initially we were just 5 people and I had the expansion approved to 7 people, the chief and 6 councillors. I always wanted to have a good representation of the community, women, young people, older people, but it doesn't always happen like that. Because young people don't seem to want to get involved until they are 35 years old in the community. Younger than that, they're not that involved. It's good when you have a good level of involvement at all levels [age groups]. Because the role of women is important in the community. They represent 51% of the community, women are in the majority [. . .] [. . .] Saying listen will ensure that there are more women. The role of women is more difficult for them because they often have two jobs, a regular job and then their family. So, it's difficult for them; that's why they don't get so involved in politics. There are more and more women (Charles, sixty-three years old, Kitigan Zibi, 1 May 2008).

In Kitigan Zibi, the number of women on the band council has been steadily increasing since the early 2000s. In the year 2000, the band council was made up entirely of men (four councillors, one chief) (Kitigan Zibi Anishinabeg, 2002: 5). In the 2002 elections, a woman was elected as councillor (Kitigan Zibi Anishinabeg, 2003: 5). The latter already had political experience as she was first elected in 1984 (Tenasco, 1986: 20). In 2004, two women were chosen by the band from the six councillor positions, among them a former elected official, Shirley Tolley (Kitigan Zibi Anishinabeg, 2005: 5). Having previously held this position appears to increase the eligibility of women candidates for reelection, as it does for men. Of the five councillor positions filled in 2006, three were filled by women, including the daughter of a former councillor (Kitigan Zibi Anishinabeg, 2006: 5). Women's representation on the band council reached equity in 2008 (flyer, Kitigan Zibi, June 14, 2008). The 2010 elections reflect the growing power of band women in official politics: four women were elected councillors out of six positions (flyer, Kitigan Zibi, June 20, 2010). Despite the increased role of women on the band council, the community has still not decided to put a woman chief in charge. The experience gained within the political structure may allow one of these women councillors to become the first chief of the band, as has been the case for other Algonquin women elected as chiefs. In general, having served as a councillor seems to be not only an asset for being elected chief, but also the logical continuation of a career in a First Nation community, as Cora Voyageur (2008: 133) explains:

> The move to the chief's office is a natural career progression for someone who has worked successfully in the reserve community. Many of my respondents served as band councillors before becoming chiefs. They had experience of the political structure, being in the public eye, and dealing with the public. Most reserve communities are small and offer limited career advancement and a limited number of positions within the administration. A woman who is thinking of running for chief may already be at the top of the hierarchy within her specific agency or portfolio. The office of chief is the most prestigious in a community with few opportunities for upward job mobility. However, tenure in the position can last as little as two years.

From one reserve to another, the entry of women into the race for chieftaincy takes place at various times. It was in 2006, at the retirement of Chief Jean-Guy Whiteduck, that women ran for chief for the first time in the history of the River Desert Band (Susan, forty-seven years old, Kitigan Zibi, February 10, 2008). The end of Chief Whiteduck's thirty-year term provided an opportunity for political renewal and the chance for any candidate to win the election in the absence of the longtime favourite. Of the four candidates for chief in the 2008 election, two were women, Marlhene Carle and Claudette D. Commanda-Côté (flyer, Kitigan Zibi, June 14, 2008). Marlhene Carle did not take over the position of chief but was nevertheless elected as a councillor. Marlhene Carle and Claudette D. Commanda-Côté did not run for chief in the 2010 elections (flyer, Kitigan Zibi, June 20, 2010). They were, however, elected as councillors. No women were running for chief in the 2012 elections (flyer, Kitigan Zibi, May 10, 2012). The absence of women candidates for chieftaincy does not signify a lack of female interest in politics. Rather, it is an unfavorable circumstance for the election of a woman leader or any other candidate. Indeed, the 2012 election campaign featured Gilbert Whiteduck, the incumbent leader elected by acclamation in the previous election, and his brother, former leader Jean-Guy Whiteduck.

In Kitigan Zibi, an Anishinabe woman's election campaign is no different from that of her male counterpart. A review of the women candidates' election announcements published in the flyer for the 2008 and 2010 elections shows that none of them highlighted women's causes in their messages to the community. Rather, the candidates addressed the band as a whole on subjects of common interest: rights, justice, freedom, security, health, education, culture, language and natural resources. In fact, it was not as a voice for women that the candidates wanted to be elected, but rather as an individual representing the community. Furthermore, if the election announcements were not primarily aimed at women's concerns, perhaps it indicates a change in the way women perceive their roles in politics: no longer only as representatives of a discriminated gender. According to Andrea (forty years old) and Diane (forty-three years old) (Kitigan Zibi, January 17, 2008), both involved with women in the community, women and men are equal on their reserve. Thus, the egalitarian electoral discourse of women candidates would be more focused on current community priorities. As was the case for men, being solicited by one's peers, having a key position in the community, having a school education and being related to former elected officials are also criteria for selecting women candidates for the band council. However, one criterion seems to have changed over the years in Kitigan Zibi: language. According to Andrea (Kitigan Zibi, January 17, 2008), one of the reasons for electing a close relative as councillor in the early 1970s and early 1980s was that she was fluent in the three languages spoken in the community. Once indispens-able, the qualities of an interpreter are no longer relevant today since Algon-quin is obsolete and the working language at the band council is English. The women of Kitigan Zibi occupy a growing place in band politics. As pioneers, they are role models for generations of women to come. How can the political role of Anishinabe women be more highly valued and how can we prepare the next generation of women leaders?

THE MISS IN KITIGAN ZIBI:
AMBASSADORS, ROLE MODELS, AND FUTURE LEADERS

Women in official politics are not the first public female role models to show leadership. In our work on the competitions for queens, princesses, misses, and majorettes among the Amerindian women of Quebec in the twentieth and twenty-first centuries, Marie-Pierre Bousquet and I (2014) found, among other things, that these elections provided First Nations women with access to leadership and recognized their role, and even their responsibility, in trans-mitting culture and values. In fact, these contests were organized on the occa-sion of "social leadership" activities supervised by the parish. For some First Nations queens and princesses, the role of ambassador of their culture did not end at the end of their respective mandates. Jeannette Corbière,[24] Kahn-Tineta Horn,[25] and Alanis O'Bomsawin,[26] are among the women whose role as a First Nation princess was a precursor of a public and political destiny.

If women were not at the heart of political decisions at the River Desert until recently, they were not as invisible as one might think. In a 1965 photo[27] taken in Maniwaki at the funeral of Father Joseph-Étienne Guinard, OMI (figure 4.1), we notice Micheline Mitchell, Princess of the Algonquins of River Desert, Assistant Chief John Lambert Cayer, and an Elder, gathered in front of the deceased's coffin. The role of princess appears to be that of an important ambassador for the community since she was one of the dignitaries of the reserve for the occasion. It was in the 1960s that the first competitions for queens and princesses were held on the reserve. This election took place during the Winter Carnival, which was a true cultural spectacle (Anonymous, 1965b). As Heather (forty-seven years old) said in a January 2008 interview (Kitigan Zibi, January 8, 2008), the Winter Carnival was a big event: "My parents and I would put on our best Indian costumes to go."

Chosen for their qualities, these young women seem to personify much more than a stereotypical beauty canon. In fact, in the archival photos seen at the Kitigan Zibi Cultural Centre, the Queen wears a ribbon that reads "*Ogima*," meaning "chief." It is possible to believe that the queens of these

Figure 4.1. Micheline Mitchell, Ambassador of the River Desert Women
AD with courtesy of Micheline Mitchell and the Cayer Family

competitions were honorary chiefs symbolically representing women in official ceremonies. In Kitigan Zibi, some of the elected women also later had a public destiny. Chosen Princess in 1965, Shirley Whiteduck was until recently principal of the Kitigan Zibi Kikinamadina School (Anonymous, 1965b).[28]

At River Desert, the queen pageants ended in the late 1960s and returned in 2000 with the Miss Algonquin Nation intercommunity pageant. Among the members of the founding committee are two prominent women who have continued to volunteer from mother to daughter in many community activities and cultural gatherings (including the annual pow-wow and the Little Turtles, a group of young dancers and drummers), Pauline Decontie and her daughter Robin. Pauline Decontie was not the only former band councillor to participate in Miss Algonquin Nation. Also on the organizing committee for the event was Shirley Tolley,[29] the first woman elected to the band council and a leading figure in the founding assembly of the Quebec Native Women's Association (Goyette et al., 2005: 63). These activists and pioneers in official politics in turn value the advancement of Anishinabeg women and the development of First Nations female role models. The Miss Algonquin Nation pageant promotes a societal ideal of the young contemporary Indigenous woman. This is reflected in the eligibility and evaluation criteria posted on the contest's website: ability to present herself in public and discuss a subject of interest to Indigenous peoples, knowledge of her culture (traditions, history, dance, language), pursuit of studies, a healthy lifestyle (that is, free of alcohol or drug dependency), being single with no children, and being recommended by a member of her band.[30] Symbols of the preservation of a particular Indigenous identity, the Miss Algonquin Nation is also entrusted with the responsibility of transmitting Algonquin culture and values. But these young women are also role models for their communities. Through their participation in various events off the reserve, they too are demonstrating a form of leadership on the part of First Nations women, thereby contributing to the political renewal of this genre. The journey of the 2007 Miss Algonquin Nation, Caitlin Tolley, is one example. Recipient of the Foundation for the Advancement of First Nations Youth Scholarship for her academic success, voted Youth of the Year by the First Nations & Inuit Suicide Prevention Association of Quebec and Labrador, in 2006 she received the National First Nations Role Model Award[31] from the Governor General of Canada, Her Excellency the Right Honourable Michaëlle Jean.[32] In 2010, Caitlin Tolley was spokesperson and representative of the Assembly of First Nations of Quebec and Labrador Youth Network along with Stacy Bossum.[33] On June 30, 2011, the National First Nations Health Organization (NAHO) and the National First Nations Role Model Program selected Caitlin Tolley as their representative at a reception at Rideau Hall in honor of the Duke and Duchess of Cambridge.[34] Caitlin Tolley took the opportunity to deliver a political message to the Duke and Duchess and to present a highly symbolic diplomatic gift to the First Nations:

> I had the chance to meet the Duchess, shake her hand and explain to her who I was and I took the opportunity to remind her that she was in Algonquin territory. I gave her an eagle feather and asked her to remember the historical attachment between the Crown of England and the First Nations of Canada. The Duchess of Cambridge, Catherine Middleton, warmly accepted this honour and assured me that she and her husband would keep this eagle feather during their trip to Canada and that she understood its significance.[35]

Her meeting with Prince William had the same purpose: "It was a very brief meeting because of the media presence at the reception. I gave him the same message that I gave his wife, reminding him of our close ties to the British Crown. It was a very special moment for me, a story that I will share with my people for generations to come[36]."

Reminding interlocutors that they are on First Nation territory is usually part of the contemporary discourse of Indigenous leaders, whether they are band chiefs, grand chiefs of assemblies or presidents of Indigenous associations. Caitlin Tolley's evocation of the band's political territory not only constitutes an affirmation of a national identity, but also demonstrates that the young woman has mastered Indigenous rhetoric. Caitlin Tolley also demonstrates her knowledge of First Nations diplomatic tradition of exchanging gifts by offering an eagle feather to the distinguished guests. Giving a gift under the circumstances not only binds the "giver" and the "receiver," but can also be seen as an act of empowerment, Mélissa Pflüg (1996: 492) points out. Pflüg, who has studied the contemporary rituals of the Odawa traditionalists, Algonquians from the Great Lakes region, explains: "Gift-giving, or what the Odawa refer to as 'gifting' is the primary social act that lends respect and prestige; it also reflects power" (1996: 492). Furthermore, handing over an eagle feather is significant to Indigenous peoples as it comes from the most sacred animal in traditionalist spirituality (Bousquet, 2002: 82). This sacred pan-Indian object is not available to everyone. As Marie-Pierre Bousquet (2002: 82) points out, "An eagle feather can only be held by an individual of high social prestige [. . .]" According to former Assembly of First Nations Chief Shawn A-in-chut Atleo, the eagle feather is "the highest symbol of respect and leadership" (Indian Country Today Media Network, 2011). Caitlin Tolley's role at the reception in honour of the princely couple goes beyond that of an ambassador of Algonquin culture or the cliché stereotype of the self-absorbed beauty pageant queen. The description of the meetings with Their Royal Highnesses is a testament to the young woman's activism and political leadership. First Nations women's activism is not confined to struggles to improve the rights and living conditions of Indigenous women. It also touches on the full range of Indigenous concerns and claims. Every public activity is an opportunity to voice and have their voices heard. The role of spokesperson for Indigenous causes often falls to each Indigenous person who lives in a Euro-Canadian environment. However, it carries more weight when it comes to official duties.

The Election Campaign of a Young Leader

The election campaign of the younger generation of Anishinabeg is bringing about a political renewal of ways of doing things. After serving on the

Kitigan Zibi New Education Advisory Council in 2011,[37] Caitlin Tolley ran
for the position of councillor in the 2012 elections (flyer, Kitigan Zibi, May
10, 2012). For her political campaign, in addition to publishing an election
statement in the flyer (Kitigan Zibi, May 24, 2012), Caitlin Tolley invited
band members to a talking circle. A talking circle is a speaking ritual where
participants, placed in a circle, take turns speaking without time constraints
or interruption. In addition to highlighting her community involvement, her
studies in political science at the University of Ottawa, her political experience at decision-making tables, and the importance of developing young
leaders to meet the community's future challenges is at the heart of her election statement. It is interesting to note the emphasis placed on this training, as
it appears to be an absorption of advocacy from government programs of the
1940s that pursued the goal of training young First Nations leaders. Caitlin
Tolley's election speech demonstrates her mastery of "non–First Nations"
and formal rhetoric, an essential criterion for any eligible candidate.

The holding of talking circles is a recent means of political campaigning
in Kitigan Zibi. However, the link between talking circles and politics is not
new, as talking circles were originally used as a parliamentary procedure by
the Woodland tribes in the American Midwest (Wolf and Rickard, 2003: 30).
The resurgence of talking circles in politics seems to be the logical continuation of the trend observed since the 1980s for this method of communication
popularized by the development of sentencing circles[38] and healing circles[39]
in First Nations communities. Through the sentencing circle, judge, victim,
offender, and community member express, share and participate in the imposition of sanctions by developing culturally appropriate recommendations
and decisions (Jaccoud, 1999: 89–90). The healing circle is a therapeutic
method that aims to restore balance to an individual struggling with certain
social disorders (Jaccoud, 1999: 86–87). These practices are part of the pan-
Indian current adopted by First Nations peoples of Quebec, where "the notion
of circle is one of the foundations of Amerindian philosophy. The circle sym-
bolizes equality, globality, the land and the life cycle" (Sioui, 1992, in Jaccoud, 1999: 87). The week prior to the Caitlin Tolley talking circle, a talking
circle of Kitigan Zibi Elders was held. In the flyer advertisement of May 17,
2012 inviting members to participate in the event, the following quote from
Dave Chief, Oglala Lakota, explaining the talking circle was included: "The
Circle has healing power. In the Circle, we are all equal. When in the Circle,
no one is in front of you. No one is behind you. No one is above you. No
one is below you. The Sacred Circle is designed to create unity." This notion
of equality and the search for unity are relevant in the context of a political
campaign talking circle. In this electoral circle, candidate and voter are symbolically on an equal footing, whereas, as discussed in the previous chapter,

at the local level there is a gap between those elected to the band council and the population. The talking circle seems to attempt to bridge this distance by including the participation of band members in debates on current affairs and perspectives typical of electoral issues and discourses. The talking circle depicts a First Nation political universe that is idealized, since, nowadays, the notion of egalitarianism no longer characterizes the Algonquian world. The profile of the research services of the Kitigan Zibi Cultural Centre, posted online on the Virtual Museum of Canada website, testifies not only to the growing importance of talking circles in the community but also to their cultural significance: "We also encourage talking circles or other culturally related forms of communication."[40] Anishinabeg values are also honored within the circle: listening, consensus, solidarity.

Due to a lack of sufficient candidates, the last Miss Algonquin Nation contest was held in 2009. Several reasons may explain the decrease in participation in this contest: difficulty for young girls to meet the criteria, significant investment of time and money, lack of follow-up in the recruitment and preparation of future participants. It is also conceivable that there was a lack of interest from other communities in the contest because the seven queens elected in the nine years of this contest were from Kitigan Zibi. Nevertheless, it is relevant to continue to document the journey of former participants in order to demonstrate the commitment in the public scene, access to leadership, empowerment, edification, and advancement of young First Nations women as a result of such cultural activities promoting the status of First Nations women. Among the women councillors elected in the June 2012 elections in Kitigan Zibi is Miss Algonquin Nation 2007, Caitlin Tolley.

CONCLUSION

The marginalization of Indigenous women from the formal political system has led them to conduct *politics in the cracks* locally through the creation of parallel channels, sometimes informal and original, and sometimes through local organizations. Through their recovery of institutions and their integration into political, administrative, educational, and cultural structures, Anishinabeg women have challenged the relationships of domination and subordination within the band and demonstrated their capacity for action (authority, creativity, knowledge, and know-how). In politics, women's empowerment can be seen, as they are increasingly asserting themselves as band councillors and thus in collective decision-making. The rise of First Nations women in politics is not solely related to the development of feminism in Canada in general. Anishinabeg women increasingly possess "power over," "power to," and "power with" (Charlier, 2006: 93). Access to these powers has increased as a result of interstitial female leadership emerging from an Indian Homemaker's Club, informal organizations, mobilization against family violence and violence against First Nations women in general, and women's contests. The political role of band women is not limited to the formal structure. Through their socio-political, symbolic, and even diplomatic actions, the Algonquin women of the River Desert have demonstrated interstitial leadership in social governance, growing autonomy, and a political culture specific to this genre. Paradoxi-cally, these women still embody traditional qualities that were typical of an Algonquian leader: being flexible, unifying, and peacemakers. The institution-alization and bureaucratization of politics through the imposed band council structure has contributed to the erosion of these traditional roles attributed to the chief. However, elected women and female public figures seem to adhere to a classic model of the personification of a chief or sub-chief as traditional female authority figures holding cultural knowledge, while representing through their gender's access to positions of power and authority within the reserve a modernity that resonates beyond the local level.

NOTES

1. Since the publication of the French edition of this book (Morissette, 2018), it is clear that research on Indigenous women has gained momentum and interest in Que-bec, particularly at the Université du Québec en Abitibi-Témiscamingue (UQAT), which hosts the Mikwatisiw—the Research Laboratory on Indigenous Women's Issues—and was recently appointed the Canada Research Chair in Indigenous Women's Issues.

2. See, among others, the interviews conducted with Evelyne O'Bomsawin and Bibiane Courtois, presidents of the Quebec Native Women's Association during the 1970s and 1980s, published in the journal *Recherches amérindiennes au Québec* (Morissette, 1983, 1984).

3. Survey conducted in 1991 among fifty-six women from various Nations in Quebec on the importance they attached to politics. It offers, among other things, the opinions of women elected as chiefs and councillors.

4. Survey conducted in 1991 in nine Innu communities in Quebec, involving 350 women from three generations (Rock, 1992: vii). The results were the subject of a publication and a video: *Montagnaises de parole / Eukuan ume ninan ententamat*.

5. Among contemporary organizations, Lajoie (2009) focuses on the Assembly of First Nations of Quebec and Labrador, the Quebec Native Women's Associa-tion (QNW), Native Friendship Centres and the creation of the Council of Elected Women.

6. The arguments put forward by Eleonor Leacock suggesting the loss of the egali-tarian status of Indigenous women due to European interference are not unanimously

accepted in the academic world because of the choice of passages from the *Jesuit Relations* used by the author.

7. For a review of the literature on the situation of First Nations women in Canada see, among others, Dion Stout and Kipling (1998). For a review of the literature on violence experienced by First Nations women see Montminy et al. (2010).

8. Mailloux refers in particular to Quéniart and Jacques (2001, 2002), Passy (1998), and Ladrière (1967, 1997).

9. On the notion of empowerment in psychology see Rappaport (1984), Bernstein et al. (1994), and Zimmerman (1995).

10. "Waseya" means sunrise (Decontie, 1991: 17).

11. As a result of this mobilization, the *Indian Act* was amended in 1985 by amendment C-31, which now allows First Nations women to retain their Indian status when marrying a non-First Nations person and those who had lost it to regain it. But amendment C-31 still maintained inequalities between First Nations women and men: that is why amendment C-3, which aims for greater gender equity by allowing the grandchildren of women who have regained their status to be registered on the Indian register, was made to the *Indian Act* in 2011. Eligibility for Indian status remains inequitable for Indian women and their descendants. Women are still fighting the battle.

12. See Roark-Calnek (1993), Leroux (1995), and Lamothe (1997).

13. Her Story, http://library.usask.ca/herstory/commun.html, accessed March 2, 2011.

14. Alberta and British Columbia are the only provinces to have had sterilization laws in place from the late 1920s to the early 1970s (Stote, 2012: 120). However, this legislation, which initially targeted the mentally retarded, was extended to the other provinces through an amendment to the *Indian Act* in 1951 that gave each province the power to determine who are mentally incompetent Indians within its territory according to its own criteria (Stote, 2012: 120–21). Several illegal acts of sterilization, that is without the patient's consent or for nonmedical reasons, have been committed against able-bodied First Nations women with the knowledge of the Indian Health Service (Stote, 2012: 126).

15. At the provincial level, Monik Sioui also included status, language, and religion among the vectors of division among First Nations women in Quebec (speech May 15, 1977, in Morissette, 1982: 113). Economic status (being rich or poor) and living environment (isolated reserve, urban environment) are also criteria of disunity according to Sioui (Morissette, 1982: 113).

16. In Canada, there were 582 cases of missing or murdered First Nations women and girls in 2010 (NWAC, 2010: 1). NWAC, in collaboration with the Sisters in Spirit research project, has provided an alarming assessment of the situation in two reports released in 2009 and 2010. Amnistie internationale Canada (2004) has also conducted research on racism, discrimination, marginalization, violence, and human rights violations against Indigenous women and continues to denounce the treatment of law enforcement officials in cases of disappearances of First Nations women and the lack of a protocol for action by Canadian authorities to address violence against Indigenous women. The National Inquiry into Missing and Murdered Indigenous Women and Girls called for by Laurie Odjick, Bridget Tolley, and several Canadian

organizations and international bodies (Ivison 2013a, 2013b) was finally established and began its work on September 1, 2016. Despite the 231 calls for justice of its final report, changes are slow in coming and the situation of Indigenous women and girls is hardly improving.

17. Based on *Storytelling: Gladys' Story*, retrieved from the NWAC website https://www.nwac.ca, accessed March 9, 2013.

18. On December 6, 1989, an armed individual fired on the women of this school, killing fourteen people.

19. For a more detailed biography of Canada's first woman band chief, see Cora Voyageur (2008, 26–44).

20. Information taken from a personal communication with Marie-Pierre Bousquet.

21. Past Chiefs and Councils, retrieved from Timiskaming First Nation website http://atfn.ca, accessed May 15, 2012.

22. Past Chiefs and Councils, retrieved from Timiskaming First Nation website http://atfn.ca, accessed May 15, 2012.

23. Verbal source from the Kitcisakik Anicinapek Council, July 3, 2012.

24. A member of the Wikwewikong First Nation (Ontario), Jeannette Corbière was elected Indian Princess of Canada by the National Indian Council (NIC) in 1965 (Anonymous, September 1965a: 7; Goyette et al., 2005: 37). Her legal battle (the Lavell Case), which began in the early 1970s to regain her Indian status after marrying a non-First Nations man, earned her great notoriety.

25. A Native of Kahnawake, Kahn-Tineta Horn was the first woman to be awarded the title of Indian Princess of Canada by the NIC in 1963 (Rutherdale and Miller, 2006: 156; Anonymous, September 1963: 3, in Bousquet and Morissette, 2014: 381). A defender of Indigenous causes, Kahn-Tineta Horn remained a political activist, particularly during the Oka crisis (Bousquet and Morissette, 2014: 382).

26. Elected Princess of Odanak in the early 1960s, Alanis O'Bomsawin made First Nations' realities widely known through her film work (Bousquet and Morissette, 2014: 382–83). A prominent activist, she received several honours for her commitment, including Officer of the Order of Canada (2014: 383).

27. Photo found at the Archives Deschâtelets. Missionary to the First Nations and Canadian settlers, Father Guinard, OMI (1864–1965), became very well known among many parishioners in the regions where he worked.

28. Retrieved from the Kitigan Zibi Anishinabeg website http://kzadmin.com, accessed May 23, 2012.

29. Retrieved from the Kitigan Zibi Anishinabeg website http://kzadmin.com, accessed February 16, 2013.

30. Retrieved from the Kitigan Zibi Anishinabeg website http://kzadmin.com, accessed May 24, 2012.

31. In 1984, Health Canada established the National First Nations Role Model Program. This program was redesigned in 2002 to include greater input from First Nations, Inuit and Métis peoples across the country. Since then, the National First Nations Health Organization (NAHO) has been responsible for reviewing and administering the program (from NAHO's website, accessed December 17, 2012). In 2012,

the federal government terminated NAHO's funding and the organization was forced to cease operations. Its website is no longer available.

32. Retrieved from the websites of the Governor General of Canada, Her Excellency the Right Honourable Michaëlle Jean, http://archive.gg.ca; the First Nations & Inuit Suicide Prevention Association of Quebec and Labrador website, http://www.dialogue-pour-la-vie.com; and the National First Nations Health Organization website accessed on October 19, 2009.

33. According to the February 14, 2010, archives available on the National Capital Region youth forum blog, Forum jeunesse de la région de la Capitale-Nationale, http://fjrcn.org, accessed on May 23, 2012.

34. Retrieved from the National First Nations Health Organization (NAHO) website, accessed May 23, 2012.

35. Source: la Gatineau retrieved from http://www.placeauxjeunes.qc.ca, accessed May 23, 2012.

36. Source: la Gatineau retrieved from http://www.placeauxjeunes.qc.ca, accessed May 23, 2012.

37. Retrieved from the Kitigan Zibi Anishinabeg website http://kzadmin.com, accessed May 23, 2012.

38. On sentencing circles see in particular the work of Jaccoud (1999), Spiteri (2001) and Cameron (2006).

39. On the subject of healing circles see, among others, the work of Lajeunesse (1993), Ross (1994) and LaPrairie (1998).

40. Retrieved from http://www.virtualmuseum.ca, accessed May 24, 2012.

Conclusion

The purpose of this research was to describe the scope of First Nations participation in the Canadian political context. In addition, it sought to determine whether First Nations peoples hold a margin of power within the formal political structure imposed on them, the band council. To this end, the interstitial leadership of the Algonquins of Kitigan Zibi was studied, as it is the key to a political practice in the cracks that confers marginal power to First Nations. The ethnographic approach countered the idea of a lack of leadership and power among Algonquians that was too often prevalent in scholarly literature, in the subtexts that animate government policy, in newspaper reports, and in popular discourse. In this study I took a critical look at the politics of Algonquin peoples, avoiding implicit comparisons with standard models of the political dimension, and letting First Nations voices speak for themselves.

THE VARIOUS POWERS AT THE HEART OF THE MANY FACETS OF AN OPEN AND FLEXIBLE LEADERSHIP

The analysis of the Algonquin political universe has shown that leadership "in the cracks" does not materialize in a single model, a single form, and a typical incarnation within a restricted framework. The leadership category is open and flexible for Algonquins. The term *chief*, which American ethnologists used as a general category (Descola, 1988: 821–22), has proven to be rather rigid, and in fact it includes a diversity of sociopolitical leaders: hunting group chiefs, wampum keepers, hereditary chiefs, so-called traditional chiefs, band chiefs, sub-chiefs, chiefs elected under the *Indian Act*. Leadership was not linked solely to chieftaincy among the Algonquins, because the shamans had, beyond the charge of relations with the supernatural world, a

157

disciplinary power and a recognized authority that allowed them to provide moral direction and regulation of the band. The gradual disappearance of hunting group chiefs, hereditary chiefs, sub-chiefs, and shamans in the twentieth century does not mean the end of the diversity of sociopolitical leaders among the Algonquins. In contemporary times, leadership is not limited to the political and administrative direction of the band and confined to the role of elected chief and councillor under the *Indian Act*. The existence of leaders engaged in the public scene within women's groups, community support networks, local organizations, and mobilization movements against violence and social ills testifies to the presence of "power over," "power to," and "power with" (Charlier, 2006: 93) in paths parallel to formal politics.

THE FIRST NATION CHIEF: MAYOR AND HEAD OF STATE

An anthropology of mayors and heads of state applied to chiefs and councillors has been an effective methodology for understanding the embodiment of official power on reserve in a context of social and political change. In the selection of formal leadership there is a negotiation of the cultural overlap of competing criteria and dual visions (Euro-Canadian and First Nations). The conditions, rules, and qualities that designated an Algonquian chief before and after the imposition of a Euro-Canadian political system, before and after the gradual takeover of band control and governance "from below," are no longer the same. The same is true for the other elected officials, the councillors. The end of some traditional skills has given way to new criteria and the emergence of a new formal Indian-style leadership. "Bottom-up" governance has led to a gradual opening of the political process and a social mix. The barrier of generations and then of gender was broken in official politics. Now elected to the band council, women and youth are no longer on the margins of power. This new representation redefines the identity and political culture of the band by including new authority figures in the First Nations chieftaincy. Political leadership has taken on a new color by opening up to the abilities and skills of various individuals to bring together and guide the community and to make decisions regarding its governance. Nevertheless, these new figures of legal authority emerged from interstitial leadership practiced in an informal space and were granted legitimacy because they had previously held a certain moral authority. However, not all actors in informal politics wish to become actors in official politics. If there are still authority figures outside the official sphere, some traditional representations also remain in formal politics.

Mayors, heads of state, and First Nations elected officials are cultural symbols, but the latter are symbols exogenous to the official system of the

State to which they belong. Symbolically, for the Anishinabeg, the band chief represents the Algonquin political culture and not the Euro-Canadian political culture. The function of a formal chief in a bureaucratic system is juxtaposed with an Algonquin cultural role and status—that is, certain functions normally managed by "hidden" and "traditional" dynamics to the formal structure. The contemporary chief exercises both formal power and/or counterpower to the government. Whether he is a manager or an activist, the band chief practices politics "in the cracks" every day in order to satisfy both the requirements of Indian Affairs through the operation of the band council structure and the demands of his band. This governance has brought about a change in the way we think about Algonquin society because its leadership is intruding at the interstice between the formal system and the cultural limits of the chief's role, creating a new dynamic. This ambiguity reflects the interstitial leadership exercised by the chief, who finds himself at the margin of his political culture by redefining his activities and acquiring legal authority, while continuing to represent traditional Algonquin authority in a new imposed political system. In his role as an intermediary with the Euro-Canadian authorities, the chief interprets or even manipulates messages or instructions from the State, hence his room for maneuver. The chief's mastery of rhetoric and other "non-Indigenous" technologies, as well as the cultural references of his people, is a typical embodiment of contemporary First Nation power. Although the band council is a political borrowing, band members often perceive it as an endogenous political entity because of the traditional representation they still associate with the role of the chief. In so doing, they reinforce bureaucratic leadership and support the imposed political structure. Despite the appearance that the traditional role of the chief is only sometimes ritualistic, his eligibility, selection as leader, and ways of doing politics have retained an Anishinabe color.

THE PRESERVATION OF A POLITICAL IDENTITY DESPITE THE ACCULTURATION ATTEMPTS OF COLONIAL AGENTS

The control of a band's formal political affairs by colonial agents did not result in full control of its internal political dynamics and membership. The written protest of the controversial election of Pakinawatik's successor, the actions of Simon-John Makate-inini known as John Bull and his family, the removal of Chief John B. Chabot by Indian Affairs, the unsuccessful visit to the Indian Affairs offices in Ottawa by band members, the protest movement formed by Pien Kijemite and the political practices in the margins of the band council by four family "clans" are evidence that some River Desert

Algonquins were not passive in the face of the imposition of Euro-Canadian laws and ways of doing things. These various political demonstrations and actions prove to be a daily form of resistance to the new ways of doing politics established by the *Indian Act*, tricks and tactics used to try to change the formal system by questioning the power of Indian Affairs. This resistance is also part of the strategies of power at the margins. Analysis of the Anishinabe daily life has shown that First Nations peoples are not content to endure, do not react as victims, do not necessarily have a culture of "whining," and do not just react but also act. Confronting Euro-Canadians has cemented the community because it is in mobilization and political action that Anishinabe identity and political culture flourish and become visible locally to various observers inside and outside the band. However, protest and resistance are not the sole driving force behind First Nations leadership and politics. In fact, political leadership among the Kitigan Zibi Anishinabeg is also based on various representations (traditional, spiritual, symbolic) that have enabled the Algonquins to preserve a political identity despite certain ruptures and transformations introduced into their society by the colonizers.

In order to control Indian politics and shape it to suit the political demands of reserve life, Euro-Canadian authorities not only used intermediaries such as missionaries and Indian agents, but also attempted to produce and train a type of Euro-Canadianized First Nation chief—that is, to create a First Nation leadership that would suit them and represent the State. For the federal government, the community development of a reserve depended on the chief. Therefore, it was essential for the authorities to educate the leaders to technically develop the reserves according to the Euro-Canadian village model and its community life. Residential schools and Indian leadership courses aimed at this political acculturation of Euro-Canadian standards to First Nations leaders by teaching the staging of Euro-Canadian power through decorum and protocol, election rituals, investiture ceremonies, and simulated demonstrations of political assembly. Applying Marie Roué's (2004: 130) line of thought on the borrowing of landscaping techniques from the Cree of Chisasibi to the political world, this work has shown that the borrowing of political models or non-Indigenous ways of doing things in terms of First Nation governance does not mean an appropriation of the Euro-Canadian semantic context. Since Algonquians are aware of the choice of an *Other* way, there is no cultural loss, but a reappropriation and reinterpretation. If they were unaware of the process, the Canadian authorities' acculturation objective would have been achieved. As Roué (2004: 130) stated: "Ends and means must be thought of separately." The ambiguities, contradictions, and paradoxes of the everyday political life of a First Nation band are not only the result of the encounter of an *Other* political universe, but also the result of the evolution and reconstruction of a traditional sociopolitical system and its internal dynamics related to power, of a redefinition of the authority and legitimacy of politics. Reserve politics is not a concrete thing, but rather a dynamic in a given time and place, with the cultural overlap of various political traditions and forms of authority, through various spaces (imposed or symbolic) and institutions (formal and informal). The chief and other leaders are at the heart of this dynamic at the margins, at the heart of the development and political emancipation of their band.

ALGONQUIN UNDERGROUND POLITICAL DYNAMICS

The observation of a relationship with the State, or the absence of one, is a key to understanding the day-to-day political functioning of the band. Beyond the legal reference to the band, the traditional band's political ways of doing things remain through its articulation and its relational dynamics between its members. Alliances and social networks with diverse bases (based, for example, on family or friendship ties, on religious or spiritual beliefs, on shared experiences, such as the attendance to residential school) persist, in which favors and resources are exchanged. The unequal circulation of resources, such as privileged access to goods, jobs, and services, particularly by the chief and elected officials, contributes to the formation of a silent hierarchy, internal division, and social fragmentation of Algonquian bands. The Anishinabe chief is no longer the equal of all. The transfer of power to the local level has created new opportunities that define a new Algonquin political dynamic that is much more oriented toward individual choice. We are witnessing the creation of "secret" networks that make it possible to evacuate traditional dynamics of sharing that have become "underground." This access to and control of resources by individuals holding official political office also explains the attraction and growing number of candidates vying for the position of councillor. Division within bands is not a new phenomenon. The grouping of individuals on reserve was not a homogeneous cohort, but rather an amalgamation of several micro-groups which, despite their cultural similarities, had sometimes divergent ways of doing things and points of view. Different religious and cultural visions led to opposing political views at Kitigan Zibi and the emergence of factions. An analysis of the conflict in the mid 1920s between the Pien Kijemite group, who wanted a return to traditional culture and the abolition of the *Indian Act*, and other band members who followed the precepts of the Catholic Church and wished to remain faithful to the system established by this same law, calls for caution in the face of the imposition of a conservative or progressive label on a group of individuals. Denis Gagnon

(2007) demonstrated this in his analysis of the incorporation of Saint Anne into Innu cosmology. Individuals or groups that are apparently the most progressive sometimes use an allogenic system to preserve Indigenous ways of doing things. Getting the most out of a system sometimes means taking part in it and putting oneself in uncomfortable positions to question its structure, even redefining it or exploiting it from its "cracks."

WOMEN'S EMPOWERMENT

Colonization had contributed to the decline in the political role, power, and status of Algonquian women. Marginalized, oppressed, and vulnerable, First Nations women gradually questioned relations of domination and subordination by organizing and mobilizing in informal networks before becoming active in the public scene and entering formal politics. First Nation women's leadership emerges from a situation in the "cracks" on the margins of that of First Nation men, parallel to the formal structure. Through the emergence of new meeting places and places of power, community engagement and activism, and the reappropriation of the management of the disorders that afflict them, Anishinabeg women have countered their political alienation and contributed to the growth of their gender. Valuing and defining the contemporary role of reserve women as leaders and reengaging them in the public scene has resulted in increased participation of reserve women in power relations. Female interstitial leadership exists on First Nation reserves with its own colors and nuances. The public female role models for leadership are diverse (queens, princesses, misses, band councillors, activists, organization presidents, volunteers) and contribute to political renewal of this genre. The empowerment of women, their participation in collective decision-making as well as their sociopolitical, symbolic and even diplomatic actions demonstrate a political culture specific to this gender. The presence of a new generation of young First Nation women in band council positions is a testament to the advancement of the status of First Nations women and the growing place of women in official politics.

THE SUSTAINABILITY OF
ALGONQUIN CHIEFS AND LEADERS

At Kitigan Zibi, past chiefs are always visible and present in both private and public spaces: books about them, photos, commemorative plaques, references to an affiliation with a past chief in self-presentation. This omnipresence of the chiefs is a testimony to the importance of the leaders and the political history of the band in the daily identity, as well as to the cultural continuity of actors in traditional Anishinabe politics and the political survival of the group. This perpetuation of Algonquian leaders remains fragile. After the death of William Commanda in 2011, no individual has been recognized as the new wampum keeper. The protection, conservation and interpretation of wampum belts is a social responsibility that requires specific skills. Ten years have passed, and the absence of a potential successor reflects the difficulty in identifying a suitable individual for this role. Is the sustainability of this traditional leadership role and form in jeopardy? Once again, Algonquin leadership is facing the challenge of modernity and, as usual, it will have to be flexible, even reinvent itself, in order to endure. Algonquins are continually renewing themselves politically within their system. This is not an effect of acculturation, hybridity, or modernity, but rather tradition. This flexibility is a characteristic of the political culture and interstitial leadership of the Kitigan Zibi Anishinabeg.

INDIGENOUS DECOLONIZATION
IN THE CANADIAN CONTEXT

It is clear that the political development (local and national) of the original inhabitants is limited by the Canadian State. The creation of an autonomous postcolonial First Nation political entity within a postcolonial Canadian federalism is not a spontaneous process. Despite a lack of full independence, the process of decolonization of Algonquians is ongoing as embryonic forms of postcolonial practices exist on reserves. On the political level, the band council apparatus imposed by the Euro-Canadian authorities is at once incorporated, deeply questioned, and reappropriated by each band. Combining Indigenous references and Euro-Canadian political demands is not a simple process, but rather the result of reflection and selection of elements or behaviors to the detriment of others. In addition to the growing operational autonomy that has been underway for fifty years, the bands are rebuilding and renewing themselves politically by recreating in an original way their political and national cultures that had been weakened by the presence and constant interference of colonial agents within First Nation societies. The indigenization of band councils is a first step toward the indigenization of the State. The attachment of traditional functions and dynamics to the formal structure is the beginning of "bottom-up" governance. The latter renews from within, through dialogue, the relationship between First Nations leaders and representatives of the State, giving local actors room for maneuver. The instrumental use of State requirements also gives them a field of action. The First Nation chief is no longer a "Puppet Chief,", to borrow Frideres's (1998) expression, but the leader of a local First Nation lobby group, a band. The development of the electoral code by the Kitigan Zibi Band is an affirmation of their self-government. The political independence of the Kitigan Zibi Anishinabeg has already begun. The Algonquins have grasped the incompatibilities of the two systems—white and First Nation—to define a new territory, in the "cracks," which becomes their domain.

THE NEED FOR AN
INDIGENOUS POLITICAL ANTHROPOLOGY

Despite the contribution of this study to this field of research, the electoral anthropology of First Nations bands remains to be done. The development of this field at this stage of Indigenous history on Canadian soil is imperative because the march toward the political autonomy of First Nations has already begun, and it is pertinent to document the path of the leaders of the postcolonial path. It is important to take a closer look at the newly elected officials in contemporary politics on First Nations reserves, especially women and youth, because their presence bears witness to a political revolution among Algonquians and can help to understand the behaviors and political situations specific to each band. Gender and age in politics are determining factors and sometimes so discriminatory that some individuals may prefer to exercise counterpower in unofficial parallel channels.

Finally, at the end of this writing, the need for an Indigenous political anthropology emerges. The current struggles and issues of First Nations cannot be understood without an increased interest in the daily and contemporary exercise of power in First Nations communities. Despite the fact that each reserve is subject to the same rules of the Canadian government, the heterogeneity of the communities, their distinct history, the variety of their forms of leadership and their different relationships with the authorities suggest the presence of a political culture specific to each band. In this plural First Nations context, where the future of the *Indian Act* is increasingly being questioned, several strategies may prove adequate to deal with the Canadian State and open equally distinct postcolonial avenues. Like many other First Nations societies, the Kitigan Zibi Anishinabeg Band still occupies its traditional political territory today. No Algonquin leader has ceded rights to this territory. Reelected in 2015 after a nine-year absence from public politics, Chief Jean-Guy Whiteduck filed a motion at the Ontario Superior Court of Justice in December 2016 claiming unceded ancestral lands in downtown Ottawa. It is the chief's responsibility to negotiate and guide the band on a postcolonial path where, I hope, the government will truly negotiate on a nation-to-nation basis. This task now falls to the youngest elected chief of Kitigan Zibi, thirty-year-old Dylan Whiteduck, elected on August 29, 2020. It is a political revolution for the Kitigan Zibi Anishinabeg to have such a young individual at the head of the band. A new political path is once again taking shape in Kitigan Zibi.

Appendix One

Band Council Powers[1]

Powers of the Council
By-laws
81 (1) The council of a band may make by-laws not inconsistent with this Act or with any regulation made by the Governor in Council or the Minister, for any or all of the following purposes, namely,

(a) to provide for the health of residents on the reserve and to prevent the spreading of contagious and infectious diseases;

(b) the regulation of traffic;

(c) the observance of law and order;

(d) the prevention of disorderly conduct and nuisances;

(e) the protection against and prevention of trespass by cattle and other domestic animals, the establishment of pounds, the appointment of pound-keepers, the regulation of their duties and the provision for fees and charges for their services;

(f) the construction and maintenance of watercourses, roads, bridges, ditches, fences and other local works;

(g) the dividing of the reserve or a portion thereof into zones and the prohibition of the construction or maintenance of any class of buildings or the carrying on of any class of business, trade or calling in any zone;

(h) the regulation of the construction, repair and use of buildings, whether owned by the band or by individual members of the band;

(i) the survey and allotment of reserve lands among the members of the band and the establishment of a register of Certificates of Possession and Certificates of Occupation relating to allotments and the setting apart of reserve lands for common use, if authority therefor has been granted under section 60;

(j) the destruction and control of noxious weeds;

(k) the regulation of bee-keeping and poultry raising;

(l) the construction and regulation of the use of public wells, cisterns, reservoirs and other water supplies;

(m) the control or prohibition of public games, sports, races, athletic contests and other amusements;

(n) the regulation of the conduct and activities of hawkers, peddlers or others who enter the reserve to buy, sell or otherwise deal in wares or merchandise;

(o) the preservation, protection and management of fur-bearing animals, fish and other game on the reserve;

(p) the removal and punishment of persons trespassing on the reserve or frequenting the reserve for prohibited purposes;

(p.1) the residence of band members and other persons on the reserve;

(p.2) to provide for the rights of spouses or common-law partners and children who reside with members of the band on the reserve with respect to any matter in relation to which the council may make by-laws in respect of members of the band;

(p.3) to authorize the Minister to make payments out of capital or revenue moneys to persons whose names were deleted from the Band List of the band;

(p.4) to bring subsection 10(3) or 64.1(2) into effect in respect of the band;

(q) with respect to any matter arising out of or ancillary to the exercise of powers under this section; and

(r) the imposition on summary conviction of a fine not exceeding one thousand dollars or imprisonment for a term not exceeding thirty days, or both, for violation of a by-law made under this section.

Power to restrain by order where conviction entered

(2) Where any by-law of a band is contravened and a conviction entered, in addition to any other remedy and to any penalty imposed by the by-law, the court in which the conviction has been entered, and any court of competent jurisdiction thereafter, may make an order prohibiting the continuation or repetition of the offence by the person convicted.

Power to restrain by court action

(3) Where any by-law of a band passed is contravened, in addition to any other remedy and to any penalty imposed by the by-law, such contravention may be restrained by court action at the instance of the band council.

R.S., 1985, c. I-5, s. 81; R.S., 1985, c. 32 (1st Supp.), s. 15; 2000, c. 12, s. 152.

82 [Repealed, 2014, c. 38, s. 7]

Money by-laws

83 (1) Without prejudice to the powers conferred by section 81, the council of a band may, subject to the approval of the Minister, make by-laws for any or all of the following purposes, namely,

(**a**) subject to subsections (2) and (3), taxation for local purposes of land, or interests in land, in the reserve, including rights to occupy, possess or use land in the reserve;

(**a.1**) the licensing of businesses, callings, trades and occupations;

(**b**) the appropriation and expenditure of moneys of the band to defray band expenses;

(**c**) the appointment of officials to conduct the business of the council, prescribing their duties and providing for their remuneration out of any moneys raised pursuant to paragraph (a);

(**d**) the payment of remuneration, in such amount as may be approved by the Minister, to chiefs and councillors, out of any moneys raised pursuant to paragraph (a);

(**e**) the enforcement of payment of amounts that are payable pursuant to this section, including arrears and interest;

(**e.1**) the imposition and recovery of interest on amounts that are payable pursuant to this section, where those amounts are not paid before they are due, and the calculation of that interest;

(**f**) the raising of money from band members to support band projects; and

(**g**) with respect to any matter arising out of or ancillary to the exercise of powers under this section.

Restriction on expenditures

(**2**) An expenditure made out of moneys raised pursuant to subsection (1) must be so made under the authority of a by-law of the council of the band.

Appeals

(**3**) A by-law made under paragraph (1)(a) must provide an appeal procedure in respect of assessments made for the purposes of taxation under that paragraph.

Minister's approval

(**4**) The Minister may approve the whole or a part only of a by-law made under subsection (1).

Regulations re by-laws

(**5**) The Governor in Council may make regulations respecting the exercise of the by-law making powers of bands under this section.

By-laws must be consistent with regulations

(**6**) A by-law made under this section remains in force only to the extent that it is consistent with the regulations made under subsection (5).

R.S., 1985, c. I-5, s. 83; R.S., 1985, c. 17 (4th Supp.), s. 10.

Recovery of taxes

84 Where a tax that is imposed on an Indian by or under the authority of a by-law made under section 83 is not paid in accordance with the by-law, the Minister may pay the amount owing together with an amount equal to one-half of one per cent thereof out of moneys payable out of the funds of the band to the Indian.

R.S., c. I-6, s. 84.

85 [Repealed, R.S., 1985, c. 17 (4th Supp.), s. 11]

By-laws relating to intoxicants

85.1 (1) Subject to subsection (2), the council of a band may make by-laws

(a) prohibiting the sale, barter, supply or manufacture of intoxicants on the reserve of the band;

(b) prohibiting any person from being intoxicated on the reserve;

(c) prohibiting any person from having intoxicants in his possession on the reserve; and

(d) providing for exceptions to any of the prohibitions established pursuant to paragraph (b) or (c).

Consent of electors

(2) A by-law may not be made under this section unless it is first assented to by a majority of the electors of the band who voted at a special meeting of the band called by the council of the band for the purpose of considering the by-law.

(3) [Repealed, 2014, c. 38, s. 8]

Offence

(4) Every person who contravenes a by-law made under this section is guilty of an offence and liable on summary conviction

(a) in the case of a by-law made under paragraph (1)(a), to a fine of not more than one thousand dollars or to imprisonment for a term not exceeding six months or to both; and

(b) in the case of a by-law made under paragraph (1)(b) or (c), to a fine of not more than one hundred dollars or to imprisonment for a term not exceeding three months or to both.

R.S., 1985, c. 32 (1st Supp.), s. 16; 2014, c. 38, s. 8.

Publication of by-laws

86 (1) The council of a band shall publish a copy of every by-law made by the council under this Act on an Internet site, in the *First Nations Gazette* or in a newspaper that has general circulation on the reserve of the band, whichever the council considers appropriate in the circumstances.

Copies of by-laws

(2) The council of a band shall, on request by any person, provide to the person a copy of a by-law made by the council.

For greater certainty

(3) For greater certainty, publishing a by-law on an Internet site in accordance with subsection (1) does not discharge the council of a band from its obligation under subsection (2) to provide a copy of the by-law to any person who requests one.

Coming into force

(4) A by-law made by the council of a band under this Act comes into force on the day on which it is first published under subsection (1) or on any later day specified in the by-law.

Duration of publication — Internet site

(5) A by-law that is published on an Internet site under subsection (1) must remain accessible in that manner for the period during which it is in force. R.S., 1985, c. I-5, s. 86; 2014, c. 38, s. 9.

NOTE

1. Source: Canada 2020, *Indian Act.*

Appendix Two

Organizational Chart of the Abitibiwinni First Nation

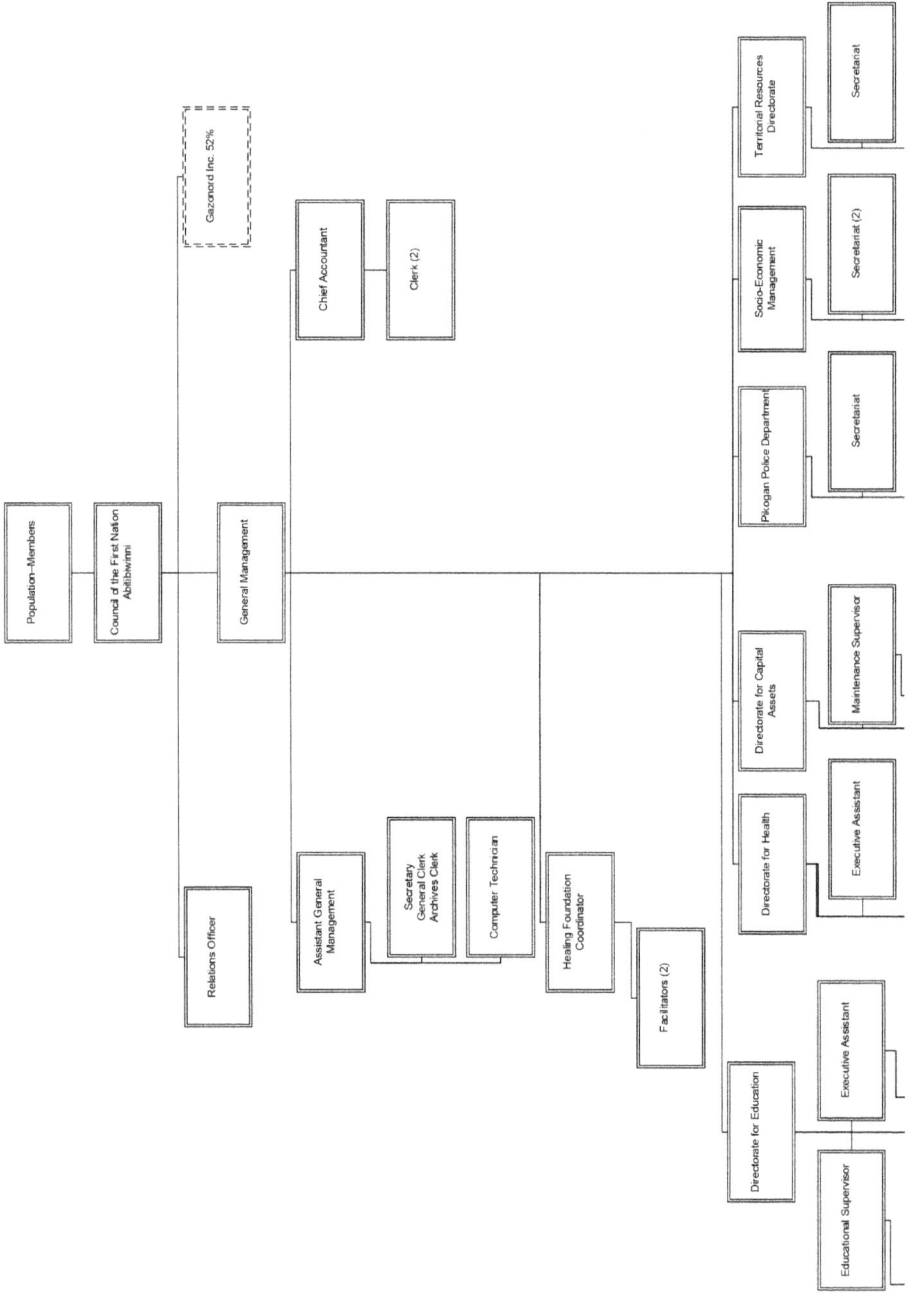

- Population—Members
- Council of the First Nation Abitibiwinni
  - Relations Officer
  - General Management
    - Gazoronord Inc. 52%
    - Chief Accountant
      - Clerk (2)
    - Assistant General Management
      - Secretary General Clerk Archives Clerk
      - Computer Technician
    - Healing Foundation Coordinator
      - Facilitators (2)
    - Directorate for Education
      - Educational Supervisor
      - Executive Assistant
    - Directorate for Health
    - Directorate for Capital Assets
      - Executive Assistant
      - Maintenance Supervisor
    - Pikogan Police Department
      - Secretariat
    - Socio-Economic Management
      - Secretariat (2)
    - Territorial Resources Directorate
      - Secretariat

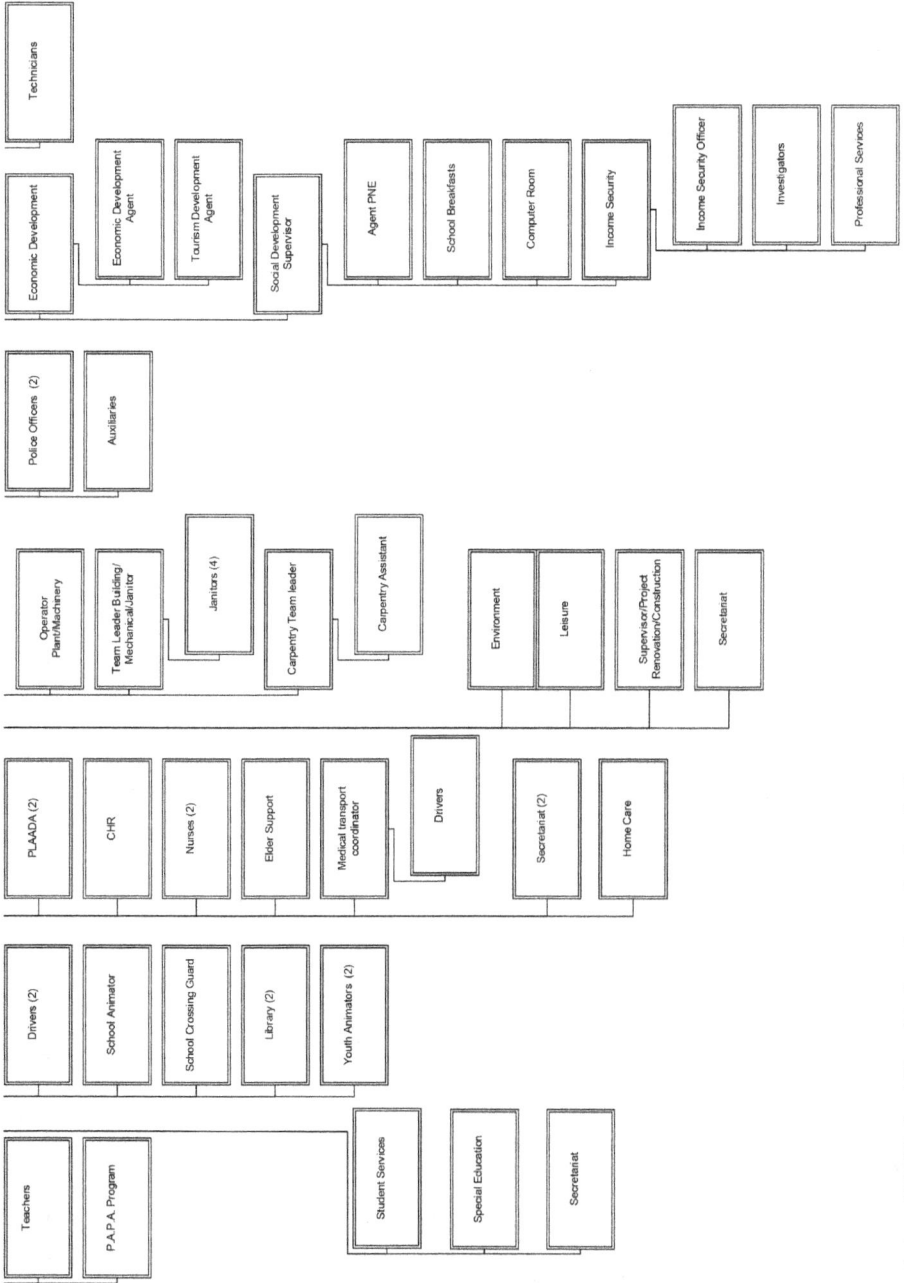

Figure A.1. Abitibiwinni First Nation Organizational Chart
Source: Expo Pikogan

Teachers
P.A.P.A. Program
Student Services
Special Education
Secretariat

Drivers (2)
School Animator
School Crossing Guard
Library (2)
Youth Animators (2)

PLAADA (2)
CHR
Nurses (2)
Elder Support
Medical transport coordinator
Drivers
Secretariat (2)
Home Care

Operator Plant/Machinery
Team Leader Building/Mechanical/Janitor
Janitors (4)
Carpentry Team leader
Carpentry Assistant
Environment
Leisure
Supervisor/Project Renovation/Construction
Secretariat

Police Officers (2)
Auxiliaries

Technicians
Economic Development
Economic Development Agent
Tourism Development Agent
Social Development Supervisor
Agent PNE
School Breakfasts
Computer Room
Income Security
Income Security Officer
Investigators
Professional Services

Bibliography

4-H. Accessed August 31, 2010. http://4-h.org.

Abélès, Marc. *Jours tranquilles en 89: Ethnologie politique d'un département français*. Paris: Odile Jacob, 1989.

Abélès, Marc. "Mises en scène et rituels politiques – une approche critique." *Hermès*, 8–9, no. 1–2 (1991): 241–59.

Abélès, Marc. "Anthropologie politique de la modernité." *L'Homme* 32, no. 121 (January–March 1992): 15–30.

Abélès, Marc. *Anthropologie de l'État*. Paris: Payot & Rivages, 2005.

AD, Archives Deschâtelets. Nos missionnaires oblats et leur œuvre auprès des Algonquins du Témiscamingue et de la Gatineau by François Marquis, n.d., JA 61. A64R 27, Ottawa.

AD, Archives Deschâtelets. *Lettre du père Guinard au Department of Indian Affairs*. July 20, 1933, Oskélanéo. HEB 6964. E83Z.78., Ottawa.

Alcoholics Anonymous. Accessed August 31, 2010. http://www.aa.org.

Alfred, Gerald Taiaiake. *Peace, Power, Righteousness: An Indigenous Manifesto*. Don Mills, ON: Oxford University Press, 1999.

Amnistie internationale Canada. *On a volé la vie de nos sœurs: Discrimination et violence contre les femmes autochtones au Canada*. Ottawa: Amnistie internationale, 2004.

ANC, Archives nationales du Canada. 1922, *Lettre datée du 3 novembre 1922. Du père Étienne Blanchin, o.m.i., adressée au Département des Affaires indiennes (Ottawa)*. RG 10, vol. 7764, dossier 27074-5 (lettre manuscrite de 14 pages).

Anderson, Kim. "Leading by Action: Female Chiefs and the Political Landscape." In *Restoring the Balance: First Nations Women, Community and Culture*, edited by Gail Guthrie Valaskakis, Eric Guimond, and Madeleine Dion Stout, 99–123. Winnipeg, University of Manitoba Press, 2009.

Anonymous. "Emile Joanis, former Maniwaki Mayor, Dies." *The Evening Citizen*, February 3, 1943, no. 195: 15.

Anonymous. "Quebec, Maritime Indians Meeting at Loretteville: Homemakers Convention." *The Indian Missionary Record,* Ottawa: Published by the Missionary Oblates of Mary Immaculate, vol. 17, no. 2 (August-September 1953): 3.

Anonymous. "Cours de formation de chefs sociaux." *The Indian Missionary Record,* Ottawa: Published by the Missionary Oblates of Mary Immaculate, 17, no. 6 (June 1954a): 8.

Anonymous. "Cours de formation de chefs sociaux." *The Indian Missionary Record,* Ottawa: Published by the Missionary Oblates of Mary Immaculate, 17, no. 5 (May 1954b): 7.

Anonymous. "Photo of the Homemaker's Club Convention, Held Last Summer at Loretteville, P.Q. Huron Reservation." *The Indian Missionary Record,* Ottawa: Published by the Missionary Oblates of Mary Immaculate, 16, no. 15 (February 1954c): 1.

Anonymous. "Convention des Cercles de Ménagères Indiennes." *The Indian Missionary Record,* Ottawa: Published by the Missionary Oblates of Mary Immaculate, 17, no. 10 (December 1954d): 12.

Anonymous. "On étudie un conflit de cultures." *Vie indienne, Organe des Indiens d'expression française,* Montréal: Commission oblate des œuvres indiennes et esquimaudes, 1, no. 2 (1957): 6–7.

Anonymous. "Nouvelles brèves. Nouveau curé chez les Indiens de Maniwaki." *Vie indienne, Organe des Indiens d'expression française,* Montréal: Commission oblate des œuvres indiennes et esquimaudes, 2, no. 4 (1959a): 7.

Anonymous. "Importante réunion à Maniwaki." *Vie indienne, Organe des Indiens d'expression française,* Montréal: Commission oblate des œuvres indiennes et esquimaudes, 2, no. 4 (1959b): 3.

Anonymous. "Ouverture du nouveau pensionnat indien de Pointe-Bleue." *Vie indienne, Organe des Indiens d'expression française,* Montréal: Commission oblate des œuvres indiennes et esquimaudes, 2, no. 8 (1960a): 3.

Anonymous. "Semaine d'étude pour les chefs indiens sociaux du Québec." *Vie indienne, Organe des Indiens d'expression française,* Montréal: Commission oblate des œuvres indiennes et esquimaudes, 2, no. 7 (1960b): 7.

Anonymous. "Parade étudiante à Pointe-Bleue." *Vie indienne, Organe des Indiens d'expression française,* Montréal: Commission oblate des œuvres indiennes et esquimaudes, 2, no. 12 (1961a): 3–4.

Anonymous. "Chez les Montagnais de Pointe-Bleue: Son Excellence Mgr Marius Paré bénit le nouveau pensionnat." *Vie indienne, Organe des Indiens d'expression française,* Montréal: Commission oblate des œuvres indiennes et esquimaudes, 2, no. 10 (1961b): 1.

Anonymous. "Nouvelles du pensionnat de Sept-Îles." *Vie indienne, Organe des Indiens d'expression française,* Montréal: Commission oblate des œuvres indiennes et esquimaudes, 2, no. 16 (1962): 3.

Anonymous. "Miss Indienne du Canada." *Vie indienne, Organe des Indiens d'expression française,* Montréal: Commission oblate des œuvres indiennes et esquimaudes, 2, no. 19 (September 1963): 3.

Anonymous. "Princesse Canada." *Vie indienne, Organe des Indiens d'expression française*, Montréal: Commission oblate des œuvres indiennes et esquimaudes, 3, no. 3 (September 1965a): 7.

Anonymous. "Mlle Linda Odjick, reine des Algonquins de Maniwaki." *Le Droit*, January 25, 1965b:16.

ARDIA (Annual Report of Indian Affairs). *Martin à Dewdney, 15 août 1889.* Pt. I., December 31, 1889, p. 35.

Arendt, Hannah. *La crise de la culture*. Paris: Folio, 1972.

Armitage, Peter. "The Religious Significance of Animals in Innu Culture." *Native Issues* 4, no. 1 (1984): 50–56.

Armitage, Peter. "Religious Ideology among the Innu of Eastern Quebec and Labrador." *Religiologiques* no. 6 (1992): 63–110.

Assiniwi, Bernard. "La femme indienne: Interview de Mme Mary Commanda." In À l'indienne, 15–25. Ottawa: 1972.

Aubert, Laura, and Mylène Jaccoud. "Genèse et développement des polices autochtones au Québec: Sur la voie de l'autodétermination." *Criminologie* 42, no. 2 (2009): 101–19.

BAC (Bibliothèque et Archives Canada). *Maniwaki Reserve, Agent John White requesting Authority for the River Desert Indians to hold an election of Chiefs*, RG 10, volume 1934, dossier 3567.

BAC (Bibliothèque et Archives Canada). *River Desert Agency, Maniwaki Reserve, Request by three Chiefs of the Band to have another agent appointed in place of Patrick Moore as he lives too far from the Desert village.* RG 10, vol. 2066, dossier 10, 270.

Balandier, Georges. "Les relations de dépendance personnelle en Afrique noire." *Cahiers d'études africaines* 9 (3), no. 35 (1969): 345–49.

Baribeau, Jean. "Les missions sauvages du haut Saint-Maurice au xixe siècle." Master's thesis, Université du Québec à Trois-Rivières, 1978.

Barth, Fredrik, ed. "Introduction." In *The Role of the Entrepreneur in Northern Norway*. Bergen: University of Norway, 1963.

Bass, Bernard M., and Ruth Bass, eds. *The Bass Handbook of Leadership: Theory, Research and Managerial Applications*. New York: Free Press, 2008.

Beaudet, Christiane. "De la production domestique à l'artisanat: Les transformations des savoir-faire chez les Montagnaises de La Romaine" Master's thesis, Université Laval, 1987.

Beck, Horace P. "Algonquin Folklore from Maniwaki." *Journal of American Folklore* 60, no. 237 (1947): 259–64.

Bédard, Hélène, *Les Montagnais et la réserve de Betsiamites, 1850–1900.* Coll. Edmond-de-Nevers, no. 7. Québec: Institut québécois de recherche sur la culture, 1988.

Bélanger, Paul R., and Louis Maheu. "Pratique politique étudiante au Québec." *Recherches sociographiques* 13, no. 3 (1972): 309–42.

Bernstein, Edward, Nina Wallerstein, Ronald Braithwaite, Lorraine Gutierrez, Ronald Labonté, and Marc Zimmerman. "Empowerment Forum: A Dialogue between

Guest Editorial Board Members." *Health Education Quarterly* 21, no. 3 (1994): 281–94.

Bertrand, Jacques. "Les relations administratives entre le ministère des Affaires indiennes et du Nord Canada et les Conseils de bande." PhD diss., Université catholique de Louvain, 2010.

Bhabha, Homi K. *The Location of Culture*. London: Routledge, 1994.

Black, Meredith Jean. "Nineteenth-Century Algonquin Culture Change." In *Actes du vingtième congrès des Algonquinistes*, edited by William Cowan, 62–69. Ottawa: Carleton University, 1989.

Blok, Anton. "Peasants, Patrons, and Brokers in Western Sicily." *Anthropological Quarterly* 42, no. 3 (1969): 155–70.

Bohaker, Heidi, and Franca Iacovetta. "Making Aboriginal People "Immigrants Too": A Comparison of Citizenship Programs for Newcomers and Indigenous Peoples in Postwar Canada, 1940s–1960s." *The Canadian Historical Review* 90, no. 3 (2009): 427–61.

Boissevain, Jeremy. "Maltese Village Politics and Their Relation to National Politics." *Journal of Commonwealth Political Studies* 1, no. 3 (1962): 211–22.

Boissevain, Jeremy. "Patronage in Sicily." *Man* 1, no. 1 (1966): 18–33.

Boissevain, Jeremy. *Friends of Friends: Networks, Manipulators and Coalitions*. Oxford: Basil Blackwell, 1973.

Bouchard, Serge, ed. Mémoires d'un simple missionnaire. *Le père Joseph-Étienne Guinard, O.M.I., 1864–1965*. Coll. Civilisation du Québec. Québec: Ministère des Affaires culturelles, 1980.

Bousquet, Marie-Pierre, and Anny Morissette. "Inscrire la mémoire semi-nomade dans l'actualité sédentaire: Les églises de Pikogan et de Manawan." *Archives de sciences sociales des religions*, 141 (2008): 9–32.

Bousquet, Marie-Pierre, and Anny Morissette. "De la bière, du fort ou du vin: Peut-on boire sans ivresse chez les Amérindiens?" *Drogues, santé et société* 8, no. 1 (2009): 123–63.

Bousquet, Marie-Pierre, and Anny Morissette. "Reines, princesses, Miss et majorettes: Une construction de la féminité chez les Amérindien(ne)s du Québec (20ᵉ– 21ᵉ s.)." In Éros et *tabou: Sexualité et genre chez les Amérindiens et les Inuit*, edited by Frédéric Laugrand and Gilles Havard: 359–407. Québec: Septentrion, 2014.

Bousquet, Marie-Pierre. "'Quand nous vivions dans le bois': Le changement spatial et sa dimension générationnelle; L'exemple des Algonquins du Canada." PhD diss., Université de Paris X-Nanterre, and Université Laval, 2001.

Bousquet, Marie-Pierre. "Les Algonquins ont-ils toujours besoin des animaux indiens? Réflexions sur le bestiaire contemporain." *Théologiques* 10, no. 1 (2002): 63–87.

Bousquet, Marie-Pierre. "La production d'un réseau de sur-parenté: Histoire de l'alcool et désintoxication chez les Algonquins." *Drogues, santé et société* 4, no. 1 (2005): 129–73.

Bousquet, Marie-Pierre. "A Generation in Politics: The Alumni of the Saint-Marc-de-Figuery Residential School. In *Papers of the Thirty-Seventh Algonquian Confer-*

ence, edited by Hans Christoph Wolfart, 1–17. Winnipeg: University of Manitoba, 2006.

Bousquet, Marie-Pierre. "Régler ses conflits dans un cadre spirituel: Pouvoir, réparation et systèmes religieux chez les Anicinabek du Québec." *Criminologie* 42, no. 2 (2009): 53–82.

Bousquet, Marie-Pierre. "Êtres libres ou sauvages à civiliser? Éducation, Amérindiens et pensionnats indiens au Québec, des années 1950 à 1970." *Revue d'histoire de l'enfance irrégulière* 14 (2012): 163–92.

Bovee, Steven. "Leading in the Cracks." *The Leading Edge*. Accessed March 11, 2013. https://go.roberts.edu/leadingedge/all.

Brizinski, Peggy M. "Les femmes dans le Nord: Problématique et devenir." *Recherches amérindiennes au Québec* 10, no. 4 (1981): 261–68.

Brownlie, Robin. "Man on the Spot: John Daly, Indian Agent in Parry Sound 1922–1939." *Journal of the Canadian Historical Association* 5, no. 1 (1994): 63–86.

Brownlie, Robin. *A Fatherly Eye: Indian Agents, Government Power, and Aboriginal Resistance in Ontario, 1918–1939*. Don Mills: Oxford University Press, 2003.

Brunelle, Patrick. "Un cas de colonialisme canadien: Les Hurons de Lorette entre la fin du XIXᵉ siècle et le début du XXᵉ siècle." Master's thesis, Université Laval, 1998.

CAM (Conseil des Atikamekw et des Montagnais), dir. *Montagnaises de parole/Eukuan ume ninan ententamat*. Québec: Conseil des Atikamekw et des Montagnais, 1992. Printed book and Video.

Cameron, Angela. "Sentencing Circles and Intimate Violence: A Canadian Feminist Perspective." *Canadian Journal of Women and the Law/Revue Femmes et droit* 18, no. 2 (2006): 479–512.

Canada. *Acte conférant certains privilèges aux bandes les plus avancées des Indiens du Canada en vue de les former à l'exercice des pouvoirs municipaux*, Statuts du Canada, c. 28 (47 Vict.), 1884.

Canada. *Acte pour amender et refondre les lois concernant les Sauvages*, Statuts du Canada, c. 28 (43 Vict.), 1880.

Canada. *Acte pour amender et refondre les lois concernant les Sauvages*, Statuts du Canada, c. 28 (47 Vict.), 1884.

Canada. *Acte pour amender et refondre les lois concernant les Sauvages. Acte pour amender et refondre les lois concernant les Sauvages*, Statuts du Canada, c. 18 (39 Vict.), 1876.

Canada. *Acte pourvoyant à l'émancipation graduelle des Sauvages, à la meilleure administration des affaires des Sauvages*, Statuts du Canada, c. 6 (32–33 Vict.), 1869.

Canada. *Annual Report of the Department of Indian Affairs for the Year Ended 31 December 1883*. Ottawa: Maclean, Roger & Co., 1883.

Canada. *Annual Report of the Department of Indian Affairs for the Year Ended 31 December 1884*. Ottawa: Maclean, Roger & Co., 1884.

Canada. *Annual Report of the Department of Indian Affairs for the Year Ended 31 December 1885*. Ottawa: Maclean, Roger & Co., 1885.

Canada. *Department of Citizenship and Immigration Report of Indian Affairs Branch for the Fiscal Year Ended March 31, 1952*. Ottawa: Department of Citizenship and Immigration, 1952.

Canada. *Indian Treaties and Surrenders, from no. 281 to 483.* Ottawa: Imprimeur du Roi, 1912.

Canada. *Loi modifiant la Loi sur les Indiens (loi C-31)*, Statuts du Canada, C-I-5 (33–34 Elizabeth II), 1985.

Canada. *Loi des Indiens, C. 29 (15 Geo. VI)*, 1951.

Canada. *Loi sur les Indiens*, QS-3621-020-BB-A2., 2020.

Canada. *Rapport de la Commission royale sur les peuples autochtones*, Éditions du gouvernement du Canada, Vol. I: *Un passé, un avenir.* Vol. II: *Une relation à redéfinir.* Vol. III: *Vers un ressourcement.* Vol. IV: *Perspectives et réalités.* Vol. V: *Vingt ans d'action soutenue par le renouveau*, Ottawa: Travaux publics et Services gouvernementaux Canada (rapport Erasmus-Dussault), 1996. Accessed July 22, 2009. http://www.collectionscanada.gc.ca/webarchives/20071115211319/http://www.ainc-inac.gc.ca/ch/rcap/sg/sgmm_f.html

Canada. *Rapport de la Division des Affaires indiennes pour l'année financière terminée le 31 mars 1958.* Ottawa: Department of Citizenship and Immigration, 1958.

Canada. Affaires autochtones et Développement du Nord Canada. Accessed June 8, 2012; March 8, 2013 and February 5, 2018. http://www.aadnc-aandc.gc.ca.

Canada. Affaires indiennes et du Nord Canada, "Première Nation de Kitigan Zibi." http://www.ainc-inac.gc.ca. Accessed July 20, 2009.

Canada. Archives publiques du Canada, R.G. 10, Red Series, vol. 1934, 3541, 1934.

Canada. Chambre des communes. *L'autonomie politique des Indiens au Canada*, rapport du comité spécial. Ottawa: Centre d'édition du gouvernement du Canada, Approvisionnements et Services Canada (rapport Penner), 1983.

Canada. Ministère des Affaires indiennes et du Nord Canada (MAINC). *Manuel de procédures comptables pour les Indiens et les Inuits*, Bureau régional de Québec, Procédure 12.1. Ottawa, ON: Ministère des Affaires indiennes et du Nord Canada, n.d.

Canada. Ministère des Affaires indiennes et du Nord Canada. *La politique indienne du gouvernement du Canada* (white paper), 1969.

Canada. Ministère des Affaires indiennes et du Nord Canada. *Rapports annuels*, Ottawa: Approvisionnements et Services Canada, 1972–1973.

Canada. Ministère des Affaires indiennes et du Nord Canada. *Rapports annuels*, Ottawa: Approvisionnements et Services Canada, 1973–1974.

Canada. Ministère des Affaires indiennes et du Nord Canada. *Rapports annuels*, Ottawa: Approvisionnements et Services Canada, 1979–1980.

Canada. Ministère des Affaires indiennes et du Nord Canada. *Rapport: une source d'information pour rehausser l'efficacité des conseils*, 2003.

Canada. Minister of Northern Affairs and National Resources. *Department of Northern Affairs and National Resources Annual Report Fiscal Year, 1965–1966.* Ottawa, ON: Minister of Northern Affairs and National Resources, 1965–1966.

Canada. Secrétariat d'État. *À nous la parole: Les femmes autochtones du Canada.* Ottawa, 1975.

Canada. Sénat. Élections chez les Premières Nations: *Une question de choix fondamental.* Rapport du Comité sénatorial permanent des peuples autochtones. Ottawa: Sénat, 2010.

Canada. Senate. *Proceedings of the Standing Senate Committee on Aboriginal Peoples*, Issue 15—Evidence, November 24, 2010. Accessed February 5, 2018. https://sencanada.ca.

Cardinal, Harold. *The Unjust Society: The Tragedy of Canada's Indians.* Edmonton: Hurtig, 1969.

Carrière, Gaston, OMI. *Le roi de Betsiamites: Le père Charles Arnaud, o.m.i. (1826–1914)*. Ottawa: Éditions de l'Université d'Ottawa, 1958.

Carrière, Gaston, OMI. *Planteur d'Églises, J.-B. Honorat, oblat de Marie-Immaculée*, Montréal: Rayonnement, 1962.

Carrière, Gaston, OMI. *Histoire documentaire de la Congrégation des Missionnaires Oblats de Marie-Immaculée dans l'est du Canada*, deuxième partie, dans la seconde moitié du XIXᵉ siècle (1861–1900), tome VII, Ottawa: Éditions de l'Université d'Ottawa, 1968.

Carrière, Gaston, OMI. *Le père Jean-Pierre Guéguen, o.m.i., 1838–1909: Un grand voltigeur: Mattawa, Kipawa, Tête du Lac, Weymontaching, Maniwaki*. Guérin: Centre d'études universitaires dans l'Ouest Québécois, 1978.

Carter, Sarah. *Capturing Women: The Manipulation of Cultural Imagery in Canada's Prairie West*. Montréal: McGill-Queen's University Press, 1997.

Cercles de fermières du Québec. Accessed August 31, 2010. http://www.cfq.qc.ca.

Chanel, Armand. "Citoyenneté et civilité aujourd'hui: Quelques éclaircissements." *DEES*, no. 118 (1999): 69–75. Accessed March 30, 2018. http://pst.chez-alice.fr/svtiufm/citoyen.htm.

Charest, Paul. "La prise en charge donne-t-elle du pouvoir? L'exemple des Atikamekw et des Montagnais." *Anthropologie et sociétés* 16, no. 3 (1992): 55–76.

Charlier, Sophie. "L'empowerment des femmes dans les organisations de commerce équitable: Une proposition méthodologique." In Économie solidaire et commerce équitable: acteurs et actrices d'Europe et d'Amérique latine, edited by Claude Auroi and Isabel Yépez del Castillo, 87–109. Leuven: UCL Presses universitaires de Louvain, 2006.

Chaumel, Gilles. "Manouane choisit la liberté." *Rencontre* 15, no. 2 (Winter 1993–1994): 11–13. Québec: Secrétariat aux affaires autochtones.

Cheater, Angela P, ed. "Power in the Postmodern Era." In *The Anthropology of Power: Empowerment and Disempowerment in Changing Structures*, 1–12. London: Routledge, 1999.

Clatworthy, S. J., and A. H. Smith. *Population Implications of the 1985 Amendments to the Indian Act*. Ottawa: Assembly of First Nations, 1992.

Clatworthy, Stewart. "Modifications apportées en 1985 à la *Loi sur les Indiens*: Répercussions sur les Premières Nations du Québec." *Cahiers québécois de démographie* 38 (2) (2009): 253–86.

Clermont, Norman. "Les Kokotchés à Weymontachie." *Recherches amérindiennes au Québec* 8, no. 2 (1978): 139–46.

Clermont, Norman. *Ma femme, ma hache et mon couteau croche: Deux siècles d'histoire à Weymontachie*. Coll. "Civilisation du Québec no 18, série Cultures amérindiennes. Québec: Ministère des Affaires culturelles, 1982.

Club Richelieu international. Accessed August 31, 2010. http://www.richelieu.org.

Club Rotary International. Accessed August 31, 2010. http://www.rotary.org.

Clubs 4-H du Québec. Accessed August 31, 2010. http://www.clubs4h.qc.ca.

Collerette, Pierre. "Le leadership et ses processus." In *Pouvoir, leadership et autorité dans les organisations*, edited by Pierre Collerette, 153–86. Québec: Presses de l'Université du Québec, 1991.

Comité des fêtes du 150ᵉ anniversaire de Maniwaki. *Album souvenir du 150ᵉ anniversaire* de Maniwaki 1851–2001, Maniwaki: Comité des fêtes du 150ᵉ, 2001.

Communauté Atikamekw de Manawan. Accessed September 7, 2010. www.manawan.com.

Conseil du statut de la femme. *Rencontre entre vous et nous: Entretiens avec des élues autochtones du Québec*, Québec: Gouvernement du Québec, 2010.

Conseil tribal de la nation algonquine Anishinabeg. Accessed July 16, 2009, and March 8, 2013. http://www.anishinabenation.ca.

Cooper, John M. "The Obedjiwan Band of the Têtes de Boule." *Anthropos*, no. 21 (1926a): 616–17.

Cooper, John M. "The Tête de Boule of the Upper St. Maurice, Abstract." *Journal of the Washington Academy of Sciences* 16, no. 5 (1926b): 138.

Craig, Susan. "Qui prend mari prend pays? A study of women's role in ethnic boundary in a native community in Quebec." Master's thesis, Université Laval, 1987.

Cuoq, Jean-André. Études philologiques sur quelques langues sauvages de l'Amérique. Montréal: Dawson Brothers, 1886.

Damas, David. "The Diversity of Eskimo Societies." In *Man the Hunter*, edited by Richard B. Lee and Irven Devore, 111–17. Chicago: Aldine Publishing Co, 1968.

Daugherty, Wayne, and Dennis Madill. *Indian Government under Indian Act Legislation 1868–1951*, Ottawa: Treaties and Historical Research Centre, 1980.

Davidson, D. S. "Notes on Tête de Boule Ethnology." *American Anthropologist* no. 30 (1928): 18–46.

Day, Gordon. "Nispissing." In *Handbook of North American Indians, vol. 15: Northeast*, edited by Bruce Graham Trigger, 787–91. Washington: Smithsonian Institution, 1978.

Day, Gordon, and Bruce G. Trigger. "Algonquin." In *Handbook of North American Indians, vol. 15: Northeast*, edited by Bruce Graham Trigger, 792–97. Washington: Smithsonian Institution, 1978.

Decontie, Jacqueline. "La maison Waseya." *Rencontre* 12, no. 4 (June 1991). Québec: Secrétariat aux affaires autochtones.

Denoncourt, Thierry. "Les Algonquins réclament l'Abitibi-Témiscamingue, l'Outaouais et une partie de l'Ontario." *La Frontière, Le Citoyen Abitibi-Ouest* and *Le Citoyen Rouyn-Noranda*, 2013. Accessed March 8, 2013. https://www.lafrontiere.ca.

Descola, Philippe. "La chefferie amérindienne dans l'anthropologie politique." *Revue française de sciences politique* 38, no. 5 (1988): 818–28.

Desgent, Jean-Marc, and Guy Lanoue. *Errance: Comment se pensent le Nous et le Moi dans l'espace mythique des nomades septentrionaux sekani*. Coll. Mercure, no. 142. Ottawa: Musée canadien des civilisations, 2005.

Desmarais, Danielle, Carole Lévesque, and Dominique Raby. "La contribution des femmes naskapies aux travaux de la vie quotidienne à l'époque de Fort McKenzie." *Recherches féministes* 7, no. 1 (1994): 23–42.

Dickson-Gilmore, Jane. ""This Is My History, I Know Who I Am": History, Factionalist Competition, and the Assumption of Imposition in the Kahnawake Mohawk Nation." *Ethnohistory* 46, no. 3 (1999): 429–50.

Dion Stout, Madeleine, and Gregory D. Kipling. *Aboriginal Women in Canada: Strategic Research Directions for Policy Development.* Ottawa: Condition feminine Canada, 1998.

Dion Stout, Madeleine, and Gregory D. Kipling. *Peuples autochtones, résilience et séquelles du régime des pensionnats.* Ottawa: Fondation autochtone de guérison, 2003.

Dominique, Richard. *Le langage de la chasse: R*écit autobiographique de Michel Grégoire, montagnais de *Natashquan.* Sillery: Presses de l'Université du Québec, 1989.

Ducas, Michel. "Salomé Mackenzie nouveau chef de Lac-Simon." *L'Écho abitibien,* February 8, 2011. Accessed May 15, 2012. https://www.lechoabitibien.ca.

Duffault, François Pierre. "Vigile en mémoire des autochtones disparues." *Le Droit,* October 4, 2009. Accessed March 9, 2013. http://www.lapresse.ca/le-droit/actualites/ailleurs-au-pays-et-dans-le-monde/200910/04/01-908372-vigile-en-memoire-des-autochtones-disparues.php.

Dumont, Micheline, and Nadia Fahmy-Eid, ed. *Les couventines: L'éducation des filles au Québec dans les congrégations religieuses enseignantes 1840–1960.* Montréal: Boréal, 1986.

Dupuis, Renée. *La question indienne au Canada.* Montréal: Éditions Boréal, 1991.

Dupuis, Renée. "L'avenir du Québec et les peuples autochtones." *Les peuples autochtones et l'avenir du Québec, l'activité politique autochtone. Choix* (Série Québec-Canada) (Institut de recherche en politiques publiques) 1, no. 10 (June 1995a): 20–33.

Dupuis, Renée. *Les revendications territoriales des Autochtones au Québec.* Montréal: McGill-Queen's University Press, 1995b.

Dupuis, Renée. *Tribus, peuples et nations: Les nouveaux enjeux des revendications autochtones au Canada.* Montréal: Éditions Boréal, 1997.

Dyck, Noel, ed. *Indigenous Peoples and the Nation-State.* St. John's: Institute of Social and Economic Research & Memorial University of Newfoundland, 1985.

Dyck, Noel. *What Is the Indian "Problem": Tutelage and Resistance in Canadian Indian Administration.* St. John's: Institute of Social and Economic Research & Memorial University of Newfoundland, 1991.

Einhorn, Arthur. "Iroquois-Algonquin Wampum Exchanges and Preservation in the Twentieth Century: A Case Study for In Situ Preservation." *Man in the Northeast,* no. 7 (1974): 71–86.

Eisenstadt, Shmuel N., and Luis Roniger. *Patrons, Clients, and Friends: Interpersonal Relations and the Structure of Trust in Society.* Cambridge: Cambridge University Press, 1984.

Ezzo, David A. "Female Status in the Northeast." In *Papers of the Nineteenth Algonquian Conference*, edited by William Cowan, 49–62. Ottawa: Carleton University, 1988.

Fantoni, Beatrice. "First Nations Franchise: Buying In or Selling Out?" *Capital News Online*, 2010. Accessed February 17, 2011. http://www.capitalnews.ca.

Fecteau, Katia, and Bernard Roy. *Paroles et pouvoir de femmes des Premières Nations*, Sainte-Foy, QC: Presses de l'Université Laval, 2005.

Feit, Harvey. "Les animaux comme partenaires de chasse. Réciprocité chez les Cris de la Baie-James." *Terrain*, no. 34 (March 2000): 123–42.

Fenton, William N. "Leadership in the Northeastern Woodlands of North America." *American Indian Quarterly* 10, no. 1 (1996): 21–45.

First Nations and Inuit Suicide Prevention Association of Quebec and Labrador. Accessed October 19, 2009. http://www.dialogue-pour-la-vie.com.

Fiske, Jo-Anne. "Native Women in Reserve Politics: Strategies and Struggles." *Journal of Legal Pluralism*, no. 30 (1990): 121–37.

Fiske, Jo-Anne. "Colonization and the Decline of Women's Status: The Tsimshian Case." *Feminist Studies* 17, no. 3 (1991): 509–35.

Flanagan, Thomas. *First Nations? Second Thoughts*. Montréal: McGill-Queen's University Press, 2000.

Flanerry, Regina. "Gossip as a Clue to Attitudes" *Primitive Man* 7, no. 1 (1934): 8–12.

Flanerry, Regina. "The Shaking-Tent Rite among the Crees and Montagnais of James Bay." *Primitive Man*, no. 12 (1939): 11–16.

Fortin, Jean, OMI. *Coup d'œil sur le monde merveilleux des Montagnais de la Côte-Nord*. Sept-Îles, QC: Institut culturel et éducatif Montagnais, 1992.

Forum jeunesse de la région de la Capitale-Nationale. Accessed May 23, 2012. http://fjrcn.org.

Foucault, Michel. *Surveiller et punir: Naissance de la prison*. Paris: Gallimard, 1975.

Foucault, Michel. *The Foucault Reader*, edited by Paul Rabinow. Harmondsworth, UK: Penguin, 1984.

Francis, Daniel, and Toby Morantz. *Partners in Furs: A History of the Fur Trade in Eastern James Bay, 1600–1870*. Montréal: McGill-Queen's University Press, 1983.

Frazer, James-George. *The Golden Bough*. London: Macmillan, 1890.

Freeman, Milton. "Tolerance and Rejection of Patron Roles." In *Patrons and Brokers in the East Arctic*, edited by Robert Paine, 34–54. St. John's: Institute of Social and Economic Research & Memorial University of Newfoundland, 1971.

Frenette, Jacques. *Le pays des Anicinabe: La revendication territoriale globale de la nation algonquine*. Énoncé de revendication documenté et rédigé par Jacques Frenette pour le Conseil de bande. Réserve algonquine de Maniwaki: Miméo, 1988.

Frenette, Jacques. "Kitigan Zibi Anishinabeg. Le territoire et les activités économiques des Algonquins de la rivière Désert (Maniwaki) 1850–1950." *Recherches amérindiennes au Québec* 23, nos. 2–3 (1993): 39–51.

Frideres, James. *Native Peoples in Canada, Contemporary Conflicts.* Fifth edition. Scarborough, ON: Prentice Hall, 1998.

Furniss, Elizabeth. *Victims of Benevolence: The Dark Legacy of the Williams Lake Residential School.* Vancouver: Arsenal Pulp Press, 1995.

Gaffield, Chad, ed. "Société, culture et développement institutionnel: 1826–1886." In *Histoire de l'Outaouais*, 207–50. Québec: Institut québécois de recherche sur la culture, 1994.

Gagnon, Denis. "Sainte Anne et le pouvoir manitushiun: L'inversion de la cosmologie mamit innuat dans le contexte de la sédentarisation." In *La nature des esprits dans les cosmologies autochtones/Nature of Spirits in Aboriginal Cosmologies*, edited by Frédéric B. Laugrand and Jarich G. Oosten, 449–77. Coll. Mondes autochtones. Québec: Presses de l'Université Laval, 2007.

Gagnon, Éric. "Engagement social, engagement identitaire—Parcours de femmes." *Service social* 44, no. 1 (1995): 49–67.

Galarneau, Claude. *Les collèges classiques au Canada français (1620–1970).* Montréal: Éditions Fides, 1978.

Gaudreau, Guy, OMI, and Danièle Miny. "À tort et à raison." *Apostolat* 74, no. 4 (July–August 2003): 6–13.

Geertz, Armin W. "Hopi Indian Witchcraft and Healing: On Good, Evil and Gossip." *American Indian Quarterly* 35, no. 3 (2011): 372–93.

Gélinas, Claude. "Jean-Baptiste Boucher, le négatif du chef atikamekw par excellence au XIXᵉ siècle." In *Anthropologie et histoire. Actes du quatrième colloque du Département d'anthropologie*, edited by Norman Clermont, 27–37. Montréal: Université de Montréal, 1998.

Gélinas, Claude. *La gestion de l'étranger. Les Atikamekw et la présence eurocanadienne en Haute-Mauricie, 1760–1870.* Sillery: Septentrion, 2000.

Gélinas, Claude. "La création des réserves atikamekw (1895–1950), ou quand l'Indien était vraiment un Indien." *Recherches amérindiennes au Québec* 32, no. 2 (2002): 35–48.

Gélinas, Claude. "La Mauricie des Abénaquis au XIXᵉ siècle." *Recherches amérindiennes au Québec* 33, no. 2 (2003a): 44–56.

Gélinas, Claude. *Entre l'assommoir et le godendart: Les Atikamekw et la conquête du Moyen-Nord Québécois 1870–1940.* Sillery: Septentrion, 2003b.

Gélinas, Claude. "Les missions catholiques chez les Atikamekw (1837–1940): Manifestations de foi et d'esprit pratique." *Études d'histoire religieuse*, 69 (2003c): 83–99.

Gidmark, David. *The Indian Crafts of William and Mary Commanda.* Toronto: McGraw-Hill Ryerson Limited, 1980.

Godbout, Jacques T. "La communauté retrouvée?" *Recherches sociographiques* 28, nos. 2–3 (1987): 407–14.

Gouverneur général du Canada. Accessed October 19, 2009. http://archive.gg.ca.

Goyette, Christian, with the collaboration of Geneviève Polèse, Manon Lévesque, Christian Iorio, and Carole Lévesque. "Retour sur le colloque: *Itinéraires d'égalité*." Organisé par DIALOG et Femmes autochtones du Québec Inc., Montréal,

February 22–24, 2005: 1–78. Accessed December 5, 2011. http://www.reseaudia-log.ca/DocsPDF/SyntheseFev2005.pdf.

Graymont, Barbara, ed. *Fighting Tuscarora: The Autobiography of Chief Clinton Rickard*. Syracuse, NY: Syracuse University Press, 1973.

Green, Joyce. "Autodétermination, citoyenneté et fédéralisme: Pour une relecture autochtone du palimpseste canadien." *Politique et sociétés* 23, no. 1 (2004): 9–32.

Guay, Christiane, and Thibault Martin. "L'ère/l'aire de la gouvernance autochtone: Le territoire en question." *Revue canadienne des sciences régionales* 21, no. 3 (2008): 637–50.

Guilbeault-Cayer, Émilie. "De l'assimilation à l'intégration? Discussion sur l'*empowerment* des Autochtones pendant le Comité mixte sur la Loi des Indiens de 1946." *Bulletin d'histoire politique* 24, no. 3 (2016): 82–97.

Guinard, Joseph-Étienne, OMI. *Mémoires*. Montréal: Ms. Maison des Oblats, 1945.

Guinard, Joseph-Étienne, OMI. *Les noms indiens de mon pays: Leur signification, leur histoire*. Montréal: Rayonnement, 1960.

Guyon, Stéphanie. "L'entrée en politique d'un village amérindien de Guyane: Eth-nographie d'un conflit entre autorité coutumière et mairie." In *Luttes autochtones, trajectoires postcoloniales (Amérique, Pacifique)*, edited by Bastien Bosa and Eric Wittersheim, 57–84. Paris: Karthala, 2009.

Hawthorn, Harry B., and Marc-Adélard Tremblay. Étude sur les Indiens contempo-rains du Canada: *Besoins et mesures d'ordre économique, politique et éducatif*, vols. 1 and 2, Ottawa: Indian Affairs Branch, 1967.

Helm, June. "Bilaterality in the Socio-territorial Organization of the Arctic Drainage Dene." *Ethnology* 4, no. 4 (1965): 361–85.

Her Story. Accessed March 2, 2011. http://library.usask.ca/herstory/commun.html.

Hessel, Peter. *The Algonkin Tribe, The Algonkins of the Ottawa Valley: An Historical Outline*. Arnprior, ON: Kichesippi Books, 1987.

Hirbour, René. "Étude de trois niveaux d'intégration sociale d'une société de chasseurs-cueilleurs: *Kitchezagik Anichenabe*." Master's thesis, Université de Montréal, 1969.

Holmes, Joan et al. *Without Prejudice: Kitigan Zibi Anishinabeg Global Research Project*. Gatineau, QC: Indian and Northern Affairs Canada, Specific Claims Branch, 1999.

Hudon, Raymond, and Stéphanie Yates. "Lobbying et patronage: Mode de médiation en contexte démocratique." *Canadian Journal of Political Science/Revue cana-dienne de science politique* 41, no. 2 (2008): 375–409.

Huot, Richard. "La nation algonquine dénonce l'emprisonnement stratégique du chef algonquin!" Centre des médias alternatifs du Québec, December 24, 2008. Accessed March 8, 2013. http://archives-2001-2012.cmaq.net/es/node/31765.html.

Indian Country Today Media Network. *Atleo Blessing Helps Bid Final Farewell to Jack Layton*. August 27, 2011. Accessed May 30, 2012. http://indiancountryto-daymedianetwork.com/2011/08/27/atleo-blessing-helps-bid-final-farewell-to-jack-layton-49525.

Indigenous Services Canada Website. Accessed November 3, 2020. https://www.sac-isc.gc.ca/,

Ivison, John. "Conflicting Numbers on Missing Aboriginal Women Another Reason an Inquiry Is Needed." *National Post*, February 13, 2013a. Accessed March 9, 2013. http://nationalpost.com.

Ivison, John. "Inquiry into Missing First Nations Women Right Thing for Tories Both Politically and Morally." *National Post*, February 13, 2013b. Accessed March 9, 2013. http://nationalpost.com.

Izard, Michel. "Colonisation." In *Dictionnaire de l'ethnologie et de l'anthropologie*, edited by Pierre Bonte and Michel Izard, 160–63. Paris: Presses Universitaires de France, 2002.

Jaccoud, Mylène. "Les femmes autochtones et la justice pénale." *Criminologie* 25, no. 1 (1992): 65–85.

Jaccoud, Mylène. "Les cercles de guérison et les cercles de sentence autochtones au Canada." *Criminologie* 32, no. 1 (1999): 79–105.

Jamieson, Kathleen. "Plus ça change, plus c'est pareil? Les femmes autochtones et la question du gouvernement indien autonome et du droit coutumier." *Recherches amérindiennes au Québec*, 14, no. 3 (1984): 65–74.

Jenness, Diamond. *The Ojibwa Indians of Parry Island. Their Social and Religious Life.* Anthropological Series 17, Bulletin 78. Ottawa: National Museum of Canada, 1935.

Joly de Lotbinière, Pauline. "Des wampums et des "petits humains." Récits historiques sur les wampums algonquins." *Recherches amérindiennes au Québec* 23, nos. 2–3 (1993): 53–68.

Justice for Missing and Murdered Indigenous Women. "Petition: Inquiry into the death of Gladys Tolley." July 25, 2009. Accessed March 9, 2013. http://www. missingjustice.ca.

Justice pour les victimes de bavures policières. "22 octobre 2012: Justice pour les victimes de bavures policières: 3ᵉ vigile commémorative." October 2012. Accessed March 9, 2013. http://22octobre.wordpress.com.

Kaufman, Robert R. "The Patron-Client Concept and Macro-politics: Prospects and Problems." *Comparative Studies in Society and History* 16 (1974): 284–308.

Kelm, Mary-Ellen. *Colonizing Bodies: Aboriginal Health and Healing in British Columbia 1900–50.* Vancouver: UBC Press, 1998.

Kitigan Zibi Anishinabeg. *Activity Report and Financial Statements: Year in Review 2001–2002.* 2002. Accessed May 23, 2013. http://www.kzadmin.com/assets/aar/ KZ_ActivityReport2001-2002_pt1.pdf.

Kitigan Zibi Anishinabeg. *Activity Report and Financial Statements: Year in Review 2002–2003.* 2003. Accessed May 23, 2013. http://kzadmin.com/Reports/66_Activity_Report_2002-2003_13062011.pdf.

Kitigan Zibi Anishinabeg. 150th Commemoration, 150 Taso Pibonezimagad Kitigan Zibi 1853–2003. Kitigan Zibi: Kitigan Zibi Anishinabeg, 2003, DVD.

Kitigan Zibi Anishinabeg. *Activity Report and Financial Statements: Year in Review 2004–2005.* 2005. Accessed May 23, 2013 http://kzadmin.com/Reports/68_Activity_Report_2004-2005_13062011.pdf.

Kitigan Zibi Anishinabeg. *Activity Report and Financial Statements: Year in Review 2005–2006.* 2006. Accessed May 23, 2013. http://kzadmin.com/Reports/69_Activity_Report_2005-2006_13062011.pdf.

Kitigan Zibi Anishinabeg flyer. March, April, June 2008, June 2010, May 2012, Kitigan Zibi.

Kitigan Zibi Anishinabeg Band Council. *Draft Community Election Code*. 2010. Accessed September 8, 2010. http://www.kza.qc.ca.

Kitigan Zibi Anishinabeg. Accessed December 15, 2010, May 23–24, 2012, and February 16, 2013. http://www.kza.qc.ca.

La Rusic, Ignatius. *La négociation d'un mode de vie. La structure administrative découlant de la Convention de la Baie-James: L'expérience initiale des Cris*, Montréal: Groupe de l'orientation, de la recherche et de l'évaluation du ministère des Affaires indiennes et du Nord canadien, 1979.

Labrecque, Marie-France. "Des femmes de Weymontachie." *Recherches amérindiennes au Québec* 14, no. 3 (1984a): 3–16.

Labrecque, Marie-France. "Développement du capitalisme dans la région de Weymontachie (Haute-Mauricie): Incidences sur la condition des femmes attikamèques." *Recherches amérindiennes au Québec* 14, no. 3 (1984b): 75–87.

Ladrière, Jean. *L'engagement*. Bruxelles: Centre national de pastorale familiale, 1967.

Ladrière, Jean. *L'éthique dans l'univers de la rationalité*. Bruxelles: Fides, 1997.

Lajeunesse, Thérèse. *Community Holistic Circle Healing: Hollow Water First Nation*. Ottawa: Solliciteur général et ministère des Approvisionnements et Services, 1993.

Lajoie, Andrée. *Le rôle des femmes et des aînés dans la gouvernance autochtone au Québec*. Montréal: Thémis, 2009.

Lamothe, Bernard. *Fragments de la vie quotidienne des Atikamekw de Manawan: Problèmes sociaux, solidarité et entraide*. Québec: Groupe de recherche hypothèse, 1997.

Lanoue, Guy. "La désunion fait la force: Survie et tension chez les Sekani de la Colombie-Britannique." *Anthropologie et sociétés* 14, no. 2 (1990): 117–41.

Lanoue, Guy. "Changement et continuité: Le passé et la construction d'un avenir dans les sociétés athapascanes septentrionales." *Recherches amérindiennes au Québec* 28, no. 3 (1998): 3–10.

Lanoue, Guy. "Canadian First Nations and the State: The Irony of Hegemony." *Societal and Political Psychology International Review* 2, no. 2 (2011): 89–93.

Lapointe, Eugène, OMI. *La ferme de 200 acres des Oblats de Maniwaki (acquisition et vente)*. Unpublished manuscript, October 22, 2007, typescript.

LaPrairie, Carol. "Native Women and Crime: A Theoretical Model." *The Canadian Journal of Native Studies* 7, no. 1 (1987): 121–37.

LaPrairie, Carol. "The "New" Justice: Some Implications for Aboriginal Communities." *Revue canadienne de criminologie/Canadian Journal of Criminology* 40, no. 1 (1998): 61–79.

Larose, François. "*Éducation indienne au Québec et prise en charge scolaire:* De l'assimilation à la souveraineté économique et Culturelle." 2 vols. PhD diss., Université de Genève, 1998.

Larsen, Tord. "Negotiating Identity: The Micmac of Nova Scotia." In *The Politics of Indianness, Case Studies of Native Ethopolitics in Canada*, edited by Adrian Tanner, 37–136. St. John's: Institute of Social and Economic Research, 1983.

Laurin, Serge. "Les 'troubles d'Oka,' ou l'histoire d'une résistance (1760–1788)." *Recherches amérindiennes au Québec* 21, nos. 1–2 1991: 87–92.

Lavell-Harvard, D. Memee, and Jeannette Corbiere Lavell. *Until Our Hearts Are on the Ground: Aboriginal Mothering, Oppression, Resistance and Rebirth.* Toronto: Demeter Press, 2006.

Lavoie, Michel. "Politique sur commande: Les effets des commissions d'enquête sur la philosophie publique et la politique indienne au Canada, 1828–1996." *Recherches amérindiennes au Québec* 37, no. 1 (2007): 5–23.

Lawrence, Bonita. *Fractured Homeland: Federal Recognition and Algonquin Identity in Ontario,* Vancouver: UBC Press, 2012.

Leacock, Eleonor. *The Montagnais "Hunting Territory" and the Fur Trade,* Memoir 78. Menasha, WI: American Anthropological Association, 1954.

Leacock, Eleonor. "Status among the Montagnais-Naskapi of Labrador." *Ethnohistory* 5, no. 3 (1958): 200–209.

Leacock, Eleanor. "Women's Status in Egalitarian Society: Implications for Social Evolution." *Current Anthropology* 19, no. 2 (1978): 247–75.

Leacock, Eleanor, ed. "Women's Status in Egalitarian Society: Implications for Social Evolution." In *Myths of Male Dominance, Collected Articles on Women Cross-Culturally,* 133–82. New York: Monthly Review Press, 1981.

Lebel, Sylvie. "Relations interculturelles entre les Atikamekw et les colons canadiens en Mauricie entre 1870 et 1910." Master's thesis, Université du Québec à Trois-Rivière, Université Laval, 2003.

Lee, Richard B., and Irven Devore, eds. *Man the Hunter.* Chicago: Aldine Publishing Co., 1968.

Lemieux, Vincent. *Parenté et politique: L'organisation sociale dans l'île d'Orléans.* Coll. Droit, science politique. Québec: Les Presses de l'Université Laval, 1971.

Lemoine, Georges, OMI. *Dictionnaire français-algonquin,* Chicoutimi, QC: G. Delisle, Bureaux du journal *Le Travailleur,* 1909.

Lepage, Pierre. *Mythes et réalités sur les peuples autochtones.* Québec: Commission des droits de la personne et des droits de la jeunesse, 2002.

Leroux, Jacques. "Le tambour d'Edmond." *Recherches amérindiennes au Québec* 22, nos. 2–3 (1992): 30–43.

Leroux, Jacques. "Les métamorphoses du pacte dans une communauté algonquine." *Recherches amérindiennes au Québec* 25, no. 1 (1995): 51–69.

Leroux, Jacques, Roland Chamberland, Edmond Brazeau, and Claire Dubé. *Au pays des peaux de chagrin: Occupation et exploitation territoriales à Kitcisakik (Grand-Lac-Victoria) au xxe siècle.* Québec: Les Presses de l'Université Laval and Gatineau: Le Musée canadien des civilisations, 2004.

Leslie, John, and Ron Maguire, eds. *The Historical Development of the Indian Act.* Ottawa: Treaties and Historical Research Centre, Indian Affairs and Northern Development, 1978.

Lévesque, Carole. "D'ombre et de lumière: L'association des femmes autochtones du Québec." *Nouvelles Pratiques sociales* 3, no. 2 (1990): 71–83.

Lips, Julius. "Naskapi Law (Lake St. John and Lake Mistassini Bands) Law and Order in a Hunting Society." *Transactions of the American Philosophical Society, New Series* 37, no. 4 (1947): 379–492.

Lipset, Seymour M. "Students and Politics in Comparative Perspective." *Daedalus* 97, no. 1 (1968): 1–20.

Lipset, Seymour M. "Youth and Politics." In *Contemporary Social problems*, edited by R. K. Merton and R. Nisbet, 743–91. New York: Harcourt Brace Jovanovich, 1971.

Lithman, Yngve Georg. *The Community Apart: A Case Study of a Canadian Indian Reserve*. Winnipeg: University of Manitoba Press, 1984.

Long, J. Anthony. "Political Revitalization in Canadian Native Societies." *Canadian Journal of Political Science/Revue canadienne de science politique* 23, no. 4 (1990): 751–73.

Lucas, Lucille. "10ᵉ anniversaire du Pensionnat Indien d'Amos." *Vie indienne, Organe des Indiens d'expression française* (Commission oblate des œuvres indiennes et esquimaudes) 3, no. 6, (1966): 1, 4–5.

Magee, Kathryn. "'For Home and Country': Education, Activism, and Agency in Alberta Homemakers' Clubs, 1942–1970." *Native Studies Review* 18, no. 2 (2009): 27–49.

Mailhot, José. "La glorification du mâle dans le vocabulaire cri et Montagnais." *Recherches amérindiennes au Québec* 8, no. 4 (1983): 291–97.

Mailhot, José. *Au pays des Innus, les gens de Sheshatshit*. Reprint, Montréal: Recherches amérindiennes au Québec, 1999.

Mailloux, Carole. "La position et l'engagement des femmes de deux communautés innues." PhD diss., Université de Montréal, 2004.

Maracle, Sylvia. "The Eagle Has Landed: Native Women, Leadership and Community Development." In *Strong Women Stories: Native Vision and Community Survival*, edited by Kim Anderson and Bonita Lawrence, 70–80. Toronto: Sumach Press, 2003.

Marinier, René. "La mission du lac des Deux-Montagnes." *Cahiers d'histoire des Deux-Montagnes* 3, no. 4 (1980): 27–39.

Mason, Arthur. "The Rise of an Alaskan Native Bourgeoisie." Études/Inuit/Studies 26, no. 2 2002: 5–22.

McDougall-Whiteduck, Gina. "Le silence rompu." *Rencontre* 13, no. 2 (Winter 1991): 15. Québec: Secrétariat aux affaires autochtones.

McGregor, Ernest C. *Algonquin Lexicon* [Algonquin-English]. Maniwaki: River Desert Education Authority, n.d.

McGregor, Ernest C. *Algonquin Lexicon* [Algonquin-English]. Maniwaki: River Desert Education Authority, 1987.

McGregor, Ernest C. *Algonquin Lexicon* [Algonquin-English]. Maniwaki: Kitigan Zibi Education Council, 1994.

McGregor, Stephen. *Since Time Immemorial: "Our Story": The Story of the Kitigan Zibi Anishinabeg*. Kitigan Zibi: Kitigan Zibi Education Council, 2004.

Memel-Fotê, Harris. 1991. "Des ancêtres fondateurs aux pères de la nation. Introduction à une anthropologie de la démocratie." *Cahiers d'*études africaines 31, no. 123 (1991): 263–85.

Memmi, Albert. *Portrait du colonisé*. Précédé du Portrait du colonisateur, et d'une préface de Jean-Paul Sartre. Coll. Folio actuel. Paris: Gallimard, 2008

Merry, Sally E. "Resistance and the Cultural Power of Law." *Presidential Address, Law and Society Review* 29, no. 1 (1995): 11–27.

Merry, Sally E. "Law, Culture, and Cultural Appropriation." *Yale Journal of Law and the Humanities* 10 (1998): 101–29.

Métis Culture. Accessed March 20, 2013. http://www.telusplanet.net/dgarneau/metis25.htm.

Michaud, Monique. "La Police amérindienne: Un défi sans cesse renouvelé." *Rencontre* 8, no. 1 (September 1986): 8–9. Québec: Secrétariat aux affaires autochtones.

Miller, Bruce G. "Women and Politics: Comparative Evidence from the Northwest Coast." *Ethnology* 31, no. 4 (1992): 367–83.

Miller, J. R. *Skyscrapers Hide the Heavens. A History of Indian-White Relations in Canada*. Revised edition. Toronto: University of Toronto Press, 1991.

Miller, J. R. *Shingwauk's Vision: A History of Native Residential Schools*. Toronto: University of Toronto Press, 1996.

Miller, J. R., ed. "Canada and the Aboriginal Peoples, 1867–1927." In *Reflections on Native–Newcomer Relations: Selected Essays*, 171–92. Toronto: University of Toronto Press, 2004.

Milloy, John S. *A National Crime: The Canadian Government and the Residential School System, 1879 to 1986*. Winnipeg: University of Manitoba Press, 1999.

Miny, Danièle. "Expansion oblate: L'effet d'une traînée de poudre." *Apostolat*, 66, no. 5 (September–October 1995): 12–13.

Miny, Danièle. "Une belle rencontre." *Apostolat* 79, no. 4 (July–August 2008): 23.

Missions de la Congrégation des Missionnaires Oblats de Marie-Immaculée. Lettre de J.-M. Nédélec au supérieur général Fabre, 15 février 1864, tome 4 (1865): 167–69.

Mitchell, Marybelle. *From Talking Chiefs to a Native Corporate Elite: The Birth of Class and Nationalism among the Canadian Inuit*. Montréal: McGill-Queen's University Press, 1996.

Montminy, Lyse, Renée Brassard, Mylène Jaccoud, Elizabeth Harper, Marie-Pierre Bousquet, and Shanie Leroux. "Pour une meilleure compréhension des particularités de la violence familiale vécue par les femmes autochtones au Canada." *Nouvelles Pratiques sociales* 23, no. 1 (2010): 53–66.

Morantz, Toby. "James Bay Trading Captains of the Eighteenth Century: New Perspectives on Algonquian Social Organization." In *Actes du huitième congrès des Algonquinistes*, edited by William Cowan, 77–89. Ottawa: Carleton University, 1977.

Morantz, Toby. "Northern Algonquian Concepts of Status and Leadership Reviewed: A Case Study of the Eighteenth-Century Trading Captain System." *Canadian Review of Sociology and Anthropology* 19, no. 4 (1982): 482–501.

Morantz, Toby. *An Ethnographic Study of Eastern James Bay Cree Social Organization, 1700–1850* (Canadian Ethnological Service Paper No. 88). Ottawa: National Museums of Canada, National Museum of Man, 1983.

Morantz, Toby. *The White Man's Gonna Getcha. The Colonial Challenge to the Crees in Quebec*. McGill-Queen's Native and Northern Series, Montréal: McGill-Queen's University Press, 2002a.

Morantz, Toby. "L'histoire de l'est de la baie James au xxᵉ siècle. À la recherche d'une interprétation." *Recherches amérindiennes au Québec* 32, no. 2 (2002b): 63–70.

Morissette, Anny. *De la forêt à la réserve, la mosaïque politique d'une bande autochtone: l'exemple des Atikamekᵂ de Manawan (Québec)*. Master's thesis, Université de Montréal, 2004.

Morissette, Anny. "Composer avec un système imposé: La tradition et le conseil de bande à Manawan." *Recherches amérindiennes au Québec* 37, nos. 2–3 (2007): 127–38.

Morissette, Anny. *Le leadership interstitiel, le champ d'action des Amérindiens ou le pouvoir dans la marge: L'exemple de la communauté algonquine de Kitigan Zibi (Québec)*. PhD diss., Université de Montréal, 2013.

Morissette, Anny. *La lutte se poursuivit en cachette: Le pouvoir des chefs et des leaders de la bande algonquine de Kitigan Zibi*. Sillery: Septentrion, 2018.

Morissette, Diane. *Vitalités et regroupements chez les femmes autochtones du Québec*. Montréal: Direction régionale du Québec du Secrétariat d'État, 1982.

Morissette, Diane. "Les utopies nécessaires ou les espoirs permanents: Entrevue avec Evelyne O'bomsawin, présidente de l'Association des femmes autochtones du Québec (AFAQ)." *Recherches amérindiennes au Québec* 13, no. 4 (1983): 273–75.

Morissette, Diane. "Être présidente en toute lucidité: Entrevue avec Bibiane Courtois, présidente de l'Association des femmes autochtones du Québec (AFAQ)." *Recherches amérindiennes au Québec* 14, no. 3 (1984): 59–64.

Mulvihill, James, OMI. "Le manque de chefs chez les Indiens." *Vie indienne* 2, no. 23 (1964): 6–7 (written for Oblate News, n.d., and reproduced in the booklet *The Dilemma for Our Indian People*, n.d.).

Murdock, George Peter. "Algonkian Social Organization." In *Context and Meaning in Cultural Anthropology*, edited by Melfort E. Spiro, 24–35. New York: The Free Press, 1965.

Musée virtuel du Canada. Accessed May 24, 2012. http://www.virtualmuseum.ca.

National First Nations Health Organization (NAHO). Accessed October 19, 2009, May 23 and December 17, 2012. http://www.naho.ca.

Nicks, Trudy. "Indian Village and Entertainments: Setting the Stage for Tourist Souvenirs Sales." In *Unpacking Culture Art and Commodity in Colonial and Postcolonial Worlds*, edited by Ruth B. Phillips and Christopher B. Steiner, 301–15. Berkeley: University of California Press, 1999.

Niezen, Ronald. "Telling a Message: Cree Perceptions of Custom and Administration." *Canadian Journal of Native Studies* 13, no. 2 (1993): 221–50.

Niquay, Thérèse. "Le rôle sacré des femmes." *Rencontre* 13, no. 2 (Winter 1991): 4–5. Québec: Secrétariat aux affaires autochtones.

Northouse, Peter G., ed. *Leadership: Theory and Practice*. Thousand Oaks, CA: Sage, 2012.

NWAC (Native Women's Association of Canada), ed. *Les voix de nos sœurs par l'esprit: Rapport aux familles et aux communautés*. Ottawa: Association des femmes autochtones du Canada, 2009.

NWAC (Native Women's Association of Canada). *Ce que leurs histoires nous disent.* Ottawa: Association des femmes autochtones du Canada, 2010.

NWAC (Native Women's Association of Canada). *Storytelling: Gladys' Story.* Accessed March 9, 2013. https://www.nwac.ca.

O'Meara, John. Reviewed work by Ernest McGregor. "Algonquin Lexicon." *International Journal of American Linguistics* 59, no. 1 (1993): 108–13.

Orfali, Philippe. "La flamme de l'espoir survit à l'indifférence." *Le Droit*, October 5, 2012. Accessed March 9, 2013. http://www.lapresse.ca/le-droit/politique/sur-la-colline-parlementaire/201210/05/01-4580636-la-flamme-de-lespoir-survit-a-lindifference.php.

Ortner, Sherry B. "Resistance and the Problem of Ethnographic Refusal." *Comparative Studies in Society and History* 37, no. 1 (1995): 173–93.

Ottawa. *Proceedings of the Standing Senate Committee on Aboriginal Peoples Issue 18—Evidence.* October 7, 2009, Ottawa. Accessed September 8, 2010. http://www.parl.gc.ca/Content/SEN/Committee/402/abor/18ev-e.htm?Language=E&Parl=40&Ses=2&comm_id=1.

Ottawa, Gilles. *Les pensionnats indiens au Québec: Un double regard.* Québec: Cornac, 2010.

Ouellette, Françoise-Romaine. "Les cris du Québec, des sous-prolétaires." *Recherches amérindiennes au Québec* 6, nos. 3–4 (1977): 7–15.

Ouimet, Lucie, dir. *Ojigkwanong—Rencontre avec un sage algonquin.* Office national du film du Canada, 2000. Video.

Paine, Robert, ed. *Patrons and Brokers in the East Arctic.* St. John's: Institute of Social and Economic Research, Memorial University of Newfoundland, 1971.

Papillon, Martin. "Vers un fédéralisme postcolonial? La difficile redéfinition des rapports entre l'État canadien et les peuples autochtones." In *Le fédéralisme canadien contemporain: Fondements, traditions, institutions*, edited by Alain-G. Gagnon, 461–85. Montréal: Les Presses de l'Université de Montréal, 2006.

Papillon, Martin. "Towards Postcolonial Federalism? The Challenges of Aboriginal Self-Determination in the Canadian Context." In Contemporary Canadian Federalism, edited by Alain G. Gagnon, 405–27. Toronto: University of Toronto Press, 2009.

Pariseau, Claude-L. "Les troubles de 1860–1880 à Oka: Choc de deux cultures." Master's thesis, McGill University, 1974.

Passy, Florence. *L'action altruisme: Contraintes et opportunités de l'engagement dans les mouvements sociaux.* Genève: Librairie Droz, 1998.

Peelman, Achiel, OMI. "Les Missionnaires oblats et les cultures amérindiennes au 19e siècle: Les oblats en Oregon (1847–1860)." Études d'histoire religieuse 62 (1996): 31–47.

Penobscot Cultural and Historic Preservation. Accessed March 9, 2013. http://www.penobscotculture.com/.

Petrullo, Vincent M. "Decorative Art on Birch-Bark from the Algonquin River du Lièvre Band." *Indian Notes* 6 (1929): 225–42.

Pflüg, Mélissa A. "'Pimadaziwin' Contemporary Rituals in Odawa Community." *American Indian Quarterly* 20, no. 3–4 (1996): 489–513.

Pharand, Sylvie. *Des services d'aide en violence conjugale en réponse aux besoins des femmes autochtones*, Montréal: Presses de l'Université du Québec à Montréal, 2008.

Picard, Pierre-Albert. *Daily Journal*, Lorette, 1916–1920.

Place aux jeunes en région. Accessed May 23, 2012. http://www.placeauxjeunes. qc.ca.

Poiré, Charles-Édouard, and Hypolite Moreau. "Extrait du journal d'une mission faite en 1839, aux lacs Temiscaming et Abbitibbi, au Grand-Lac et au lac La Truite, etc." In *Rapport sur les missions du diocèse de Québec* (Association de la propagation de la foi), no. 2 (January 1840): 42–62.

Poirier, Sylvie. "Contemporanéités autochtones, territoires et (post) colonialisme: Réflexion sur des exemples canadiens et australiens." *Anthropologie et sociétés* 24, no. 1 (2000): 137–53.

Poirier, Sylvie. "Territories, Identity, and Modernity among the Atikamekw." In *Aboriginal Autonomy and Development in Northern Quebec and Labrador*, edited by Colin Scott, 98–116. Vancouver: UBC Press, 2001.

Ponting, J. Rick, and Cora J. Voyageur. "Challenging the Deficit Paradigm: Grounds for Optimism among First Nations in Canada." *Canadian Journal of Native Studies* 21, no. 2 (2001): 275–307.

Preston, Richard J. "The Wiitigo: Algonquian Knowledge and White Man Interest." In *Actes du Huitième Congrès des Algonquinistes*, edited by William Cowan, 101–7. Ottawa: Carleton University, 1977.

Preston, Richard. *Cree Narrative: Expressing the Personal Meanings of Events*. Revised edition. Montréal: McGill-Queen's University Press, 2002.

Proulx, Jean-Baptiste. "Douze cents milles en canot d'écorce ou la première visite pastorale de Mgr N.-Z. Lorrain, évêque de Cythère." *Les Missions catholiques* 23 (1891): 5–274.

Proulx, Jean-Baptiste. *Annales de la Propagation de la foi Québec pour les provinces de Québec et de Montréal*, vol. 46. Montréal: Gebhardt-Berthiaume, 1892.

Proulx, Jean-René. "Acquisition de pouvoirs et tente tremblante chez les Montagnais." *Recherches amérindiennes au Québec*, 18, nos. 2–3 (1988): 51–59.

Quéniart, Anne, and Julie Jacques. "L'engagement politique des jeunes femmes au Québec: De la responsabilité au pouvoir d'agir pour un changement de société." *Lien social et politiques* 46 (2001): 45–53.

Quéniart, Anne, and Julie Jacques. *Apolitiques les jeunes femmes? Regard sur les formes et le sens de leur engagement*. Rapport de recherche. Montréal: Presses de l'Université du Québec à Montréal, Relais-femmes-ARIR, 2002.

Radcliffe-Brown, Alfred R. "Social Organization of Australian Tribes." *Oceania Monographs*, no. 1 (1930): 34–63.

Radio-Canada. "Madame la chef." June 26, 2007. Accessed November 16, 2012. http://ici.radio-canada.ca/nouvelle/358582/femme-chef-pikogan?ref=rss.

Radio-Canada. "Kitcisakik: Un nouveau chef." December 24, 2009. Accessed January 3, 2010. http://ici.radio-canada.ca/nouvelle/458215/kitcisakik-chef.

Rappaport, J. "Studies in Empowerment: Introduction to the Issue." In *Studies in Empowerment: Steps toward Understanding and Action*, edited by J. Rappaport, C. Swift and R. Hess, 1–8. New York: Heyworth Press, 1984.

Rapport des cours de formation de leaders sociaux (RLS). Ottawa: Archives De-schâtelets, HR901, 1959.

Répertoire des élus municipaux en Outaouais de 1845 à 1975. Accessed March 1, 2013. http://craoutaouais.ca/repertoire/Web/maniwaki.html.

Résumé du cours de formation de responsables sociales "Leadership" (RRSL). Ot-tawa: Archives Deschâtelets, HR901, 1960.

Riopel, Marc. *Le Témiscamingue: Son histoire et ses habitants*. Montréal: Fides, 2002.

Roark-Calnek, Sue. "Un mariage dans le bois: Continuité et changement dans le mariage algonquin." *Recherches amérindiennes au Québec* 23, nos. 2–3 (1993): 87–107.

Robichaud, Denis. "Le directeur général (gérant de bande) et l'administration des bandes indiennes." Master's thesis, Université Laval, 1992.

Rocher, Guy. *Introduction à la sociologie générale*. Troisième édition. LaSalle, QC: Hurtubise Ltée, 1992.

Rock, Rollande. "Introduction" In *Montagnaises de parole/Eukuan ume ninan en-tentamat*. Québec: Conseil des Atikamekw et des Montagnais, 1992.

Rodon, Thierry. *En partenariat avec l'État: Les expériences de cogestion des Autoch-tones du Canada*. Québec: Presses de l'Université Laval, 2003.

Rogers, Edward S. *The Hunting Group-Hunting Territory Complex among the Mis-tassini Indians*. Bulletin no. 195, coll. Anthropological Series, 63. Ottawa: Depart-ment of Northern Affairs and National Resources, 1963.

Rogers, Edward S. "Leadership among the Indians of Eastern Subarctic Canada." *Anthropologica*, no. 7 (1965): 263–84.

Ross, Rupert. "Duelling Pradigms? Western Criminal Justice versus Aboriginal Com-munity Healing." In *Continuing Poundmaker and Riel's Quest*, edited by Richard Gosse, James Y. Henderson, and Roger Carter, 241–68. Saskatoon: Purich, 1994.

Roué, Marie. "Les trois scènes de la Confédération crie à Chisasibi (Baie James): Réunion politique, lieu de mémoire et naissance d'un musée." *Anthropologie et sociétés* 28, no. 2 (2004): 121–39.

Rousseau, Jacques. "Rites païens de la forêt Québécoise: La tente tremblante et la suerie." *Les Cahiers des Dix* 18 (1953): 129–55.

Rousseau, Jean. "Review of *Aboriginal Autonomy and Development in Northern Quebec and Labrador*, by Collin H. Scott." *Études inuit* 27, nos. 1–2 (2003): 545–49.

Routhier, Marie-Josée. "Que sont devenues les sages-femmes d'antan? L'accouchement chez les femmes attikamèques de Manouane." *Recherches amérindiennes au Qué-bec* 13, no. 4 (1984): 26–36.

Rutherdale, Myra, and Jim Miller. "'It's Our Country': First Nations' Participation in the Indian Pavilion at Expo 67." *Journal of the Canadian Historical Association/ Revue de la Société historique du Canada* 17, no. 2 (2006): 148–73.

Saganash, Diom Roméo. "Les pensionnats pour Autochtones, outils d'assimilation: Un héritage honteux." In *Le devoir de mémoire et les politiques du pardon*, edited by Micheline Labelle, Rachad Antonius and Georges Leroux, 85–99. Sainte-Foy: Presses de l'Université du Québec, 2005.

Sahlins, M. Âge de pierre, âge d'abondance: *L'économie des sociétés primitives.* Paris: Gallimard, 1976.

Said, Edward. *Orientalism.* New York: Vintage, 1978.

Saint-Onge, Anne. "Propos entre générations: Anne Saint-Onge interviewe sa mère Bernadette." *Recherches amérindiennes au Québec* 13, no. 4 (1983): 269–72.

Satzewich, Vic. "Patronage, Moral Regulation and the Recruitment of Indian Affairs Personnel, 1879–1900." *Canadian Review of Sociology and Anthropology* 33, no. 2 (1996): 144–66.

Satzewich, Vic. "Indian Agents and the 'Indian Problem' in Canada in 1946: Reconsidering the Theory of Coercive Tutelage." *Canadian Journal of Native Studies* 17, no. 1 (1997): 227–57.

Satzewich, Vic, and Linda Mahood. "Indian Affairs and Band Governance: Deposing Indian Chiefs in Western Canada, 1896–1911." *Canadian Ethnic Studies* 26, no. 1 (1994): 40–58.

Satzewich, Vic, and Linda Mahood. "Indian Agents and the Residential School System in Canada, 1946–1970." *Historical Studies in Education* 7, no. 1 (1995): 41–65.

Sauber, Mariana. "Traces fragiles. Les plaques commémoratives dans les rues de Paris." *Annales. Économies, sociétés, civilisations* 48, no. 3 (1993): 715–27.

Savard, Rémi. *L'Algonquin Tessouat et la fondation de Montréal: Diplomatie franco-indienne en Nouvelle-France*, Montréal: Hexagone, 1996.

Sawaya, Jean-Pierre. *Au nom de la loi, je vous arrête! Les Amérindiens du Québec et la Dominion Police, 1880–1920.* Québec: Septentrion, 2012.

Schreiber, Dorothee. "'A Liberal and Paternal Spirit': Indian Agents and Native Fisheries in Canada." *Ethnohistory* 55, no. 1 (2008): 87–118.

Scott, Collin H., ed. *Aboriginal Autonomy and Development in Northern Quebec and Labrador.* Vancouver: University of British Columbia Press, 2001.

Scott, James C. "Everyday Forms of Resistance." *Copenhagen Journal of Asian Studies*, no. 4 (1989): 33–62.

Scott, Richard T., and Selina Conn. "The Failure of Scientific Medicine: Davis Inlet as an Example of Socio-political Morbidity." *Canadian Family Physician*, no. 33 (July 1987): 1649–53.

Séguin, Claire. "Essai sur la condition de la femme indienne au Canada." *Recherches amérindiennes au Québec* 10, no. 4 (1981): 251–60.

Séguin, Louise. "Si les femmes décidaient." *Rencontre* 12, no. 4 (June 1991): 5–7. Québec: Secrétariat aux affaires autochtones.

Service, Elman R. *Primitive Social Organization: An Evolutionary Perspective*; New York: Random House, 1962.

Sharma, S. L. "Empowerment without Antagonism: A Case for Reformulation of Women's Empowerment Approach." *Sociological Bulletin* 49, no. 1 (2000): 19–39.

Silvermann, Sydel F. "Patronage and Community-Nation Relationships in Central Italy." *Ethnology* 4 (1965): 172–89.

Simard, Jean-Jacques. "Par-delà le Blanc et le mal: Rapports identitaires et colonialisme au pays des Inuit." *Sociologie et sociétés* 15, no. 2 (1983): 55–72.

Sioui, Georges E. *Pour une autohistoire amérindienne: Essai sur les fondements d'une morale sociale.* Montréal: McGill-Queen's University Press, 1992.

Sioui, Jules. *Lettre de Jules Sioui à la Couronne, 25 octobre 1943, Loretteville.* In *Since Time Immemorial: "Our Story." The Story of the Kitigan Zibi Anishinabeg,* by Stephen McGregor, 281. Kitigan Zibi: Kitigan Zibi Education Council, 2004.

Smandych, Russel, and Gloria Lee. "Une approche de l'étude du droit et du colonialisme: Vers une perspective autohistorique amérindienne sur le changement juridique, la colonisation, les sexes et la résistance à la colonisation." *Criminologie* 28, no. 1 (1995): 55–79.

Speck, Frank G. *Family Hunting Territories and Social Life of Various Algonkian Bands of the Ottawa Valley,* Memoirs 70, Anthropological Series 8. Ottawa: Canada Department of Mines, Geological Survey, 1915.

Speck, Frank G. *The Functions of Wampum among the Eastern Algonkian.* Memoirs of the American Anthropological Association 6, no 1 (January–Mars 1919). Lancaster, PA: American Anthropological Association, 1919. Reprint, Millwood, NY: Kraus Reprint Co., 1964.

Speck, Frank G. "Algonkian Influence upon Iroquois Social Organization." *American Anthropologist* 25, no. 2 (1923): 219–27.

Speck, Frank G. "River Desert Indians of Quebec." *Indian Notes* 4, no. 3 (1927): 240–52.

Speck, Frank G. "Divination by Scapulimancy among the Algonquin of River, Desert, Québec." *Indian Notes,* no. 5 (1928): 167–73.

Speck, Frank G. "Boundaries and Hunting Groups of the River Desert Algonquin." *Indian Notes* 6, no. 2 (1929): 97–120.

Speck, Frank G. *Naskapi. The Savage Hunters of the Labrador Peninsula.* Norman: University of Oklahoma Press, 1935.

Speck, Frank G., and Loren C. Eiseley. "The Significance of the Hunting Territory System of the Algonkian in Social Theory." *American Anthropologist,* no. 41 (1939): 269–80.

Spielmann, Roger. "'Makwa nibawaanaa': Analyse d'un récit algonquin concernant les rêves sur les ours." *Recherches amérindiennes au Québec* 23, nos. 2–3 (1993): 109–17.

Spiteri, Mélanie. "Sentencing Circles in Aboriginal Offenders in Canada: Furthering the Idea of Aboriginal Justice within a Western Justice Framework." Master's thesis, University of Windsor, 2001.

Springer, Kimberly. "The Interstitial Politics of Black Feminist Organizations." *Meridians* 1, no. 2 (2001): 155–91.

St. Louis, A. E. *Ancient Hunting Grounds of Algonquin and Nispissing Indians Comprising the Watersheds of the Ottawa & Madawaska Rivers.* Rapport déposé au Centre de la recherche historique et de l'étude des revendications, ministère des Affaires indiennes et du Nord Canada. Ottawa: n.p, 1951.

Steward, Julian H. "The Economic and Social Basis of Primitive Bands." In *Essays in Anthropology Presented to A. L. Kroeber,* edited by R. H. Rowie, 341–42. Berkeley: University of California Press, 1936.

Steward, Julian H. *Theory of Culture Change*: *The Methodology of Multilinear Evolution*. Urbana: University of Illinois Press, 1955.

Stote, Karen. "The Coercive Sterilization of Aboriginal Women in Canada." *American Indian Culture and Research Journal* 36, no. 3 (2012): 117–50.

Sultzman, Lee. "The Algonkin." Accessed February 10, 2010. http://www.snowwowl.com/peoplealgonquin.html.

Sunseri, Lina. "Sky Woman Lives On: Contemporary Examples of Mothering the Nation." In *First Voices: An Aboriginal Women's Reader*, edited by Patricia A. Monture and Patricia D. McGuire, 54–62. Toronto: Inanna Publications & Education, 2009.

Sûreté du Québec. "Les policiers autochtones à la S.Q.." *Revue de la Sûreté du Québec* 9, no. 5 (May 1979).

Talaga, Tanya. "UN to Investigate Missing Aboriginal Women." *Toronto Star*, January 26, 2012. Accessed March 8, 2013. http://www.thestar.com/news/insight/2012/01/06/un_to_investigate_missing_aboriginal_women.html.

Tanner, Adrian. "Divinations and Decisions: Multiple Explanations for Algonquian Scapulimancy." In *The Yearbook of Symbolic Anthropology*, edited by E. Schwimmer, 89–101. Montréal: McGill-Queen's University Press, 1978.

Tanner, Adrian. *Bringing Home Animals: Religious Ideology and Mode of Production of the Mistassini Cree Hunters*. St. John's: Institute of Social and Economic Research, 1979.

Tanner, Adrian. *The Politics of Indianness. Case Studies of Native Ethopolitics in Canada*. St. John's: Institute of Social and Economic Research, 1983.

Taylor, A. C. "Évolutionnisme." In *Dictionnaire de l'ethnologie et de l'anthropologie*, edited by Pierre Bonte et Michel Izard, 269–72. Paris: Presses Universitaires de France, 2002.

Teicher, Morton I. *Windigo Psychosis: A Study of a Relationship between Belief and Behavior among the Indians of Northeastern Canada*. Proceedings of the 1960 Annual Spring Meeting of the AES, American Ethnological Society, edited by Verne F. Ray, 1960.

Tenasco, Jenny. *Algonquin Chiefs of the River Desert Band*. Maniwaki, QC: River Desert Education Authority, 1986.

Tennant, Paul. "Aboriginal Rights and the Penner Report on Indian Self-Government." In *The Quest for Justice: Aboriginal Peoples and Aboriginal Rights*, edited by Menno Boldt and J. Anthony Long, 321–32. Toronto: University of Toronto Press, 1985.

Testart, A. "Chasseurs-cueilleurs." In *Dictionnaire de l'ethnologie et de l'anthropologie*, edited by Pierre Bonte and Michel Izard, 135–38. Paris: Presses Universitaires de France, 2002.

Thériault, Charles. "La langue algonquine renaît tranquillement à Kitigan Zibi." *Le Droit*, 11 October, 2011. Accessed October 21, 2013. http://www.lapresse.ca/le-droit/actualites/ville-de-gatineau/201110/10/01-4455876-la-langue-algonquine-renaittranquillement-a-kitigan-zibi.php.

Therrien, Jean-Marie. *Parole et pouvoir. Figure du chef amérindien en Nouvelle-France* (coll. Positions anthropologiques). Montréal: l'Hexagone, 1986.

Timiskaming First Nation. "Past Chiefs and Councils." Accessed May 15, 2012. http://atfn.ca.

Tobias, John L. "Protection, Civilization, Assimilation: An Outline History of Canada's Indian Policy." *Western Canadian Journal of Anthropology* 6, no. 2 (1976): 12–30. Reprinted in *As Long as the Sun Shines and Water Flows: A Reader in Canadian Native Studies*, edited by A. L. Getty and Antoine S. Lussier, 39–55. Vancouver: UBC Press, 1983.

Tollefson, Kenneth D. "The Snoqualmie: A Puget Sound Chiefdom." *Ethnology* 26, no. 2 (1987): 121–36.

TSA. "Violet Pachanos Overcoming the Traditional Gender Barrier." *Nation* 11, no. 1 (2003): 85–87. Accessed February 7, 2018. http://www.nationnewsarchives.ca.

Turner, D. H., and P. Wertman. *Shamattawa: The Structure of Social Relations in a Northern Algonkian Band*. Ottawa: National Museum of Canada, 1977.

Turpel, Mary-Ellen. "Patriarchy and Paternalism: The Legacy of the Canadian State for First Nations Women." *Canadian Journal of Women and the Law*, no. 6 (1993): 174–92.

Umfreville, Edward. *The Present State of Hudson's Bay*, London: C. Stalker, 1790.

Valaskakis, Gail G. "Les pensionnats indiens: Souvenir et reconciliation." In *Le devoir de mémoire et les politiques du pardon*, edited by Micheline Labelle, Rachad Antonius and Georges Leroux, 101–25. Sainte-Foy: Presses de l'Université du Québec, 2005.

van Binsbergen, Wim. "Les chefs royaux nkoya et l'association culturelle Kazanga en Zambie. Résistance, déclin ou folklorisation de la fonction du chef traditionnel." In *Le retour des rois: Les autorités traditionnelles et l'État en Afrique contemporaine*, edited by C. H. Perrot and F. X. Fauvelle-Aymar, 489–510. Paris: Karthala, 2003.

Viau, Roland. "Les dieux de la terre: Histoire des Algonquins de l'Outaouais, 1600–1650." In *Trace du passé, images du présent*, edited by Marc Côté and Gaëtan Lessard, 109–32. Rouyn-Noranda, QC: Cégep de l'Abitibi-Témiscamingue, 1993.

Vincent, Sylvie. "Structure du rituel: La tente tremblante et le concept de mistapew." *Recherches amérindiennes au Québec* 3, nos. 1–2 (1973): 69–83.

Vincent, Sylvie. "Les bonnes et les mauvaises alliances." *Recherches amérindiennes au Québec* 6, no. 1 (1976): 22–35.

Vincent, Sylvie. "Structures comparées du rite et des mythes de la tente tremblante." In *Actes du Huitième Congrès des Algonquinistes*, edited by William Cowan, 90–100. Ottawa: Carleton University, 1977.

Vincent, Sylvie. "Mistamaninuesh au temps de la mouvance: Notes inspirées par l'autobiographie d'une femme montagnaise." *Recherches amérindiennes au Québec*, 13, no. 4 (1983): 243–53.

Voget, Fred. "The American Indian in Transition: Reformation and Status Innovations." *American Journal of Sociology* 62, no. 4 (1957): 369–78.

Voyageur, Cora J. "The Community Owns You: Experiences of Canada's Women Chiefs." In *Out of the Ivory Tower: Taking Feminist Research to the Community*, edited by Meryn Stuart and Andrea Martinez, 228–47. Toronto: Sumach Press, 2003.

Voyageur, Cora J. "They Called Her Chief: A Profile of Chief Dorothy McDonald." In *Unsettled Pasts: Reconceiving the West through Women's History*, edited by Sarah Carter, Lesley Erickson, Patricia Roome, and Char Smith, 355–61. Calgary: University of Calgary Press, 2005.

Voyageur, Cora J. *Firekeepers of the 21st Century: First Nation Women Chiefs*. Montréal: McGill-Queen's University Press, 2008.

Voyageur, Cora J. "First Nations Women in Canada." In *Visions of the Heart: Canadian Aboriginal Issues*, edited by David Long and Olivia Patricia Dickason, 213–37. Oxford University Press, 2011a.

Voyageur, Cora J. "Out in the Open: Elected Female Leadership in Canada's First Nations Community." *Canadian Review of Sociology/Revue canadienne de sociologie* 48, no. 1 (2011b): 67–85.

Waugh, Earle H. *Dissonant Worlds: Roger Vandersteene among the Cree*. Waterloo: Wilfrid Laurier University Press, 1996.

Weber, Max. *The Theory of Social and Economic Organization*, trans. A. M. Henderson and Talcott Parsons, with an introduction by Talcott Parsons. New York: The Free Press, Macmillan Company, 1965.

Wesley-Esquimaux, Cynthia C., and Magdalena Smolewski. *Traumatisme historique et guérison autochtone*. Ottawa: Fondation autochtone de guérison, 2004.

White, Geoffrey M., and Lamont Lindstrom. *Chiefs Today: Traditional Pacific Leadership and the Postcolonial State*. Stanford, CA: Stanford University Press, 1997.

Widdowson, Frances, and Albert Howard. *Disrobing the Aboriginal Industry: The Deception behind Indigenous Cultural Preservation*. Montréal: McGill-Queen's University Press, 2008.

Wolf, Paulette Running, and Julie A. Rickard. "Talking Circles: A Native American Approach to Experiential Learning." *Journal of Multicultural Counseling and Development*, no. 31 (2003): 39–43.

Wright, Susan, ed. *The Anthropology of Organizations*. London: Routledge, 1994.

Zimmerman, M. A. "Psychological Empowerment: Issues and Illustrations." *American Journal of Community Psychology* 23, no. 5 (1995): 581–99.

Index

AANDC. *See* Aboriginal Affairs and Northern Development Canada
AANTC. *See* Algonquin Anishinabeg Nation Tribal Council
Abélès, Marc, 19, 71, 77, 105
Abitibiwinnik band, 12, 27, 114
Aboriginal Affairs and Northern Development Canada (AANDC), 16n7. *See also* Indian and Northern Affairs Canada (INAC)
Aboriginal Autonomy and Development in Northern Quebec and Labrador (Scott), 4
academic formation, Western-style residential school, 67–68
An Act for conferring certain privileges on the more advanced Bands of the Indians of Canada, with the view of training them for the exercise of municipal powers (Canada 1884). *See Indian Advancement Act* (1884)
Act for the better protection of the Lands and Property of the Indians in Lower Canada (1850), 16n9
An Act for the gradual enfranchisement of Indians, the better management of Indian affairs (Canada 1869), 1, 6

An Act to amend and consolidate the laws respecting Indians (Canada 1880): chiefs limited by, 7
adaptation period, for new chief, 104
administration. *See* bureaucracy
administrative power, political power from, 99–100
administrative takeover, of First Nations governance, 93, 95, 96, 98, 101, 106–7, 116
age, of chiefs, experience synonymous with, 43–44
agriculture, 24–25, 61
alcohol, 78, 79, 91n19
Alcoholics Anonymous, 83, 92n27
Alexander (interviewee), 41
Alexander, Shannon, 137
Alfred (interviewee), 102–3
Alfred, Taiaiake, 100–101, 113
"Algonkian Social Organization" (Murdock), 16n13
Algonquin Anishinabeg Nation Tribal Council (AANTC), 12, 13
Algonquin Chiefs of the River Desert Band (Tenasco, J.), 28, 30, 49
Algonquin Council of Western Quebec, dissension in, 12

About the Author

Dr. Anny Morissette is an assistant professor in the School of Conflict Studies at Saint Paul University. She has a PhD in anthropology from Université de Montréal. An Algonquian peoples specialist, her research has focused primarily on First Nations politics, religious pluralism, and Indian Day schools, as well as the empowerment of First Nations women.

www.ingramcontent.com/pod-product-compliance
Lightning Source LLC
Chambersburg PA
CBHW050645280326
41932CB00015B/2786